Professor Marianne Elliott, OBE
An internationally renowned his
a number of acclaimed books, i
winning biography *Wolfe Tone:* .
She has received widespread recognition for her role in the
Northern Ireland peace process, most notably serving on
the Opsahl Commission in 1993 and co-writing its report,
A Citizens' Inquiry. She was director of the Institute of Irish
Studies at the University of Liverpool for eighteen years,
before retiring in 2015. In 2000, she was awarded an OBE
for services to Irish Studies and to the Northern Ireland
peace process. In 2017 she was honoured with a Presidential
Distinguished Service Award from the Irish government.

MARIANNE ELLIOTT

Hearthlands

A memoir of the White City
housing estate in Belfast

·THE·
BLACK
·STAFF·
PRESS

For Flo Kelsey, Gerry Mulholland and Brian Dunn, and in memory of
Sheila Burns, Shane McAteer and Anna Pearson.

First published in 2017 by Blackstaff Press
an imprint of Colourpoint Creative Ltd, Colourpoint House,
Jubilee Business Park, 21 Jubilee Road,
Newtownards, BT23 4YH

With the assistance of The Arts Council of Northern Ireland

The acknowledgements on pages 249–251 constitute an extension
of this copyright page.

Printed in Berwick-upon-Tweed by Martins the Printers

A CIP catalogue for this book is available from the British Library

ISBN 978-0-85640-997-4

www.blackstaffpress.com

Frontispiece: My parents, Terry and Sheila, at Bellevue in the early 1950s.

Contents

Abbreviations

BDTUC	Belfast and District Trades Union Council
BNL	*Belfast News Letter*
BSD	*Belfast Street Directory*
BT	*Belfast Telegraph*
BWT	*Belfast Weekly Telegraph*
CAIN	Conflict Archive on the Internet (University of Ulster)
CRC	Community Relations Commission
HLG	(Ministry of) Housing and Local Government
IN	*Irish News*
IT	*Irish Times*
IW	*Irish Weekly*
Nat. Arch.	The National Archives (UK)
NIHE	Northern Ireland Housing Executive
NIHT	Northern Ireland Housing Trust
NILP	Northern Ireland Labour Party
NIPC	Northern Ireland Political Collection (Linen Hall Library)
NW	*Northern Whig*
PRONI	Public Record Office of Northern Ireland
QUB	Queen's University Belfast
RDC	Rural District Council
RUC	Royal Ulster Constabulary
UDA	Ulster Defence Association
UDR	Ulster Defence Regiment
UUC	Ulster Unionist Council
UYB	*Ulster Year Book*

Introduction

I have never subscribed to the view that the Northern Ireland Troubles of 1969–98 were inevitable. This was reinforced when I served on the 1993 Opsahl peace commission and met a group of north Belfast women. Like myself they had grown up in mixed-religion housing, only to find their communities torn apart by the Troubles and sorted into single-religion ghettoes. These women had kept in touch with friends from the old community and worried that memories of such communities would be lost, for their children would have no similar experience. Since then I have felt that this was a story that needed to be told. I knew that the body most credited with building such neighbourhoods was the Northern Ireland Housing Trust, established in 1945 to remedy the housing crisis caused by neglect and wartime bombings. At first I intended to tell the story of its work throughout Northern Ireland. However, this would have been a very large project, taking many years, and time was passing. There might not be many of the original residents left to tell their stories. This is why I decided to focus in on Belfast – where the housing crisis was worst – and in particular on the north Belfast Housing Trust estate where I grew up, the White City.

It was into this, one of the first-built mixed-religion estates, that my parents moved in 1949. By then we were a family of four including two children – my brother, aged four, and myself, aged one. Two sisters would arrive later, in 1953 and 1960. Here we lived until 1963. This book is a biography of that estate. Its title, *Hearthlands,* was devised to represent this key theme. It is also a survey of the times in which its people lived and operated. Because of my own personal connection with the estate, I was able to find former neighbours and family friends from that first generation of tenants. It started out with a notice I placed in the Ard Rí Fold in Glengormley, where my mother was then living, asking if any former White City residents would like to come together to share memories. This is how I first met Anna Pearson, one of the earliest residents of the new estate (she moved there in 1947), who had come from Donegal and remained in the White City until 2002. As with all those first residents who became my starting point, she had excellent recall and we would sit in her immaculate little flat talking about the past. One day I also met Anna's daughter, Moira Morrow, who joined in the reflections and, with another of Anna's daughters, Rosemary Walsh, has remained to help me ever since.

Thereafter I got in touch with others from that first generation – Shane and Philomena McAteer and Shane's sister Anne, by then a religious sister in Dublin. My family had never really lost touch with Shane and we all had fond memories of him as our fun-loving and infinitely generous choirmaster at St Mary's on the Hill in Glengormley. Another family friend was Flo Kelsey (who turned out to have been one of Anna's friends too) and we had a hilarious meeting – hilarious as much because of my incompetence with a rather-too-hi-tech recording device as from the various occasions on which Flo said laughingly, 'Best turn that off,' and then regaled us with some Belfast scandals, much to Anna's disapproval.

I learnt then that there is no 'one-size-fits-all' approach to memory retrieval and, since these were now my friends, I gleaned more from extended, informal conversations than set interviews. Along with my own mother, Sheila (O'Neill) Burns, Flo forms the backbone of this story. She is a remarkable woman, still the good-looking, natty dresser that I recall from my childhood; she is highly intelligent, with impressive recall and a wicked sense of humour. Until recently (July 2016) she continued to live in the White City, where she had been since 1949.

Of the next generations, I have been fortunate in having had generous input from Brian Dunn, who was born in the White City in 1951 and who today is its community officer, having been an active tenants' representative since the 1980s. Lizzy Welshman moved onto the estate on her marriage in 1955 and still lives there, as does her daughter May Doherty, who has also helped with the project. Gerry Mulholland's people had always lived in the area. He moved in as a seven-year-old in 1949, leaving when he married a local girl in 1963, but only moving to the adjacent Longlands area. Norah Van Puten lived on the estate from 1952 to 1962 and continued to live in north Belfast until 1972, when she moved to London. The Brooks sisters, May, Ena and Nessie, were our neighbours in the 1950s and 1960s. My sisters, Geraldine Walsh and Eleanor Dent, contributed their own stories, while Linda Taylor, a White City resident from 1976 to the present day, gave vital assistance in bringing me up to date with more recent developments. Many others have shared their memories with me, including some who had worked for the relevant housing authorities, and they are thanked in the acknowledgements. Others did the same, but preferred not to be named.

The first residents were young and had lived through the hardships and dangers of the Second World War. Some had lost their homes in the Belfast Blitz. Others were sharing overcrowded parental homes even after they had started their own families. Many of the men had just been demobbed from wartime service. My parents were twenty-six and twenty-nine years old when they moved onto the estate. My mother was from Kerry in the south-west of Ireland, my father from Belfast. They had met in Dublin, where my father was in the Irish army, and both had had difficult life trajectories. For some reason, which she never adequately explained, my mother had been sent away to a boarding school in Wexford – largely, it seems, to prepare her to be a farmer's wife. She hated it, not least because her other sisters, all three of them, escaped to England or America, where they had fulfilling nursing careers. My father's mother died shortly after his birth and his father remarried a much younger woman from Mayo, where they settled. My father was brought up by his mother's cousin and friend, Minnie Magee, first in the Old Lodge area of north Belfast, then in Albert Street on the lower Falls, where they had relocated during the sectarian troubles of 1935. By all accounts Mrs Magee was one of the world's genuinely kind and generous people, even though she was widowed young and had to raise a family of four, in addition to my father, in a two-up, two-down terraced house. These were our closest relatives when I was growing up.

When my parents met in Dublin, the kind of idealised future that young nationalists like my father aspired to beckoned, for he was about to receive a commission as an officer. His photo in dress uniform was proudly displayed in my childhood home. Soon, however, that dream fell apart. In the course of the required medical, it was discovered that he had contracted tuberculosis at an earlier stage of his service. He was sent home to Belfast, to the already overcrowded Magee household and a much bleaker career future. My parents married earlier than they had intended, largely because of the accommodation problems – good Catholics did not 'live in sin' in those days. This ended my mother's aspirations to a nursing career. Although she had been accepted to train in north Belfast's Mater hospital, nursing was one of those professions closed to married women. They were married in October 1944 in St Paul's Catholic Church on the Falls Road.

What happened afterwards is told in the following chapters of this book. Like the others to whom I spoke, my mother told of what it was like to acquire a tenancy of one of these state-of-the-art modern houses, of furnishing them in times of continued post-war rationing, of their new neighbours and friendships forged on the estate, and always of the new sense of space and beautiful landscape, in such contrast to their lives beforehand. This is also the story of how people related to place and neighbourhood. It does not deny the underlying sectarianism of Northern Ireland society, but shows that neighbourhood identity could be more important, particularly at a time when newspapers were rarely read and the television age was yet to come.

The neighbourhood in question is located between the Antrim, Whitewell and Serpentine Roads, immediately north-west of Greencastle and four miles from Belfast city centre. It is four miles of steady ascent towards Belfast Castle and Bellevue, and the location of these pleasure grounds was a fundamental part of the sense we had of rural living – a sense not usually associated with social housing. The climb out of town is guided by Belfast's iconic Cave Hill, which looms over the White City as one approaches it. The estate today is smaller, having been rebuilt in the 1990s after structural faults in the original design were found to be irreparable. But it is still referred to as the White City, an identifying name plaque positioned at its main entrance.

This is also a social history of Belfast in the decades before the Troubles, taking in popular pastimes, work, schooling, shopping, fashion, the arrival of the motor car and television, and above all the impact of the welfare state on working-class lives, after its introduction in the late 1940s. Then there were the not-so-ordinary events: the Curran murder of 1952 – to this day unsolved; the disastrous loss of the *Princess Victoria* in the great storm of 1953; and the stolen babies scandal of 1954–5, which involved the police forces of the whole island and was centred on an apparently respectable and hard-working family on the estate. All impacted on the White City, the last in particular opening a window onto how communities perceive and even protect their own black sheep.

The book is something of an alternative history of the institutions of Northern Ireland. It does not deny the iniquities that arose from one-party unionist rule, but it shows that the high-octane rhetoric that made its way into the press was not reflective of most people's lived experiences and that democratic values operated more often than commentators recognise. It goes behind the political decisions to chart the role of the civil servants – often a more accurate reflection of what actually happened than politicians' public statements – notably in the establishment of the Northern Ireland Housing Trust in 1945.

The Housing Trust was set up by the unionist government of the day, which often defended it against critics within the wider unionist tradition. Remarkably for a governing party with such a poor record in building social housing, the Unionist Party intended the new body to operate independently of Northern Ireland's often disreputable local councils. The trust, which built and managed the White City and similar estates all over Northern Ireland, was a rather admirable organisation. Taking its philosophy from Victorian philanthropy, it was committed to the idea that good environment as much as good housing determined working-class experience and aspirations, and it designed its estates accordingly. It also allocated housing on a needs-based, religion-blind system, so that its estates throughout Northern Ireland were mixed. This is also the story of the Housing Trust and of how its ideals informed our experiences of shared living. It is not quite so complimentary about the government's persistent failures in urban planning, however, and shows how such failures blighted ordinary lives and helped give rise to the Troubles.

The story is partly a memoir, my own recollections informing it up until 1963, when we moved. I might have stopped at that point, but

I felt that some explanation was needed for the transformation that has occurred in the religious and social profile of the White City since then. Two final chapters look at the politics of these decades, taking the community through the Troubles and showing how the estate went from being a mixed one to a Protestant, even loyalist, one. But it never entirely lost its mixed character and even today there are some Catholics remaining. They are mostly original tenants from the 1940s and as such are accepted as part of the neighbourhood community. But they are elderly and there is little likelihood of others moving in until continuing, though much-diminished, intercommunal tensions in the Greater Whitewell area become a thing of the past. Although the story of this mixed-religion estate has some relevance for societies experiencing intercommunal conflict, this is not intended to be a polemical treatise. It takes the view that the stories of these people's lives and experiences are worth telling for their own sake, particularly as their descendants may never experience such mixed-religion living, and the memories of such experiences are in danger of never being recorded. It is a history as well as a participant-observer memoir, recreating as far as possible the deep sense of place that helped define this particular community and that was and still is as much a part of its identity as any religious or political affiliation.

1

A Desirable Suburb

Place is everything … when you get there you know you belong …
you know you're kith and kin.

Colin Middleton (artist), 1967[1]

It was the outside space that I remember most about the White City – the large garden, the surrounding fields and woods, the sense of freedom and wildness. My mother believed that because our row of four houses was the last to be built on the estate, we had been the beneficiaries of the land that was left over. She was right, for early planning maps show the last four houses at the top of Portmore Hill having back gardens twice the size of others on the estate.[2] At the highest point of the estate, we also had unimpeded views over Belfast Lough and the Holywood hills. The sharp gradient from the lower slopes of the Cave Hill to the Whitewell Road was a real challenge to the planners of the 1940s, but a wondrous natural helter-skelter for generations of children. I recall a childhood full of bumps, falls, scratches and cuts, and the attendant whiff of Germolene and TCP.

The gardens were tableaux of the self-sustainability of the post-war generation. My father took particular pride in his large marrows and would share tips over the wire fence with our neighbour. The vegetable garden seemed to be a male preserve, while the front flower garden belonged to the women and children. The Housing Trust, which built the estate, went in for the kind of open-plan space often associated with North America. There was little to protect the vegetables and flowers from petty pilfering, which I do not recall, but which others do. Those at the top of the estate were also victims of early loss of light, as the sun went behind the overlooking Cave Hill.

The Cave Hill is Belfast's most iconic landmark and it towered over the estate. It figures prominently in that sense of having lived somewhere special, which is the common theme in the memories of everyone who has lived in the White City – a shared mentality shaped by environment. The French writer Guy Debord called this 'psychogeography' – the 'specific effects of the geographical environment, consciously organized or not, on the emotions and behavior of individuals'.[3] Geographers have long been aware of people's and entire nations' identification with particular landscapes and environments and of how those landscapes in turn affect lived relationships, producing a sense of belonging and shared identity.[4]

Did pride in place also extend to pride in people? Were we a community? The Housing Trust expressed the hope that their estates would grow into proper communities, though as far as I can see this too had an element of pride in place – keeping the estates nice. I also found today's older residents – who have lived on the estate for forty to fifty years or more – very protective of its environment and critical of newcomers who are less so. Their voices can be heard in a 1986 North Belfast Community Resource Centre report, following news that the estate was to be demolished and rebuilt. 'The Whitecity is a long established and traditional community,' wrote Brian Dunn, chairman of the estate's tenants' association. Residents were anxious about 'keeping the community together', some 70 per cent of respondents wanting to retain the same neighbours.[5] However, by then, 'community' did not mean quite the same as in the estate's earlier history. The Troubles had intervened and the term was well on its way to having the polarised meaning that it carries today. Anecdotally, 'the same neighbours' would have included Catholics. However, from 23 per cent in the 1971 census, the Catholic population of the White City had declined to 5 per cent in 1991, and that old 'community' was no more.

We marvel at how past ages could build those continental villages that seem to cling precariously to rocky escarpments. The sight of a modern estate such as the White City climbing up the lower slopes of the Cave Hill inspires similar wonder. Belfast is a most unlikely development, built on slob-land and intertidal mud-flats. Even today it is prone to frequent flooding. In the Protestant origin-myth, Belfast owes its creation and success to seventeenth-century planters from England and Scotland. But this is only partly true, for it already had a history of usage and settlement by various peoples by then: Ulaid, Gael and Anglo-Norman. These had the good sense to largely settle in the rising ground and surrounding hills, their presence marked by the ancient forts which were to give their names to the area's townlands.[6] This tendency would remain with wealthy Belfast people until the 1940s, when the policy of building workers' housing in the suburbs was rolled out.

The Antrim Road, along which the villas of the wealthy were located, was laid in 1827 and for a while the Belfast Charitable Society, which owned some of the land, kept an eye on anything that 'would lower the tone of the area'.[7] Beyond the lower Antrim Road lay some of the country seats of the local gentry (more accurately, Belfast's business class) and the acreage of the properties increased the further out of the city one travelled. So the extension of wealthy property up the Antrim Road followed a trend through existing demesnes and parkland.[8] Writing in 1960, social geographer Emrys Jones could still talk of the Antrim Road as north Belfast's equivalent of the affluent Malone Road, south of the city centre: 'The richer suburban spine of north Belfast continues to be the Antrim Road, its villas a reminder of the older landscape which it replaced.' This was the road along which I, and many others from the White City, travelled to school. By then the older villas were interspersed with larger numbers of the smaller, though still detached, houses of Belfast's middle class. In the 1950s the area still had the highest rateable values in the city, along with the Malone Road, even though it overlooked lower-status housing on the low-lying land of the shoreline.[9]

The surrounding hills of Belfast put a natural brake on development and it was views of housing visibly creeping up the hills in the 1950s that sparked protests about Belfast's lamentable urban-planning record.[10] Though it was a case of the penny looking down on the halfpenny, it was little wonder that White City residents felt privileged, for this was working-class housing invading the leafy suburbs of the middle and upper classes. Early residents had the expanses of Nissen huts and prefabricated bungalows on the Whitewell Road and in Greencastle to remind them of their superior living standards. Suburban housing estates, though common in England and Wales since 1918, only appeared on a 'significant scale' in Northern Ireland in 1945, and a survey carried out in 1953–4 singled out the White City as the most suburban of all the new estates.[11]

The White City lies in the townland of Ballygolan, in the parish of Carnmoney. It also fringes the lower-lying townlands of Drumnadrough and Greencastle. The author of the Ordnance Survey memoir of 1839 was impressed by the scenic contrasts of the area: 'The parish of Carnmoney presents extreme diversity of surface, and in the contrast of its bold and strongly marked features ... possesses an agreeable variety of scenery.' The name Ballygolan (Ballygoliagh), he explained, meant 'the townland of the heavy moist soil', the perfect natural ingredient for those mud marbles that we children used to make and dry in the summer sun.[12] Of the lower, eastern reaches bordering Belfast Lough, he noted 'very beautiful scenery', the shore 'fringed with planting to the water's edge. Its low grounds are exceedingly diversified and ornamented with numerous handsome residences.'[13] The higher, western side was 'bounded by the almost mountainous ridge which extends from the southern extremity ... and which rises abruptly to an elevation of from 500 to 1,200 feet ... a precipitous wall of basalt extends along the summit of the acclivity ... where it attains, in the summit of the Cave Hill, an extreme elevation of 1,185 feet above the sea. The eastern district of this hill is remarkably bold and presents a magnificent and varied profile. A precipitous and irregular wall of basalt from 50 to 250 feet high ranges along its summit.'[14]

Below the basalt of the Cave Hill scarp lies a thick layer of limestone. The chalk has been quarried since the earliest times and has given the prefix 'White' to many of the placenames in the area. In the second half of the nineteenth century a wagon-way took stone from the quarry on the side of the hill to the Shore Road, ingeniously using the steep slope to operate on a gravity-cable basis, the weight of the descending wagons pulling back the empty ones. From the Hightown Road to the Cavehill Road, cottages had been built to house the workers, colourfully known as Daddystown and Mammystown.[15] All around the Cave Hill such nineteenth-century workers' cottages survived into the 1960s and 1970s. By the 1940s they were already becoming relics of a time when the country and the town intertwined and the old countrywomen in their shawls were still recognisable in the Belfast streets. With the former gamekeeper's cottage just below the Cave Hill, they were also used as scouts' huts, and as many as fifteen scout groups operated in the north-Belfast to Glengormley area in the 1950s. By the late 1950s, empty and decaying, they started to be vandalised. The gamekeeper's cottage was burnt down in a number of arson attacks in 1957.[16]

The name 'Cave Hill' comes from the five caves cut into its face. Before that, its Irish name was Beann Mhadagáin, 'mountain of Matudan', whose father was one of the kings of the Ulaid, the ancient ruling dynasty of Ulster. The Iron-Age hillfort at the summit, now known as McArt's Fort, was his. There are also a number of smaller raths and souterrains below the Cave Hill, where refuge might have been found against the slave raiders of the day.[17] An early, rather primitive map of the Belfast area (c. 1570) describes this feature as 'hill with a cave' and 'Benmadiane', overlooking heavily wooded slopes down to the shore. The landscape is devoid of buildings except for 'Cloughnecastella', a small castle in what became Greencastle, and another at Whitehouse. These are described as 'two little piles below the Cave'.[18] Indeed, for many centuries 'the Cave' was the general designation of the area where the White City would be built in the late 1940s. Early maps show two substantial farms, Throne at the Whitewell Road end and Thronemount on the Antrim Road side, taking their names from local legend. In the eighteenth century Throne was already known as a place where 'whey and pure air' might be had and in 1872 the Throne lands were donated by mill-owner John Martin for the purpose of building a children's hospital.[19] This was the imposing Victorian edifice that adjoined the White City and proved a godsend to generations of worried parents with injured children.

The wealthy began to move out of Belfast in the eighteenth century. The area between the Cave Hill and Belfast Lough was already one of extensive parkland rather than a natural landscape. It had been laid out as such by the earl of Donegall, whose family, the Chichesters, had been granted Belfast and its surrounds in 1603. By 1611 Sir Arthur Chichester had already preserved the area as a park and hunting ground. In May 1795, it was in the Donegalls' deer park, just below where Belfast Castle stands today, that the Belfast United Irishmen hired a marquee to say goodbye to Wolfe Tone and his family before they sailed into exile in America.

F.J. Bigger, Protestant nationalist and ardent supporter of local history and culture, lived in one of those large Antrim Road villas just opposite Belfast Castle. His fascination with the United Irishmen has left us with an impressive antiquarian collection in Belfast's Central Library and he wrote frequently about the area in which he lived. He traced the route from Belfast to the Cave Hill that the 1795 group might have taken, up Buttermilk Loney, now Skegoneill Avenue, to the deer park, today's Old Cavehill Road. From there they would have progressed to the 1782 Volunteer Parade Grounds and along the steep Sheep's Path, through 'gorse banks, hazel dells, and broomy slopes to the Volunteer Well'.[20] The Volunteers were the armed wing of Protestant middle-class and gentry opposition to central (British) government, forcing a number of key constitutional reforms at the time. Both the United Irishmen and the Orange Order were later offshoots. From the Volunteer Well, the 1795 group of republicans would have been able to look down on the country residences of the leaders of enlightenment Belfast. From here the men ascended to McArt's Fort on the top of the Cave Hill to take the first oath of Irish republicanism. They were all Protestant and mostly Presbyterian, and there has remained an element of Ulster Protestant/unionist admiration for these founders of Irish republicanism, though, of course, it later became a largely Catholic tradition.

The textile workers in the area had a reputation for being 'intemperate, disorderly and unsettled'.[21] This may have been because of the largely Presbyterian character of the area, for Presbyterianism had little time for hierarchical traditions and any expected deference from lower sorts. South Antrim was one of those areas not subjected to the Ulster Plantation, with people arriving and settling from Scotland over many centuries instead. Anglican-dominated governments in Dublin and London feared and disliked these Presbyterians. Certainly, a highly attuned concept of their rights produced a number of politico-economic protests in the eighteenth century,[22] and such radicalism shaded into the United Irishmen in the 1790s: 'In the parish of Carnmoney,' recalled William Grimshaw, who had been a teenager in the 1798 period and, along with his brothers, a United Irishman, 'I never knew a man, born within its precincts, who was not a United Irishman, and, moreover, of the Protestant religion, almost wholly Presbyterians.' Such was 'the universality of the spirit of opposition to the late administration' in the parish that, when an amnesty was offered, 'not less than seven hundred persons, of adult age, took the oath of allegiance, before a magistrate, in the Presbyterian meeting-house'.[23]

The Grimshaws had been the most important landholders and industrialists in the Ballygolan, Whitehouse and Greencastle areas since the eighteenth century. William Grimshaw also tells of how his father's employees were deterred from fighting with the 1798 rebels at the Battle of Antrim for fear that his buildings and machinery would be destroyed in reprisal and the thousand handloom weavers and other workers would lose their livelihoods.[24] The area was still overwhelmingly Presbyterian in the 1830s. With Catholics now also finding employment in the mills, the Grimshaw family endowed two chapels for them at Whitehouse and Greencastle, which still served the White City estate when I lived there in the 1950s and 1960s.[25]

The Cave Hill was a regular haunt of these United Irishmen. They were young and frequently walked out from Belfast into the countryside. Thomas Russell, the handsome young officer from Cork, talked of spending happy times there with his love, Eliza Goddard. In 1794 Henry Joy McCracken had fathered a child with the daughter of gamekeeper David Bodell, who lived beside the Cave Hill. McCracken, his two brothers and others returned to take refuge there after their defeat at the Battle of Antrim during the 1798 Rebellion. His sister, Mary Ann, and sister-in-law had spent several days searching for him, walking along the shore to Whitehouse and from there up to the Cave Hill and other hills surrounding Belfast – quite a feat for young middle-class women in an area thick with soldiers and defeated rebels. Henry Joy McCracken was a hero of the common people of the area and had spent much time among them. There is certainly a sense that they helped and accommodated both him and his sisters on a hillside that was clearly more populated than in the twentieth century. Mary Ann arranged a boat to take Henry from the coast, but he was arrested on his way to the ship and, in early July, brought to Carrickfergus

Gaol. He was later executed in Belfast. Mary Ann raised the little girl, Maria, and helped her mother, Mary Bodell, and her family to reach America.[26] Little wonder, then, that the Cave Hill is often linked with tragic love or that the doomed liaison was the centrepiece of Stewart Parker's most famous play, *The Northern Star*.

The Cave Hill dominates both the physical and the imaginative landscape of Belfast. It pervades the personality of north Belfast in particular, and of all who have lived there. It towers over the White City like some great Moses figure. There was always a physical sense of looking upwards in the White City. Predictably, when brought together in 2000 to produce a quilt of their memories, its older residents chose the Cave Hill as its centrepiece. In many of the literary and historical references to the Cave Hill, the idea of access and escape to a wilder, more natural world prevails. Jonathan Swift was said to have taken the idea for *Gulliver's Travels* from it. For Derek Mahon, it could save us from 'the squinting heart' and 'perverse pride' in always feeling wronged:

> We could *all* be saved by keeping an eye on the hill
> At the top of every street, for there it is,
> Eternally, if irrelevantly, visible – [27]

People in this part of Belfast do not refer to the Cave Hill in two words, merely as a geographical name, but elide the words into 'Caavill', like a personal name. The name of its highest promontory, McArt's Fort, also is personalised as 'Napoleon's Nose'.[28] I have not been able to trace the derivation of this name, although it may have come from the owner of a villa below, just off the Antrim Road. That villa was built in 1860 by wealthy explorer and ship designer Captain William McAteer. He called it St Helena because of his admiration for Napoleon and it was said to have been a replica of the house in which Napoleon died. He went further, erecting an eight-foot-high statue of Napoleon on the roof. When the statue was blown down, damaging the roof, he re-erected it in the garden, where it became quite a curiosity, visible from the Antrim Road.[29] Knowing the irreverent wit of Belfast people, I imagine a comment on the damaged house and statue might have gone something along the lines of, 'Well, he still has

Napoleon's nose above,' and that was too good not to enter local lore. But this is quite unproven and I may be wrong, particularly since the resemblance to Napoleon's face was noted in the *Belfast News Letter* as already existing in 1845.[30]

For White City residents the Cave Hill had a permanent and proximate visual presence, weather patterns starkly visible against its greyness, often dictating moods, much as they had in Marjory Alyn's semi-autobiographical account of growing up in the White City, *The Sound of Anthems*. It also served to block more housing development, further contributing to that sense of living in a wild and wonderful place – quite the opposite of estate-living stereotypes.[31]

Such a personal relationship with this special landscape feature was not new. A famous right-of-way case in 1859 – won by an impressive cross-class campaign – illustrates this. The case was taken against one of the earl of Donegall's tenants – a newcomer, the merchant Joseph Magill – for blocking the customary right of way from the Antrim Road to the Cave Hill. Magill was the son-in-law of Andrew Nash, a naval lieutenant from Cork and a Catholic. Stationed in Belfast in 1817, he encountered Sarah Orr while riding over the Cave Hill. Through marriage he became one of the area's 'middlemen' or substantial leaseholders, in this case holding 151 acres from Donegall, and the immediate landlord of those lower down the social scale. Magill had built himself a villa, 'Martlett Towers', and a porter's lodge that straddled the old path. The Association for the Protection of the Public Rights of Way, with sixty-eight founding members including Belfast's mayor, was set up to challenge Magill. In January 1856 notice was served on him to remove the restrictions, since 'from time immemorial a right of way has existed to the Cave Hill, from the High Road between Belfast and Antrim'. The Association also gained the support of the marquess of Donegall: 'My own wish is that the people should continue to enjoy the customary resort to the Hill for amusement and recreation.'[32]

But the main force behind the campaign was the Grimshaw family. The senior member of the family, the 87-year-old James Grimshaw, was the leading figure against Magill. His father had been a Volunteer captain. He recalled mingling with the Volunteers on the hill in the 1780s and 1790s and was angry that the landmark of the Volunteer Well near the path was also blocked by Magill's outbuildings. He could remember turf being brought down the path by horse and cart to Greencastle, as well as travelling that way with his father on horseback to buy linen in Glenavy. He and others also spoke of the traditional Easter Monday fair on the Cave Hill, when as many as 20,000 would go there and tents, dancing, poteen – 'for the Belfast Mountains harboured many a still' – egg-rolling, ballad-singing and other amusements would await.[33] The traditional route to the pathway and Cave Hill ran up from Greencastle through Gray's Lane, along which traders would convey cockles, mussels and willicks (periwinkles) from the shore. Magill lost the case. There were 'wild scenes' of public celebration from people in the locality and the right to roam on the Cave Hill remained thereafter. It was during this affair that the idea of granting the grounds of Belfast Castle to the people emerged.[34]

The Cave Hill right-of-way case highlighted the changes to the landscape that were occurring in the Victorian period. In the 1830s the Ordnance Survey found a landscape that had been stripped by centuries of small-scale farming and was inhabited by poorer people than those who were now constructing villas and enclosing gardens and orchards. It noted remains of the natural woodland in the thinly scattered 'stunted brushwood' being 'eaten down by cattle, and … rapidly disappearing before the operations of the husbandman'. Cattle continue to be grazed on the Cave Hill to this day and were grazed lower down the hill until the White City was built.[35] So the leafier aspects that were so appealing in the 1940s and 1950s owed much to replanting by this class of wealthy residents who moved there in the latter half of the nineteenth century. Their parkland was already performing that role of 'Belfast's playground' that would make it such a special place for White City residents.

The second marquess of Donegall squandered most of his estate and what was left passed to the Shaftesbury family in the 1880s. Before the Antrim Road was built up, older Belfast residents recalled the Shaftesbury estate wall extending the entire length of the road, from the Old Cavehill Road to the Sheep's Path.[36] The ninth earl of Shaftesbury (1869–1961) had lengthy associations with Belfast, serving as lord lieutenant, lord mayor and chancellor of Queen's University (in 1909–23). It was to him that we were especially indebted for our own Arcadia, for in 1934 he donated Belfast Castle – by then empty and unsaleable – and some two hundred acres of demesne land to Belfast Corporation. The memorandum of agreement carried certain restrictions on the usage of the new acquisition, and, mercifully, it was decided that 'the grounds should remain an open space, available to the public'.[37] They still do. At one stage a Museum of Ulster Life and Tradition was mooted for the Belfast Castle estate, but held up by the post-war shortage of steel.[38] Given the extensive grounds and entrance fees at the museum's final home at Cultra, it is difficult to see how this would have complied with the original agreement. As it was, the idea of nearby open country, with uninhibited open access, became part of a sense of well-being emanating from the public literature of the 1950s. In its 'sightseeing by public transport', the *Belfast Official Handbook* advised:

> On this route also on the side of Cave Hill and surrounded by 200 acres of beautiful grounds, stands Belfast Castle … The Castle contains a magnificent ballroom and café, the view from which across the Belfast Lough to the County Down coast is superb in its splendour … The grounds are beautifully wooded and provide an enchanting retreat in which one may while away the hours far from the noise and bustle of the City, while the mountain air to be breathed here laden with the smell of health-giving pines, is wholly delightful.[39]

A 1937 government inquiry into the corporation's request for finance to upgrade Belfast Castle detailed the facilities:

> The Castle and its demesne of some 200 acres, situated on a steep slope rising sharply to the Cave Hill, became the property of the Corporation some two years ago, under certain conditions as to the use to which the Castle could be put. The grounds are heavily wooded, with quantities of rhododendrons and shrubs, and do not appear to be adaptable to any other purpose than that of a park with

walks and footpaths. The Castle itself [built in the late 1860s]
is a square, castellated, four-storeyed building, approached
by two long winding avenues.

The description of the castle's interior reflects previous gentry
use, the basement housing domestic offices and some staff, though
opening onto the front terraces on the east side, the ground floor the
principal day-rooms, the first floor the main bedrooms, the second
floor 'minor' bedrooms and staff accommodation. The plan was to
generate income by providing facilities for light refreshments and to
turn the main reception rooms into a ballroom, hosting three evening
and two afternoon dances per week. The entertainments manager felt
confident of 'sufficient patronage'. The grounds would not be altered,
except to repair the existing roadways and add a small car park for fifty
to sixty cars. There was some public concern, expressed by ninety-five
ratepayers, about potential damage to the grounds should the dance-
hall attract 'undesirable persons'. The report agreed that 'the grounds
are a magnificent open space and should be kept in their present natural
condition'. The general manager of Belfast Corporation Tramways,
which had oversight of the castle's finances, calmed such concerns by
pointing to the public's 'respect for property' in the nearby Bellevue
and Hazelwood pleasure gardens, and assured them 'that everything
would be done to preserve the amenities of the estate, and to see that
dancing was carried on in an orderly and proper manner'.[40]
    Thus did every photo album of local residents come to contain
pictures of families in their Sunday best, the parents posing as lords and
ladies of the manor in front of the castle, the children clutching bundles
of bluebells, which proliferated in the grounds. Since my parents were
almost pathologically law- and rule-abiding, I cannot believe they
would have allowed us to pick the flowers had it not been an accepted
practice. Indeed, in 1923 Bigger described 'the youngsters gathering
posies of primroses and blue hyacinths [bluebells]'.[41] Marjory Alyn's
young heroine describes the castle grounds as a magical forest, the
'shocking pageantry' of the crimson rhododendrons and 'strangely
muted brilliance of thousands of bluebells' inducing a kind of stupor:
'The deep blue carpet, shading to light purple in the shadows,
sprawled everywhere, around the trees and up and down the fern

banks.'[42] There were a small number of long-term leaseholders and tenants on the demesne, largely towards the Antrim Road end. In order, it seems, to retain the views and character of the area, it was forbidden to build property, unless it was of a high value and set back from the Antrim Road.

One of the objections raised to the dances at the castle was the competition they would pose to similar events in the Floral Hall, barely a mile up the Antrim Road at Bellevue. This was part of the famous Bellevue/Hazelwood park, a huge adventure playground, open to the public, which we just referred to as Bellevue. From the late nineteenth century Bellevue had been the name of the pleasure gardens further up the Antrim Road at Glengormley. The old gardens were a popular attraction for Belfast workers, partly because of the alcoholic refreshments available on Sundays, when Sunday opening for anything, let alone alcohol, was already controversial. Transport from Belfast developed to serve this extremely popular venue – first horse-drawn trams from the 1880s, then electrified ones from 1906, with over four million tram journeys recorded on that section for the summer months alone in 1934.[43]

When the Belfast Corporation Tramways Department took over the tramline in 1911, thereby releasing a site near the junctions of the Antrim and Whitewell Roads, a decision was taken to move and extend the gardens to the present Bellevue area. As the work got under way, news of the scheme was greeted with enthusiasm by the local press. It would be a place where Belfast's workers 'can enjoy themselves far from the surroundings of their toiling hours … an opportunity for revelling in real rural surroundings'. The *Belfast Evening Telegraph* was rhapsodic:

> The place is happily named Bellevue, for no more beautiful view is to be found in Ulster than the outlook towards the lough, over undulating hills, delightfully pastured valleys, wooded avenues, interspersed with charming residences and mansion houses, down to the foreshore, and on over the lough where Bangor can be seen, and on a clear day the coast of Scotland is visible. It is indeed a fitting climax to a glorious tram ride, ending as it does with a magnificent

panoramic view that bursts suddenly on the sight and charms the spectator with its beauty … When the grounds are ultimately finished and open to the public it is not too much to say that they will be one of the greatest and most unique pleasure grounds in the Three Kingdoms.[44]

In a little gem of local history, *Bellevue: Belfast's Mountain Playground*, Stewart McFetridge charts the logistical problems of developing the site. The steep lower slopes of the Cave Hill, adjoining the Antrim Road, were liable to subsidence, owing to quarry waste and scree having been dumped on top of the clay substratum. Of course, all of this added to the sense of adventure for us local children. One of the many thrills of Bellevue was the mad dash down the steep and winding steps from the playground. We would barely be able to stop before being deposited onto a perilous bend on the Antrim Road.

Despite the escalating costs, the huge amount of concrete needed to prevent subsidence of the majestic staircase linking Bellevue to the Antrim Road and the burning down of the new tea house by suffragettes in 1914, Bellevue was formally opened by the lord mayor of Belfast on 10 July 1920. Military bands regularly played in the bandstand and from 1923 another attraction was added in the form of an open-air dance floor, with tiers of seats hewn from the rocks. Until the mid-1930s, Bellevue's dances reflected the Fred Astaire age, as male dancers took to the floor in tails and starched shirts, the female dancers in silk gowns. A miniature golf course was also developed at this time. The house and grounds of Hazelwood were added to the pleasure gardens in 1923. The house was turned into a café, with glazed verandas, cabarets starting at 9 p.m. and dancing supplementing the outdoor dances until the Floral Hall was built in 1936.

The acquisition of Hazelwood also permitted the development of one of the most attractive features, as I recall – the central boating lake, with ducks to feed and pedalos for a special treat. It was excavated around a natural ancient feature called Ballygolan Fort. This was described in the 1838–9 Ordnance Survey memoirs as being on the land of Robert McFarren, 'now under tillage'; the original trench had been destroyed.[45] This seems to have been an ancient crannog or small lake dwelling. Crannogs date from the early Christian period and some were still in use in the seventeenth century. Constructing them required large quantities of wood and, since there are three in the general area, they would have made 'significant inroads into the local woodlands'.[46]

The 1830s Ordnance Survey also located two fairy-thorn bushes in the area but, given that my parents were not aware of these, and the fact that they had a heightened awareness of such old Irish fears and superstitions, the trees must have disappeared by the mid-twentieth century. A zoo, covering twelve acres to the sides of the Bellevue staircase, was added in 1934. McFetridge tells the hilarious story of the arrival of the first elephant that year. She was walked up the long ascent from Belfast docks by a very young keeper and raided the bread vans and vegetable stalls as she progressed through north Belfast up York Street and the Antrim Road. She too was experiencing that long climb out of Belfast that had challenged horse-drawn carts and trams in the past. Predictably, her search for water became urgent as the ascent steepened towards the castle, where she clambered into a horse trough and gave herself an elephant bath, much to the shock of people in passing trams and carts.[47]

The Floral Hall – Belfast's Art-Deco masterpiece – was added in May 1936. Circular and domed, with a diameter of eighty-five feet, an unobstructed floor area that could seat a thousand people and glass-roofed terraces, this would remain Belfast's pre-eminent ballroom of romance until the 1960s.[48] To such an abundance of leisure provision was added the icing on the cake, at least for the teenagers: the amusement park. Along with a miniature railway, it was initially organised and run by a Blackpool-based family, but was revamped in 1951 by legendary funfair organisers and local family, the Barrys – just in time to benefit the first generation of White City children. Although the pleasure gardens remained open throughout the war, the July holidays witnessing the normal influx and Floral Hall dances attracting 182,969 in 1943–4,[49] evening activities were restricted and the summer lights and fireworks disappeared because of the blackout. Indeed Belfast went through a bleak period during the war, the dangerous animals in the zoo having to be put down. But Sheila the elephant survived to become the star attraction of my childhood. During the Blitz, the young elephant was looked after by a keeper, Denise Austin, in her back yard on the nearby Whitewell Road. Each evening the unlikely pair would walk to the house, returning to the zoo in the morning via the Throne stores, where Sheila would be given stale bread. Though Sheila died in 1966 and Denise followed her in 1997, the story inspired Michael Morpurgo's 2010 work *An Elephant in the Garden* and, in 2016–17, the feature film *Zoo*.[50]

However, as with Belfast as a whole, the revival of pleasure activities after the war took on a new life and Bellevue entered its golden age. Fleets of trams, then trolleybuses from 1949, ferried massive crowds from Belfast city centre to Bellevue in its heyday and late transport was available for the trip back. By 1959 crowds of over a hundred thousand were being recorded at Easter, sixty thousand on Easter Monday alone.[51] A resident dance orchestra of eight musicians played nightly to a packed Floral Hall until new safety regulations in 1959 restricted the numbers to 1,250. In May 1953 fifteen thousand people turned up for Coronation Day celebrations. From 7 a.m. they queued at the Floral Hall for a live television transmission to take place at 10.15 a.m., and most had to be turned away. But they had brought picnics and, on a day when Belfast was 'basking in sunshine', were entertained by folk dancing, military bands and displays by various groups: judo, fencing, football clubs, Girl Guides, Boy Scouts, the Boys' Brigade and women's keep-fit associations.[52]

In the 1950s pictures of Bellevue and the Floral Hall graced every Northern Ireland tourist and trade booklet.[53] 'Bellevue Gardens, unrivalled for pleasure and picnics, magnificent views, picturesque scenery,' proclaimed Belfast's *Official Handbook* for 1950: 'dancing nightly' at the Floral Hall, nine holes of miniature golf, 'one of the most varied and finest collections of animals, etc., outside London', a children's playground with donkey rides and sand pit, and a moderately priced café open daily – all for a threepenny trolleybus fare from the city.[54]

In the evenings the Floral Hall and pleasure gardens were festooned with coloured lights, and dancers and courting couples could wander through the grounds. As a child I recall peeking out from behind our bedroom curtains and thinking how elegant the returning dancers looked. Whilst the castle's more formal dances were where one went when 'going steady', the Floral Hall was where one went to meet in the first place. The whole area around the Cave Hill, Belfast Castle and Bellevue was considered 'a great courting place', and figures as such in the fiction of the period and in females' recollections of being warned of the attendant dangers.[55] It was all very different from the bleak reputation that Belfast acquired. With some 127,917 dancers recorded for 1947 in the Floral Hall, and 17,194 who paid for admission to fireworks and a military band concert in July 1948, Belfast was partying in those post-war times. I never remember being bored, even in my difficult mid-teenage years. Bellevue was always to hand and as teenagers we could listen to the latest hit songs being played at Barry's and flirt with the local schoolboys hired for the summer.

Throughout the Belfast Corporation debates and correspondence concerning the Belfast Castle, Bellevue and Hazelwood sites, there is a recurrence of the idea that they 'belonged to the people' and should remain open to the public. Belfast Lord Mayor Sir Crawford McCullagh said as much at the Floral Hall's opening ceremony on 4 May 1936, though he believed that it also had to be 'a paying proposition'. 'However, it was his and his colleagues belief that a great city like Belfast could not count everything in pounds, shillings and pence … the public should realise that the hall belonged to them and not private enterprise.'[56] Certainly in the 1950s and 1960s White City children treated the area like a big open playground. It actually did also contain a traditional playground, with swings from which, if you swung high enough, you had the sensation of flying over Belfast Lough.

Bellevue intermittently ran into Sunday-closure campaigns. 'The Protestant Sunday' was what made Belfast a 'dismal' place for visitors and was a particular problem when American troops were based in Northern Ireland during World War II.[57] On Bellevue's first opening in the 1930s, seven-day operation was the policy. This was challenged in a much-publicised Belfast Corporation debate in 1956. Unionist councillor James Dixon argued that the seven-day policy had been the outcome of a secret ballot in 1933, and implied that if councillors had to face their constituents they might vote otherwise. Those proposing the closure argued from their 'heritage … handed down from their ancestors'. With fairground amusements instead of Sunday observance, argued Councillor Walsh, 'we will have a Continental Sunday worse than in England'. Those opposing the motion pointed to the contradiction of trying to close pitch and putt at Bellevue and doing nothing about the many golf courses that operated on Sundays. 'Belfast was dull enough at the best of times,' argued Councillor Marrinan. Bellevue brought a 'little brightness ... to Sunday' and he thought Councillor Dixon 'was carried away with the doctrine of Calvin'. The motion was rejected, but by a very small margin, twenty-five to twenty-two.[58] On this occasion there was cross-party opposition to Dixon's motion, including from all the women councillors as well as from the Council of Social Welfare of the Methodist Church. 'Having regard to the crowded and restricted conditions in which many citizens live, and out of concern for their health and happiness,' it approved of the opening of children's playgrounds and parks on Sundays and had no objection to Bellevue or Hazelwood.[59] But the closures eventually came in 1964 and are indelibly linked to the rise of Ian Paisley, whose new Free Presbyterian Church, backed by the Orange Order, campaigned successfully to reverse the narrowly won decision to stay open. The press satirised the controversy as symbolising the low level of political debate.[60] But Dixon's warning came to pass in the municipal elections of 1967, when those liberal unionist councillors who had voted in favour of Sunday opening were not renominated by their local association.[61]

The other physical characteristic that struck the Ordnance Survey recorder in the 1830s was 'the numerous streams which irrigate the surface of this parish ... trickling down the steep declivities ... and as they issue from a limestone bottom their water is of an excellent quality'.[62] I remember a multitude of rivulets and marshy ponds in the nearby fields where we played and our Labrador dog wallowed in the crater pond created by the 1941 bombings. There was a real boundary between the upper and lower fields, marked by a stream full of wild rushes and bridged by a fallen tree. Storms would regularly bring down trees in the area and the men of the estate would arrive with saws and hatchets to claim firewood. The tree would function also as our stage, particularly when Mickey Duffy would regularly join us from the Whitewell cottages. Though older than us, Mickey added to our range of entertainments, for he was as enamoured of the same American westerns as ourselves. From our imaginary stage he would strum an old guitar to the 1957 Australian hit song, 'Pub with No

Beer'. Just as the Ordnance Survey memoir found back in the 1830s, tiny streams still oozed from the floor of the forest, through which we children reached Bellevue, where we spent many summers climbing trees, making woodland dens and decking them with the bluebells, violets, primroses, forget-me-nots and sweet-smelling delicately pink wild roses that grew in abundance in the early summer. It made for a magical dell-like landscape for White City children – ponds full of tadpoles and wild irises; rivulets to be bridged with driftwood and stones, marking out imaginary territories. But it also made for excessive dampness in the winter and treacherous walks to bus stops up the adjacent Snaky Path, which regularly iced over and tended to flood at lower levels.

In the 1830s it was this 'incalculably valuable extent of water' that was powering thirteen mills and 'manufactories' in the parish. There had been various forms of linen production in Ulster for many centuries, the moist atmosphere lending itself to the growth of flax, its staple product. However, it was the higher end of the market that had established itself in the area by the second quarter of the eighteenth century. The production of cotton also arrived in 1784, when the first cotton mill in Ireland was built at Whitehouse by Lancashire-born Nicholas Grimshaw – the beginning of that family's lengthy association with the area.[63] Grimshaw built another mill at Greencastle three years later, and a market house in 1793. The Grimshaws seem to have been quite paternalistic, building a school, cottages and other amenities for their workers. Over the next fifty years the area was considered a model of efficient industry and good living standards for working people. They also built a quay on the lough shore, which could import coal more cheaply than if it came through Belfast and supplied the factories and bleach greens in the whole area as far as Antrim. Neat rows of houses were built for the workers, mostly on both sides of the Belfast to Carrickfergus Road, though some straggled up the ascent from Whitehouse towards the Antrim Road, along what we knew as Mill Road. Marjory Alyn's young heroine, Jennifer, described such cottages in Greencastle as they still existed until the 1950s:

> On the lough side of the Shore Road, where Aunt Nin
> lived, the land is flat, its sandy soil supporting lanes of tiny

whitewashed row houses ... Aunt Nin's house had windows
little bigger than postage stamps and walls two feet thick
that, Grandmother said, did bugger all to keep the damp
out. They'd been built over a hundred years ago, before the
great famine.[64]

Further up the Whitewell Road, between the Throne and
Church Road, were another cotton factory, a bleach green, a flax-
spinning mill (offering employment to 266 people, 175 of them
female) and associated dams. In nearby Whiteabbey, two large flax-
spinning mills, established in 1760, were employing 440 workers by
the 1830s.[65] All of Marjory Alyn's working-age female characters
worked in the local mills and I recall many White City women still
working there in the 1950s.

Grimshaw's 1805 will – leaving his lands and properties to his sons
James, Thomas and Edmund and his daughter, Mary Anne Murphy
– describes a well-cultivated landscape stretching from Greencastle
to Whitehouse and north-west to the top of the Throne Road, the
future Longlands. There are a number of substantial houses, including
his own and those inhabited by his sons, with orchards and gardens
bounded by thorn hedges and various paths. The 1832–3 Ordnance
Survey map identifies these, including those which later became the
Throne Path down from the Antrim Road, as well as the White City's
iconic walkway, the Snaky Path. Apart from the lower reaches of the
Cave Hill, the area in the 1832 map is not as wooded as I recall in the
1950s and 1960s, and is largely arable and pasture. Otherwise, the main
feature of both documents is the extensive numbers of mills, dams,
watercourses, bleach greens, soaping and dyeing houses associated
with the textile and printing concerns.[66] There is a concentration of
such concerns along the Mill Road, where we used walk with our
mother to the maternity and child-welfare clinic in the British Legion
hall.[67] The Mill Road was lined with the neat workers' cottages that
Grimshaw built and it passed by the largest of his dams, the Mill Dam.
The dam presented a constant worry to White City parents, particularly
after a four-year-old child was drowned there in 1960.[68] I also recall
stories of unwanted kitten litters being drowned in it. This industrial
archaeology would help define our space when the housing followed.

The other artery along which residents access the estate is the Serpentine Road. This tortuously winding residential road runs between the Antrim and Whitewell Roads. It does not appear on the 1832–3 Ordnance Survey map, but does on the 1901–2 map. Then it was still surrounded by open countryside. By 1920–2, however, the suburban creep of the middle classes was visible in the smaller detached villas at the top end, diminishing in size as one descended, reaching the more built-up terraces of the salaried working-class at the bottom.[69]

Within the boundaries of the Antrim, Serpentine and Whitewell Roads, the Housing Trust had given us an environment which was recognised as different from and better than what had gone before and this in turn impacted on our lived relationships. Unlike 'the mere multiplication of houses which had characterised pre-war building', these post-war planners had discovered the idea of 'neighbourhood' and sought to implement it in new estates like the White City.[70]

2

'A Benevolent Public Body': The Northern Ireland Housing Trust

[T]he Trust is a benevolent public body different from the average landlord to whom most tenants have been accustomed.

Royal Institute of British Architects, 1949.[1]

On the morning of 2 July 1969 representatives from the Northern Ireland Housing Trust appeared before the Cameron Commission, set up to investigate the outbreak of the Troubles in Northern Ireland. The trust's chairman, Herbert Bryson, had served (unpaid) on the Housing Trust since its inception in 1945 and had been instrumental in the transformation of working-class housing in Northern Ireland. Now, however, it was the discriminatory record of some local councils in Northern Ireland that was under scrutiny and he was repeatedly questioned on the religious make-up of the trust and the tenants on its estates. The trust had always prided itself on its impartiality, so this was painful for the tall, dignified and elderly man who seemed to have stepped in from another age. Was the first chairman, Sir Lucius O'Brien, Protestant, he was asked. The term sounded stark.

'He was a member of the Society of Friends and I think that qualifies as a Protestant, although I sometimes doubt it. I can speak with authority here because I am married to a Quaker.'

'How did it happen that for so long there was no Catholic member of the board?' continued his interrogator. A Catholic board member had not been appointed until 1968.

'The Board, as you know, is appointed by the minister,' answered Bryson. 'For quite a long time we pressed … for a Roman Catholic to be appointed [when vacancies came up, only for two ministers in succession to declare it] inappropriate and they would not accept our advice.'

'Inappropriate?' asked Lord Cameron. Was that not simply the conventional way of saying no?

Bryson thought not. They very probably did wish eventually to appoint a Catholic, but each time there seemed to be 'some political difficulties'.

'Are you or any of your board in a political party?'

'I am not.'

The point is made again.

'Two are Unionist. I do not know of the others and think not.'

'What of the officers? Are Catholics and Protestants employed?'

'Oh yes.' He had no precise information, 'but we do try in our housing management – that is, our women housing managers, of whom we have quite a number – to see that the balance is approximately two-thirds to one-third.'[2] And so they did, even against ultra-unionist protest.

It is a poignant encounter: the new reality of sectarian head-counting breaking into an older world, which operated on a 'whatever you say, say nothing' culture of brushing controversial issues under the carpet. There is an element of this in the history of the Housing Trust. However, it is more accurate to see this as a new harshness pitted against a culture in which people like Bryson and his colleagues genuinely tried to work neutrally, despite the restrictions. I grew up hearing a lot about the Housing Trust from my parents' generation, who owed it their opportunity for a new life.

Since the creation of the new state of Northern Ireland in 1921, the workers of Belfast had not been well served in terms of housing. 'There was no city in England, Wales or Scotland,' commented future Housing Executive chairman Charles Brett, 'whose house-building record in the inter-war years, whether in the public or private sector, or taking the two together, was worse than that of Belfast.'[3] Fears of socialism, the stranglehold of private and moneyed interests, the pusillanimity and prejudice of the local councils and class snobbery – the power of the ratepayers – made Belfast a city of slums. There was an ingrained belief that such matters should be left to private enterprise. Against all the evidence, the lord mayor of Belfast, Sir Crawford McCullagh, could still argue in January 1945 that private enterprise would resolve the housing crisis, and that it would take at least eighty years for it to do so.[4] This deference to 'private enterprise' shocked observers from Great Britain, particularly since such private housing attracted public subsidies in Northern Ireland. In fact, of the 36,483 houses built under Northern Ireland Housing Acts between 1919 and 1939, the bulk (32,644) had been built by private builders with government subsidies, only 3,839 (190 per annum) by local authorities.[5] The 1944 report into housing in Northern Ireland – the first ever such report – was critical: the 'comparatively well off were housed with the aid of public money, part of which was contributed by persons in less fortunate circumstances'.[6] Between the wars Belfast Corporation built less than a tenth of the 20,420 houses erected, and none after 1930. Despite a population increase of 425 per cent in Belfast and its surrounding townlands between the 1901 and 1951 censuses, no estates such as those in Great Britain had been built.[7] Belfast's housing stock was further reduced by the German bombardment of built-up areas in 1941. Before the war there had been 117,000 houses in Belfast. By the end of 1941, 56,000 had been damaged by the bombings and 3,200 had been entirely destroyed.

It was their experience of the suffering of people bombed out of their homes that turned Lucius O'Brien and Herbert Bryson, welfare officers in the Civil Defence Authority, into campaigners. They had a survey carried out that made 'urgent representations' to the government on the need for more houses. The result was the first ever survey of housing conditions in Northern Ireland in 1944, which estimated an immediate need for a hundred thousand new houses.[8] But that was considered an underestimate, for past neglect and recent damage meant that a further eighty thousand houses were in need of repair or improvement:[9] 'It was calculated that a complete programme of slum clearance, and provision for the abatement of overcrowding, would probably involve the building of at least 200,000 houses,' nearly two-thirds of the entire existing stock.[10] Reports by the Belfast medical officer ascribed the high incidence of tuberculosis in Belfast to poor and overcrowded accommodation.[11] Indeed, Belfast had the most overcrowding, worst lack of open space and highest infant mortality of any industrial city in the UK, Glasgow included.[12] The scale of infant mortality in Belfast – one in ten dying before the age of one – was also attributed to poor housing conditions.[13] As wartime industry began to wind down, and even before the return of demobbed servicemen and women and others from war work in Britain, some thirty thousand men and women 'paraded' through Belfast on 28 March 1945 calling for work and homes, and holding the Northern Ireland government responsible.[14] The suffering crossed sectarian boundaries, despite the old stereotype of Catholics as being poorer and underprivileged. The Blitz had caused severe damage in predominantly Protestant working-class areas.[15] On 8 September 1945 homeless women from east Belfast 'with babes in arms flocked to the Belfast City Hall' to tell their councillors about 'the terrible housing conditions in that part of the city'.[16]

Certainly the issue of homelessness and housing was uniting people in Northern Ireland as never before. Even civil servants were frustrated with the politicians. In an irreverent and critical letter about the way wartime needs seemed to have been used as an excuse to do nothing, Adrian Robinson, secretary to the minister of home affairs, wrote to the Ministry of Commerce: 'The position as I see it really is that during the 10 years before the war no slum clearance whatever was done in Belfast, and as a result, when the war came, we had an undue proportion of extremely bad housing.' After the Blitz, claims for war damage were much higher than in England because 'the housing is in such foul condition that the moment you get on to the roof to put a slate on you disappear through the roof and into the dining room on the ground floor! It seems also very relevant to me that 10,000 houses were found by the Medical Officer of Health to be unfit for human habitation as far back as 1936 and that he has been yapping about these ever since.'[17]

However, moves were afoot from within government to address the issue and even nationalists were prepared to acknowledge that there was something different about the new minister for health and local government, William Grant.[18] A former shipwright and a unionist with labour sympathies, he came to the post with a determination to cut through the 'procrastination' of the local authorities. 'Billy Grant was unique,' recalled John Oliver, then his private secretary, who was also committed to social improvement. 'He was a huge, rugged, man; a shipwright from the Queen's Island; a plain man; a man's man, a football fan; a strong teetotaller ... an Orangeman; a Labour-Unionist; a man of immense courage.' Grant would sometimes tell a self-deprecating story about a trade-union official saying, 'Billy, it's a blessing that you're a teetotaller for you're coarse enough when you're sober.' He was one of those ministers, in Oliver's recollection, 'who attract business', in that people of every creed contacted him about 'every social ailment'. He would habitually turn up at his office with his pockets stuffed with bits of paper that people had handed him. Paddy Agnew, Northern Ireland Labour Party (NILP) MP for South Armagh, who came from a Catholic background, would also send him handfuls of bits of paper from the poor of his constituency. He was 'a man who could make up his mind and then defend himself before all comers – the ideal leader for a department about to enter battle'.[19]

'I think you should remember', advised Grant's friend and former northern premier, John Andrews, 'that it was the procrastination of many of our local authorities which prevented many more houses being built under our various housing acts in prewar days.' Andrews criticised the emollient language traditional in communications between Stormont and the local authorities. There was no sense of telling them 'to get a move on' with the acquisition of land and building of houses: 'Instead of now being told that they "might consider", they should be told that they ought to consider it immediately, otherwise I am very confident that the same indefensible delay will take place in our country districts that is at present taking place in Belfast.'[20]

The Ministry of Health and Local Government was a new department and Grant was appointed minister in June 1944. Thereafter he, the prime minister, the minister of finance and a permanent secretary – Trinity College Dublin graduate Leslie Freer – operated as a task force. Sir Lucius O'Brien felt that it was only with the formation of this ministry that proper standards were finally laid down for building houses and acquiring sites.[21] Anticipating opposition, the new minister conducted a detailed investigation of possible solutions to Northern Ireland's housing problem. The Scottish Special Housing Association was considered the best model and in July 1944 Ronald Green – assistant Health and Local Government Ministry secretary, a sensible and patient man – travelled to Edinburgh to meet Norman Campbell, the Scottish association's manager. On his return he drafted a report that put forward the ministry's answer to the housing crisis – the establishment of a new body, the Northern Ireland Housing Trust.

The Scottish Special Housing Association had been set up in 1937 and, despite its building programme having been interrupted by the war, was considered a very effective body in building affordable accommodation for working-class families. Green concluded that this was what Northern Ireland needed, but with significant changes. Like Scotland, they should carefully select those to run the new organisation 'from people well known … for enthusiasm in social work … [not] because they have a name or status'. A female member was desirable, no 'titled person or social climber', but 'a woman accustomed to housework and household management … artisan or middleclass', capable of 'humane management'. The Scottish association was not directly involved in the management of the houses, which was left to the local authorities – a matter of regret to Campbell. Nor did it have compulsory acquisition powers. Green concluded that Northern Ireland needed a much more robust organisation, 'established openly by Act and not allowed to creep into the housing picture under some quasi-philanthropic guise'. Housing management was as important as housing construction and should be assumed by the new association from the start. And since the local authorities were already shaping up for a fight over their housing allocation, that allocation should go to the new association 'as a first instalment' of its building programme:[22] 'If there was a case for a Housing Association in Scotland where the local authorities were fully discharging their housing responsibilities, there can be, I feel, no question about the necessity for one here.'[23]

Green was also suspicious of certain private enterprises, for Campbell had been contacted by Belfast's auctioneers and estate agents, seeking information on the Scottish association and claiming to be concerned about the housing crisis in Northern Ireland. 'The housing problem is very acute here,' they wrote, 'and our members are very anxious to assist in providing houses for the people.' By now exchanges between the Scottish association and those involved in planning the Housing Trust were regular and friendly and Campbell copied the communication to Green, who responded by return. The

Auctioneers and Estates Agents' Institute is, he wrote, 'actively engaged in building up opposition to the Bill. As you know, there is no tradition in Northern Ireland of house ownership by public authorities, and the Estate Agents have had the factoring in their own hands almost entirely. Naturally they do not look forward with enthusiasm to the setting up of large well-run humanely managed estates.'[24] Green was to be permanent secretary at the ministry for much of the trust's life and its 'ready ally', as Charles Brett recalled.[25]

On 24 October 1944, Grant introduced the Housing Bill, which established the Housing Trust:

> Those proposals must be looked at against the tragic background of our present housing position. I am not going to throw stones at the people who allowed our housing to get into the state in which it is to-day, but neither am I going to hand out any bouquets. It is not a matter on which one can blame the Government or the local authorities, or even private enterprise; it reflects an absence in our country of public feeling about housing conditions which had long since begun to arouse the public conscience throughout the rest of the Kingdom ... between the wars the combined efforts of the State, the local authority and private enterprise built no more than half our population proportion of the houses built across the water. Thus while in 1939 the housing problem in Great Britain was well on the way to solution, here we had dropped relatively further and further behind. The Housing Report estimates our immediate need of houses at 100,000, and I was taken to task in some quarters for mentioning a figure of such magnitude. I want to say definitely that this figure of 100,000 is an understatement. It represents a building programme, which will tax all our resources for many years ...[26]

Not only was Northern Ireland not building sufficient numbers of houses, but those that were built were substandard, well below British standards: 'The need, therefore, is for many new houses and for houses generally of a much better standard than we have been accustomed to provide for our people in the past.'

Who would assume this huge task and how would it be paid for? In anticipation of objections to the new authority from the local councils, he argued, disingenuously, that they had quite enough on their hands already. They could not be expected to cope with a post-war building programme producing nearly thirty times the number of houses that were built by all the local authorities between the two wars. So a new body would be created: the Northern Ireland Housing Trust.

Grant assured members that, despite misconceptions, the Housing Trust was not designed to supersede the local councils, but to supplement them. And, as he stressed throughout the speech, the local authorities still had a statutory duty to provide houses for their 'working people'. Nor he added, somewhat tongue-in-cheek, would he be seeking its members from existing channels, for it would be unreasonable to add to the work of a man 'whose hands are already full'.[27] In other words, there would be no 'jobs for the boys', no political patronage. As for those private interests who might feel threatened, so long as building materials were in short supply, they should be directed towards public housing rather than private. However, the building industry would still be building for the state and the local councils and the whole issue of subsidy for private enterprise had been accepted in principle. Then there was the new concept of the Housing Trust's female 'Housing Managers', who would actively run the new estates:

> I am afraid that an impression has got abroad that the Trust will be operating as busybodies, prying into the homes of the people and teaching them how to cook. The science of house management – for it is a science – bears no relation at all to fancies of this kind. I want to tell the House that wherever skilled management has been undertaken in Great Britain it has added greatly to the happiness of the tenants and to the efficient running of the housing estates concerned …[28]

He concluded that houses would be provided on the basis of need. They would be financed by annual payments by the state instead of a lump-sum subsidy, and the state would remain involved to ensure that the houses were kept in good repair and condition:

> In this I hope it will in future be known as a tenant's charter. The Bill does no more than lay a sound foundation upon which we can build. Housing is a human problem, and it is as a contribution to the human needs of our people that I ask the House to support this Bill.[29]

Grant's long speech was compassionate but firm and calm, and dealt with many of the concerns already voiced. Even so, he was subjected to a good deal of peevish opposition from members of his own Unionist Party. Here the apparent threat the new Housing Trust would pose to estate agents and builders, as well as to the local councils, was the issue. The Housing Trust was also subjected to criticism along 'nanny state' lines, 'the Gestapo provision of female inspectors' going round the houses as 'spies'.[30] Nationalists picked up on the clause restricting tenancies to Northern Ireland residents of at least seven years' standing, seeing it as a design to exclude those from south of the border. Nationalist Senator J.G. Lennon denounced it as 'an insult to the Irish race', the outcome of 'blind fanatical hatred'.[31] Grant replied that this was not a party issue and that it made sense in the circumstances of the terrible shortages that those who paid – the ratepayers and taxpayers – should have preference. Even so, amendments were made, as unionists too had anxieties about the residential clause, for citizens of neutral Éire had supplied many of the farm labourers and servants during the war. But there was also a lot of good sense spoken. Even those MPs who blustered agreed on the priority of the housing issue.

On the second reading of the bill in the Senate, there were claims that it smacked of a 'socialist state'. Surely the very idea of giving the workers 'luxuries like bathrooms' was some kind of utopia. Grant expressed his amazement that bathrooms should be considered luxuries:

> Who was to enjoy the so-called luxury of a bath? Were they to be reserved for a certain section of the community?

> Were the millions of men and women who were serving
> their country on the different battlefields and in the various
> industries engaged in the war effort to be told that they
> were entitled to live as free men and women in the post war
> era, but that they could not have a bath?[32]

Green wrote to his housing friends in Scotland: 'our Bill is having
a very stormy passage. This is not the place for a lecture on the political
trends in Northern Ireland, but the misfortune is that this Bill is the
first measure to be introduced with a background of social reform by
a strongly Conservative Government.' He suggested that much of the
trouble was ill informed: 'The Committee stage alone has dragged
over a fortnight ... There has been so much trouble, misrepresentation
and opposition to the Bill and the Government's position is so
difficult.'[33] The feeling at the Health and Local Government Ministry
was to avoid amendments, which might provide the house further
opportunity to renew the controversy. An exhausted Green reported
to George Ross on 1 February 1945: 'The Housing Bill has at last
dragged its weary way through both Houses ...' They hoped to set up
the trust the following week.

In the event, the measure had cross-party and cross-community
support, despite nationalist reservations and the absence of Catholics
on the new body created by the 1945 Housing Act.[34] Indeed, given
the caustic tenor of many debates, it is notable that there was little
reference to housing south of the border – where a similar housing
report had appeared in 1943.[35] But the many amendments had reduced
the powers of the fledgling trust. It was, reflected Charles Brett, 'hotly
opposed by the Unionist old guard, who saw it as a reflection on the
competence and integrity of the local authorities, as a derogation from
the controlling powers of Stormont, and as an example of creeping
communism'. That cohort gained concessions 'which were to tie the
hands of the Trust when set up' – in particular that it was to be 'an
auxiliary to the local authorities with no powers to coerce them'.[36]

The main outcome of the 1945 Housing Act was the establishment
of a new public authority, the Northern Ireland Housing Trust,
separate from the local councils and directly responsible to the
Health and Local Government Ministry. As described in official

publications, the Housing Trust was a 'new public authority to work in co-operation with the local authorities, with the object of erecting housing accommodation for workers'.[37] Predictably, relations between the local councils and the trust would be brittle, even though the ministry was at pains to emphasise that the local authorities still had the main responsibility for building houses. Those built by the trust would be supplementary. Green had met with the Association of Rural District Councils in November 1944 to discuss their anxieties about the Housing Bill. They wanted the subsidies to come to them, rather than the trust: 'I doubt if even now some of them understand that the Trust is there to help them with a free gift of houses to the people of their district.' This, after all, was additional money and the tenants would be those taken from the councils' waiting lists. 'The feeling is perhaps that it is too good to be true.'[38] It was more than this, and Grant had implicitly recognised their irritation at the loss of this new channel for patronage.

There had been speculation about whether this new public body would be another source of 'jobs for the boys'. Grant had assured critics 'that the Trust would be composed of men and women, good types of Christian people who were willing and anxious to give their service to help their fellowmen and women'.[39] They would need to be, as these were unpaid positions. Members were initially appointed for five years, but reappointed at the end of that term. The prime minister, Sir Basil Brooke, accepted that the Housing Trust might be something of an 'unorthodox' body using unorthodox means, but given the size of the problem he thought unorthodoxy entirely justified and he promised that the government would 'put at the disposal of the Trust all the resources that can legitimately be called in to support it'.[40] John Oliver recalled how the ministry had identified housing as one of their three most urgent issues, the others being tuberculosis and the Poor Law: 'We needed new thinking, new men, new methods, new courage. And by one of those happy turns of fortune in public affairs, we got all four,' in the members of the new Housing Trust board.[41]

Their names were revealed at a press conference on 15 February 1945. The chairman, Lucius O'Brien – a Quaker, educated at Friends' school in Lisburn – had been manager of the Franklin Laundry Company, then chief welfare officer of the Belfast Civil Defence

Authority during the war. This had occupied so much of his time that he never returned to business life. O'Brien had a sound lineage in such public service. In 1934 he succeeded his father on the committee of the celebrated Belfast Charitable Society at Clifton House, eventually becoming its president in 1961.[42] He was also a trustee for the Belfast Savings Bank and several other charitable organisations. He was knighted in 1949 'for his services to the homeseekers, services which started when he became so depressed with the housing situation during the war that he gave up active business to devote all his time to improving conditions'.[43] As Mass Observation diarist Moya Woodside had also noted, the destruction of entire streets in working-class areas and the plight of thousands of refugees, walking the streets, pouring into the country towns, or 'spending their nights under hedges in the countryside', had finally alerted people to the housing and health of people living in such areas.[44]

The trust's vice-chairman, Herbert Bryson, was a director of Spence, Bryson & Co., linen manufacturers. He had served in the Royal Artillery in World War I and re-enlisted in 1940, but was released to join O'Brien on the Civil Defence Authority. The two had been particularly active in the welfare side of civil defence and set up district welfare offices to help those who had suffered in the Blitz. With O'Brien, Bryson's life was changed by the distress and terrible housing conditions in Belfast and they commissioned the 1944 survey, which directly led to the 1945 Housing Act. Eleanor Craig had been active in the Girl Guides and from 1941 was head of the Women's Voluntary Society's emergency feeding programme. She was introduced at the press conference as 'a practical housewife' who would offer suggestions for the design of the houses: 'As women have to spend most of their lives in their homes, they will be consulted through their various organisations, as to their ideas about kitchen arrangements etc.'[45] Graham Larmor was director of the Ulster Weaving Company and since 1939 had acted in an unpaid capacity as the Ministry of Supply's liaison officer in negotiating wartime textile supplies. The final member, James Duff, son of unionist senator Hugh Duff and a member of the Northern Ireland football team, was a partner in the family linen and farming business in Coagh. In public life he was vice-chair of Tyrone County Council and representative of the rural councils on planning advisory boards. Sir Lucius would remain in the chair until 1960, when he was succeeded by Bryson.[46] John G. Calvert, the civil servant who had been secretary to the Planning Advisory Board that produced the seminal 1944 report, was general manager to the Housing Trust from 1946 to 1967. W. McCaughey had been chief inspector at the Ministry of Labour and was seconded from the Health and Local Government Ministry to act as the trust's general manager for its first year.

'If ever personalities played a commanding part in the formulation of housing policy and practice, these did so,' reflected Charles Brett forty years later.[47] With an average age of forty-four, the trust was the youngest ever public body to be appointed in Northern Ireland until then and was broadly welcomed by both the nationalist and the unionist press. The nationalist *Irish News* regretted the fact that no Catholic had been appointed: 'The new members will no doubt do their work well and impartially ... But in view of the unsatisfactory record of many local authorities, the Government missed an obvious opportunity of showing it was at last in earnest by making the Trust more representative than it now is.' Even so, it welcomed the new authority and hoped it would succeed in its task of 'remedying the years of neglect' and 'failure to give the people the accommodation they need'.[48]

The trust was also a new and major employer, with 1,150 general managers and 805 deputy managers, on loan from the Ministry of Health and Local Government, along with 600 architects, 500 accountants, 320 registrars, 150 confidential shorthand typists, 101 typists and 135 clerical assistants.[49] Offices were set up at 5 Donegall Square South and there were fifty-six formal meetings in its first six weeks, in addition to daily informal ones. The new body was given a remarkable degree of latitude by government. In the formal invitation letter to O'Brien on 7 February, Grant outlined plans for the trust to build five thousand houses immediately – with few restrictions being placed on it, other than those outlined in the act – and twenty-five thousand overall in its first ten years. It was the local councils who had the main responsibility for building 'workers' houses', and the trust should cooperate with them 'as far as this can be achieved'. That said, 'the Government fully appreciates that housing is one of the most critical subjects with which it will have to deal in the years to come, and that its problems must take the very highest priority ... I should like to assure you that your general inquiries and the giving of such approvals as are necessary will be handled with the utmost expedition.' He had the full approval of the prime minister and the Ministry of Finance and any appointments of staff needed to perform the trust's duties 'would be approved without question':

> Generally, I should like you to understand that the Government has the fullest intention that the special qualifications which you and your colleagues can bring to this task will be allowed to operate untrammelled and unfettered ... every effort will be made by my Department to delegate the maximum amount of responsibility to you and your colleagues.[50]

In Belfast the trust was to build outside the city boundaries where land was available. Existing suburban residents, often in privately owned houses, were apprehensive. However, as one Finaghy resident recalled of the new housing estate, they were relieved to find it 'a nice estate, with lots of green spaces'. And this was the point. Housing Trust estates were *not* council estates. They were for the elite of the working classes, 'no ASBO types permitted', as a former senior civil servant declared to me. 'Most of the houses the Trust will build,' at least for the time being, O'Brien told the press conference on 15 February, 'will inevitably be occupied by the better-paid workers, leaving the houses they vacate to relieve over-crowding among the worst housed sections of the people.' This was the process of 'filtering up', he explained, since 'the worst housed families are generally those least able to pay for better accommodation'.[51]

The main need was for three-bedroomed houses, well built and reasonably spacious, with every reasonable modern convenience. When the proposed better standard of housing was discussed at Stormont, there was some patronising sniffiness. Senator J.G. Leslie (unionist) called it 'a Utopian scheme ... What they wanted in Northern Ireland was houses, not elaborate pleasure gardens.'[52] There was also the objection to bathrooms for the working class noted earlier.

In fact, as the trust's first report explained, in this respect as in others, subsidised houses built in Northern Ireland in the 1920s and 1930s were inferior to those in England, which generally followed the recommendations of the Tudor Walters Report of 1918 of not more than twelve houses per acre, each standing in its own garden.[53] Such housing followed the garden-suburb traditions of the Bourneville, Port Sunlight and Welwyn Garden City models. There were no such traditions in Northern Ireland. In Belfast densities of forty to sixty houses per acre were normal and densities were as high as seventy to eighty in some central areas.[54] 'Also,' as Sir Lucius explained in 1951, 'the strong non-party public opinion in Great Britain in favour of improved housing, based on many reports and wide discussions, had not been aroused in Northern Ireland … So that Northern Ireland was really starting in 1945 where Great Britain had started in 1919.'[55]

The trust sought, too, to build estates of character. There would be no standard plan or house. Adopting the recommendations of the 1944 report, it would build houses designed to achieve the maximum natural light, and as much attention would be paid to external as internal space. Each site would be treated as a separate entity and dwellings would be designed to harmonise with the district. Green spaces became a central aspect of trust planning. The new estates would grow into real communities, with community buildings, shops, schools and 'ample open spaces for recreational purposes'. They should not be 'traversed' by main traffic routes, and staggered junctions to slow traffic would further ensure child safety. There was no experience of such estate planning in Northern Ireland and this resulted in some early delays.

Considering all the controversy over relations with the local authorities and private enterprise, the trust was at pains to point out that the councils were responsible for providing most of the houses and that the trust could not work except in cooperation with them, to the extent also of taking its tenants from local-authority lists. In the placing of contracts, it followed the recommendations of the Simon Report of 1944, usually inviting tenders by public advertisement, or occasionally, when speed was necessary, by private negotiation after the prices had been checked. It was also careful to list in its reports all the private contractors so employed and to involve all the related professional associations.

Given the urgency of its task and post-war shortages of building materials, the trust was empowered to build unconventional structures. It investigated precedents in England and Scotland, particularly those approved by the Burt Committee, which had been appointed by the British Ministries of Works and Health. The trust was very anxious to use local materials and labour. Three forms were chosen as suitable for Northern Ireland. The Orlit type would be used for the Whitewell estate, colloquially known as the White City. Hugh Turtle and Harold Campbell, directors of McLaughlin and Harvey Ltd, had investigated the suitability of this type of building; samples of local building material had been sent for testing to the Orlit Works in England and found workable. Accordingly, in July 1945 Orlit Ltd was invited to establish a factory at Lisburn and production started in March 1946. The first three hundred houses were destined for the Whitewell/White City estate. The Orlit house consisted of precast reinforced concrete 'members', covered externally with concrete slabs and cavity walls. Since they were made in the factory, they could be erected quickly onsite. The texture and colour of the slabs forming the external walls were also considered pleasing to the eye.[56]

Perhaps the most innovative – at least for Northern Ireland – aspect of Housing Trust estates was the idea of estate management and exclusively female managers. This was the Octavia Hill system, in operation in Britain and still the keystone of estate management in Northern Ireland today. Octavia Hill was a Victorian philanthropist who was inspired by the ideas of Robert Owen and John Ruskin and pioneered the kind of working-class housing management adopted by the Housing Trust. The emphasis was on mutual responsibilities – prompt rent payment and good maintenance of property and environment by the tenants, efficient and humane management, personal contact and scrupulous implementation of repairs and maintenance by the housing body. The weekly rent visit was an essential part of this. The promotion of open spaces, gardens and the idea of community – the careful choice of tenants – all became part of Housing Trust ethos.[57]

At a very early stage the trust appointed trained women housing managers, through the Ministry of Labour, women's services and the universities. Eight women were selected, and by arrangement with the Society of Women Housing Managers they were sent for training to England on housing estates owned by the Ecclesiastical Commissioners in London, Liverpool Improved Houses Ltd, National Model Dwellings Co. Ltd, London, the housing departments of the Boroughs of Paddington and Southall, Hemel Hempstead Urban District Council and Chester Corporation. The training was quite onerous, involving business accountancy, construction methods and maintenance and housing and social-service law. Thereafter they had to pass the examination for the Certificate of Housing Estate Management of the Chartered Surveyors' Institute, and all this while carrying out day-to-day duties on the estates. The first batch of eight were then to train others in Northern Ireland. Given that the trust was to build twenty-five thousand houses in the following ten years, as its first report commented, 'it will be readily seen that an interesting and important field of work is being opened up to the women of the Province'.[58]

Building the houses was just a beginning for the trust. Housing management was just as important:

> The Trust's women housing managers, who are trained in the Octavia Hill system, have much more to do than merely collect rents. Often they have to advise families on such matters as their weekly budgets or how to make the best use of the modern equipment provided. Most tenants come from poor and overcrowded dwellings and have never before had a home of their own. The women housing managers even have to trace any fault in the house, deal with the minor ones and report all the more serious defects. They have to see that the Trust's duties as landlord are scrupulously carried out and to convince the tenants that they also have duties to the landlord's property and to the amenities of the estate. In all this they have to create a feeling of mutual confidence between the Trust and the tenants and to demonstrate that the Trust is a benevolent public body different from the average landlord to whom most tenants have been accustomed.[59]

Through the housing managers the trust took great care in helping the new tenants make what was a considerable adjustment from their previous living conditions: 'The wise advice of the Housing Manager … may mean the difference between success and failure in the family's adjustment to new conditions.'[60]

These, then, were not 'sink' estates. Careful 'selection' of tenants, 'persons who will be appreciative of better housing conditions',[61] was followed up by weekly visits from the housing manager. Tenants had to be 'workers' as defined by the 1945 act and also meet its residence qualification. The act made quite a point about 'workers' as opposed to 'labourers' and 'working classes' in earlier acts. Workers included 'all persons working for wages; persons not working for wages but working at some trade or handicraft without employing others … and persons whose income in any case does not exceed an average of eight pounds a week'.[62] In the areas in which the trust was building, it would take names from those on local-authority waiting lists and apply a 'points system'. Ex-servicemen and bombed-out families went to the top of the list, but 'need' was 'the decisive test for securing a house', and determination of need was 'one of the most important duties of the Housing Manager'. Other factors to be taken into account were 'the size of the family; the extent to which their present occupation is overcrowded; whether they are sharing with another family or families; whether their present conditions are unsatisfactory; lacking, for example, a WC, or a water supply inside the house; also, any special health consideration, such as the presence of T.B.' The housing manager would assess the application forms sent to the local authority, decide on the most needy, then visit the family. She would then be 'in a position by personal contact with the family in its environment, to form a sound opinion on the merits of the case'. A sub-committee of the trust would then assign the houses on the basis of the manager's reports.[63] As the trust's programme was rolled out, this inevitably became a task of considerable magnitude, some ten thousand visits having been made by the housing managers by the time of the 1948–9 report.

The trust faced a daunting task. Unlike local authorities in England in 1945, it had no sites purchased and partially developed before the war broke out, and no technical or administrative staff experienced in planning and building large-scale public-housing projects. And, while there was a large unskilled workforce, there was a serious shortage of skilled labour. As a result the wages of skilled labourers were higher than anywhere else in Britain, except London. There was also a shortage of building materials. War-damage reconstruction and the building of factories and schools had stretched brick-building capacity to the limit, while much of the material and equipment had to be imported from England. Unlike many Great British housing authorities, the trust had to bear the full cost of land, roads, fencing and administrative overheads. Finance also was problematic. The trust was funded by a government loan to be repaid at current interest rates, half-yearly over sixty years. As houses were completed and passed by the ministry inspectors, the ministry then paid a subsidy, based on the Scottish subsidy, which was higher than that in England. So, apart from the subsidy, the rents, when they started to come in, had to cover the costs. The trust had to balance its firm desire to keep rents low – in a population with a lower ability to pay than in England – with its need to pay off the loans. Very early on (1948) it suffered the serious blow of rising interest rates and then a huge jump in building costs.

The trust was very conscious of the limited ability of workers to pay high rents, as well as rates. It agonised about the impact of rising costs and evictions for non-payment of rent were rare: 'It is generally accepted that a man cannot pay more than a fifth or a sixth of his income in Rent and Rates, and therefore the saving of even a shilling in rent quite literally opens the door to a whole new group.'[64] Rather than raise rents, the trust chose to economise on house size and design. Such a solution attracted the attention of housing authorities in England, also struggling with rising costs. In the spring of 1949 legendary British town planner Sir Frederic Osborn, chairman of the Town and Country Planning Association in Britain, and Eric Bird, editor of the *Journal of the Royal Institute of British Architects*, came to Northern Ireland and wrote glowingly of the work of the trust.[65]

The White City houses were 945 square feet in area. The downsized 'Austerity' houses were 800 square feet. The new designs also had a combined WC and bathroom located on the ground floor, with smaller kitchens, hallways and living rooms. But no compromises would be made in house densities and spacious layout. Bird thought the 14s. rent high and so did the trust, which tried unsuccessfully to have it reduced.[66] I wonder whether White City residents ever realised how hard the Housing Trust had fought on their behalf. The location of the White City in three different local authorities also caused confusion over rates valuations. Some houses in Merston Gardens, Ballyroney Hill and Mulderg Drive fell into the higher-rated Belfast City authority; indeed, the boundary cut right through a number of them.[67] The final rate valuation for the estate was £23 for most houses, with the rents of 14s. per week for three-bedroom houses and two-bedroom flats and 15–16s. for the larger houses.[68]

Given such obstacles, the trust's early progress was impressive. From taking over an unfurnished office in February 1945, it had created the new organisation and placed the first building contracts by August. Within eighteen months it had carried out the surveys and site acquisitions, provided roads and services and placed contracts for over three thousand houses on fourteen different sites. By the fourth year, with rents coming in, it had covered all its expenses. In the years 1948 and 1949 the Housing Trust was the most productive housing organisation in the whole of Northern Ireland and was held up as an example by the Health and Local Government Ministry to show how 'incompetent' and 'dilatory' were the local councils.[69] It was in these golden years that the Housing Trust built the White City.

Charles Brett was very critical of the Cameron Commission. It was 'superficial and subjective' and did not conduct any very thorough research. He also criticised the lazy commentators and writers who simply cited Cameron without checking (a criticism that I fully endorse).[70] Brett did, however, agree that a minority of councils discriminated and the unionist government did nothing about it. The commission's case histories of discrimination against Catholics in the allocation of public housing were taken from those areas that had generated most complaints, and scholarly opinion supports Cameron's accusations against them.[71] Less well known is the coolness that existed between unionist governments and such councils. There was particular frustration with 'the backward rural districts', as Grant called Fermanagh, followed by Tyrone and Londonderry.

Much of this was because of their clear reluctance to build working-class housing and their complaints against the Housing Trust, which was doing so. As noted earlier, Grant and his team were also perfectly well aware of the issue of corruption and 'leverage' in the allocation of housing and it was made very clear from the outset that the trust would resist all such pressure: 'tenants will definitely not be selected as a result of letters of recommendation or pressure of any kind', the inaugural press conference was told. 'Members of the Trust are determined not to be moved by any influence from any quarter.'[72] The people behind the creation of the Housing Trust had good reason to suspect the various private interests that clamoured against it. An earlier inquiry, highlighting corruption and jobbery in Belfast Corporation in the awarding of contracts and land deals, had not been acted upon.[73] Meanwhile, housing records throw up any number of examples of popular belief that unionist politicians and councillors could be influenced.

'Putting in a word' on behalf of supplicants for houses was very widespread. Available records suggests that this was common in the Protestant community. But the practice was rife among Catholics too and there are recollections of parish priests and other so-called 'busy' people also 'putting in a word'. I found this belief common among those early Catholic residents of the White City that I spoke with, even though it was their application forms and visits by trust managers that would have decided matters. A search of Belfast Corporation records for these years shows a rash of supplications to influential people from all quarters, but particularly from serving policemen and ex-servicemen, including an effort in August 1947 to secure Princess Elizabeth's intervention through her lady-in-waiting. Royal Ulster Constabulary (RUC) headquarters was rather cloak-and-dagger about its own activities, talking about efforts to 'sow the seed' when they met anyone from the housing authorities and how it would be a good thing to have a few police living in the new Housing Trust estates. There was, of course, a real issue of accommodation when police officers were transferred to Belfast. But Belfast Corporation was not in the same discriminatory league as those councils west of the Bann, which were the focus of Cameron's findings, and in the cases I have looked at (at least for the immediate post-war years), the points system was adhered to and police and ex-servicemen alike turned down because there were simply not enough houses. However, as Brett observed, the points system was being applied in a 'somewhat primitive' fashion, as the housing scandal of the early 1950s would expose.[74]

Annie Copeland was one of these 'busy' people, who wrote voluminously and colourfully to the Belfast Corporation Housing Department, threatening to expose shady practice if she were not given a house. Her MP, Harry Midgley, contacted the Housing Trust on her behalf in October 1948 and was told, frostily, that she was not an urgent case.[75] Nor was she, and she was taking bribes to influence the City Hall's Estate Department into fraudulently granting corporation houses. The housing inquiry set up to investigate the case found against her. And, although it did not find clear evidence against Belfast Corporation, it did highlight unsupervised and sloppy procedures that facilitated such practices. Moreover, visitations to applicants to check on their claims, as was Housing Trust policy, were not being carried out.[76]

John Oliver recalled of his time with the Health and Local Government Ministry 'a notable absence of religious controversy in administrative affairs' in this 'positive era', a conclusion which my study of his department largely endorses.[77] Sir Lucius was annoyed when the kind of string-pulling noted above was tried on himself. On the basis of a complaint from the North Armagh Unionist Association on 27 March 1950, the Ulster Unionist Council (UUC) established a sub-committee to investigate the Housing Trust. The resolution followed a meeting in Portadown, where Rev. H.W. Coffey, MBE, MA, seconded by John Holmes, JP, proposed:

> That we the Office-bearers, Delegates and members of Annaghmore, Breagh, Drumcree, Killyman, Tartaraghan and Tullyroan Branches of the North Armagh Unionist Association, at a combined meeting held in Clontilew Orange Hall, Birches, Portadown, on Monday 27th March 1950, protest most strongly against the action of our Ulster and Protestant Government in permitting the appointment of a Roman Catholic to be in charge of the allocation of the houses built in County Tyrone, County Fermanagh, South Derry and a large part of the County of Armagh under the Northern Ireland Housing Trust. We feel that all our endeavours to increase the Unionist majority have been brought to nought by the action of this unacceptable person

who has for instance allocated over 90% of the houses in Keady district (County Armagh) to Roman Catholic Republicans. We demand her immediate withdrawal from this position of responsibility.[78]

The resolution was passed unanimously.

The UUC set up a special sub-committee to look at the Housing Trust. It was made up of members from Armagh, Tyrone, Fermanagh and Derry, but not Belfast, unless we can count its chairman, the former unionist MP for Dock, Captain G.A. Clark, then living in Helen's Bay in north Down, one of Northern Ireland's most affluent areas. Investigations were conducted into the religion of Housing Trust tenants, though this can only have been anecdotal, as the trust did not gather such information. E.T. Herdman, Tyrone representative on the above sub-committee, wrote in advance of its meeting:

We are working hard to get a more satisfactory allocation of houses in this area [Sion Mills] ... I hope you got my list of selected Unionist Applicants for the Trust Houses ... so I hope we may be able to slip in a few more of the Right Sort ... it is of vital political importance that these people should get houses.[79]

Other such representations echoed the language used at Stormont against the female managers. 'We will not tolerate this,' wrote the Fermanagh Unionist Association to Captain Terence O'Neill (future unionist prime minister, then parliamentary secretary to the Ministry of Health and Local Government) on 20 May 1950. 'Two women inspectors go round this district selecting their tenants,' they complained. They are 'Hitlers in the way in which they manage the whole affair here', another 'string in the fiddle they are playing to bring us into the Irish Republic'. Detailed information was gathered on these female 'Hitlers' and the districts for which they were responsible. Of the six senior housing managers, two were found to be 'RC', but the Protestantism of one of the others was deemed suspect as she was considered a communist. Of their assistants, twenty-one were Protestant and nine Roman Catholic.

A UUC delegation waited on Sir Lucius on 23 May and reported it to be a very helpful and constructive meeting. The representations and religious head-counts were read out, though the actual figures showed the representations of the North Armagh Unionist Association to have been wildly exaggerated (Keady, for example, having twenty-one Protestants and twenty-eight Catholics). The correspondence reflects the fact that trust houses were considered superior and that perhaps was a factor behind the complaints, for many of the Protestants were already 'adequately housed', as Sir Lucius explained. The delegation seemed largely happy with their meeting and advised the local associations that they should accept responsibility for helping applicants obtain houses by early and correct applications, and then follow up with practical advice.[80]

The internal ministry and cabinet papers show how politically controversial housing allocation was. The Fermanagh Unionist Association accused the then-minister for Health and Local Government, Dame Dehra Parker, of 'opening the back door to disloyalty'; the spokesperson, Thomas Nelson, went on to claim 'that this Protestant Government should have set up the Housing Trust in the interests of the Protestant population. Had he realised that they were going to house Catholics he would never have supported the Trust.' The town's mayor had even visited Sir Lucius and suggested that some of the agitation would cease if his son 'were fixed up with a house'. All of this was reported to the cabinet in a letter from Dame Dehra, in which she clearly thinks the complainants are being unreasonable and she doubts, if the controversial estate were handed over to the local council, that it would ever finish building it.[81] As always in Northern Ireland there is another side to such stories and, in fairness, the seminal 1944 report, *Housing in Northern Ireland: Interim Report of the Planning Advisory Board*, recorded Fermanagh and Tyrone as having the most overcrowded living conditions in the province.[82] The trust continued to be suspected of being too sympathetic to Catholics by grass-roots unionists, but it was a government creation and the unionist government continued its support. Another UUC delegation about the trust in February 1951 was told by Prime Minister Brooke that he would not be responsible for discrimination against the minority and hinted that they were, after all, responsible to a socialist (Labour) government in London.[83]

The record of the Housing Trust was generally a very fair one and most commentators thought it made a real beneficial difference to working people in Northern Ireland during its existence. John Oliver pays tribute in his autobiography. The two areas in which he felt the Health and Local Government Ministry was most successful were in housing and the treatment of tuberculosis, of which Northern Ireland had the highest incidence in the UK. The Housing Trust he considered 'a high watermark in British housing':

> The members of the five-member board took a close personal interest, visiting sites, approving layouts and supervising management methods ... And they were stern moralists in financial matters – Gladstonian liberals, we used to say, in their repugnance to anything savouring of deficit financing. They had indeed a remarkable financial record. To some people they may have seemed paternalistic – to some they have seemed self-satisfied; they certainly had their detractors among the local authorities – but all in all their achievements stand up to most criticisms and it was tragic to see the Trust subsumed into the bigger Housing Executive in 1971.[84]

3

The New Estate

The good siting, the superb landscaping and the distinctive house-types of the housing trust represent a high watermark in British housing.

John Oliver, *Working at Stormont.*[1]

In the early years of the 1939–45 war few in Belfast thought the city faced enemy bombardment. Plans to evacuate children had attracted only a third of those eligible and they started drifting back when nothing happened. Government was slow to provide air-raid shelters, only 25 per cent of Belfast's population having access to them.[2] People of the Whitewell area were rather dismissive of air-raid warnings. They were seen as a nuisance and exercises were often ridiculed by spectators. After Easter Tuesday 1941 this all changed. Just before midnight on 15 April the drone of enemy aircraft could be heard approaching from Knockagh Hill, the most prominent high landmark locally on the shores of Belfast Lough. They dropped flares over the Whitewell Road, and the whole area 'seemed brighter than at noon in summer-time'. Then came the parachute mines. One fell on Veryan Gardens – a densely occupied street of relatively new working-class housing – the crash shattering the whole neighbourhood. Another fell on open ground on the Whitewell Road, destroying much of the air-raid wardens' post. As the wardens recovered, they looked up the Whitewell Road and saw hundreds of panic-stricken people, many of them injured, running down towards the post. James Hawthorne from the Serpentine Road had been a constable on duty at the RUC barracks in Greencastle that night and had been on his way to a house in Dandy Street, which was breaking the blackout, when the flares lit up the district: 'I remember looking up and seeing a parachute carrying a land mine drifting slowly down ... I did not have to visit the house in Dandy Street – the bombs had done my job for me.' He also recalled the streets becoming filled with 'thousands of screaming and terrified people, all rushing towards the safety of the hills and the countryside'.[3] Many of the casualties had to be placed in fields or ditches. Schoolrooms were opened as rest centres for the homeless. There were no air-raid shelters in the area. The Rev. Finlay Maguire opened St Ninian's Church on the Whitewell Road to people of the area, 'both Catholic and Protestant'.

There were many small fires, as the blast entered the chimneys and scattered coal fires into the rooms. A human chain of buckets was set up from the now water-filled fifteen-foot crater in Veryan Gardens. One fire was in number 45, where four generations of the Danby family were wiped out. The head of the household, Arthur, aged thirty-five, was an air-raid warden and died on his own doorstep, where he had been posted by the senior warden. His parents had only recently travelled over from England to avoid the bombings there.

As the end-of-raid siren sounded at 4.54 a.m. and dawn broke, a scene of 'desolation and grievous loss' greeted the helpers. An ambulance was being loaded with wounded people in Veryan Gardens and at the other side of the crater a lorry was loading the dead and transporting them to a temporary mortuary at Erskine's Felt Works in Greencastle. A small boy was found wandering on the Whitewell Road. His house at number 128 had been completely demolished and his parents and grandmother killed. His baby sister was found alive, buried by soil, the hood of her Tan-Sad (baby buggy) protecting her. But all the adults in the house had been killed. The boy was identified as Hugh Doherty of Veryan Gardens.[4] A toddler was found alive after being buried in rubble for nearly twelve hours. The *Belfast Telegraph* – which had printed all the Belfast papers because their plants had been destroyed – ran a campaign to discover his identity.

The following day another toddler was found wandering in the fields near Veryan Gardens. He was Brendan McKay, only survivor of the McKay family from Dandy Street.[5] Soon crowds of spectators gathered. There were worries about identity cards found in the area getting into the wrong hands and houses being entered illegitimately. The list of valuables collected in pillowcases from each house tell the story of a thrifty working-class people, with savings books and insurance policies, and in one case savings of £11 hidden in a laundry bag in the kitchen. Senior air-raid warden, Alfred Ambrose, also recalled the strange sight of the stairway, a jar of jam, a bottle of sauce and half a dozen eggs undamaged in a house that otherwise had been totally demolished. Despite the wardens' best efforts to retain people's furniture and effects in the street near their houses, they were all mixed together in the salvage vans.

All that day there was a constant stream of traffic down the Serpentine Road, for the Antrim Road was blocked near Ben Madigan Park. North Belfast, including the Antrim Road area, was one of the worst hit by the Easter Tuesday raids, numbers 5 right up to 334 suffering varying degrees of damage.[6] I recall many stories from my childhood, since significant numbers of White City residents were from these areas: the bombs that dropped on the Waterworks and Newington area; the shelter that had taken a direct hit there; the bodies laid out in the Falls Baths. Shane McAteer's family had lived on the Cavehill Road, opposite the Waterworks. They had survived an earlier bombing on 7–8 April by hiding under the stairs, where most people chose to hide in the absence of shelters.[7] The following day the family fled – the parents by lorry with their belongings, the children walking the two miles to Great Victoria Street station. Had they stayed they would almost certainly have perished on Easter Tuesday night (15–16 April), when a hundred German bombers destroyed their area. They at least had family to go to, in the country nearby (Randalstown). Those who had no one took refuge in the surrounding hills. The vehicles coming down the Serpentine Road that night were full of people fleeing to the country from the Belfast Blitz and the wardens stopped those with a little space to ask them to take some of the homeless from the Whitewell area. For weeks afterwards Moya Woodside continued to pass lorries and cars stacked with bedding and furniture on the roads out of Belfast, as well as people walking out each night to sleep in the fields and returning in the morning.[8]

The Antrim Road residents had requested that the dangerous animals in the zoo be put down. Alex McClean, head of the ARP. Veterinary Section, helped by an RUC constable from Glengormley and a Home Guard sergeant, was preparing to do so when the

15 April raid occurred. From the height he could see the bombers flying up the Antrim Road and turning round to make further attacks.[9] When hospitals were checked and the final count was made, 46 people had been killed in Veryan Gardens and the Whitewell Road and 2 on the Serpentine Road; 118 had been injured and 128 houses had been damaged or destroyed. Further raids on the night of 4–5 May killed another 30 in Greencastle and the lower Whitewell Road. Alfred Ambrose, reporting on these awful events, remarked ruefully, 'The people of Greencastle now respect the Air Raid Warden.'[10]

The Belfast Blitz killed 1,100, damaged 56,000 buildings and transformed the local landscape of the future White City. 'Vacant space' in the street directories described significant portions of the worst-affected areas into 1948, when replacement houses started to appear.[11] Thorburn Road had taken a direct hit in the raid of 1941, and an unexploded bomb remained in the open space later considered for a children's playground. Bomb craters pockmarked the surrounding fields. One in the upper field became a much-prized play area for White City children, filled with water irises and reeds, a glorious mud-hole for family dogs. Claims for damage and rebuilding programmes continued right into the 1950s. Work started early to rebuild the bombed areas on the Whitewell Road and lower Serpentine (January–February 1945). That month, too, the gas-lamps came on again for the first time since being blacked out at the beginning of the war.[12]

The legacy of the war pervades this biography of place. People lived with rationing and shortages for many years. There was a terrible dearth of civilian clothing after it ended. Department stores listed 'utility' prices and the number of coupons required to purchase clothes, which remained under wartime rationing until 1949.[13] In July 1946 the minister of commerce put out an appeal for empty jam-jars and bottles, such was the shortage in the food and other industries.[14] People from the area recalled paying for cinema tickets in jam-jars. Sugar rationing was removed in 1953 but many other foodstuffs, such as butter, margarine, bacon, cheese and meat, were rationed far into the 1950s. A butcher on the Shore Road despaired about producing sausages with so little meat content when meat rations were further reduced in 1951.[15] Wartime control of coal only ended in July 1958.[16]

Fruit was such a luxury that it filled children's stockings at Christmas.

White City people travelling into Belfast via the Shore Road would pass many blitzed sites. The damaged Midland Hotel only reopened in May 1951; the flax mill on York Street, destroyed in 1941, was still in the process of being rebuilt in October 1951; the big empty site as they entered the city between Donegall Street, York Street and St Anne's Cathedral remained desolate throughout the 1950s.[17] As they progressed they found a toothless city with big gaps where there once were buildings, now being used for that modern-day problem of car parking, then just beginning to exercise the Belfast planners.

There was of course another side to the story – the new availability of unused space on which the public could imprint their imagination. One such space was the Saturday-morning market that had taken over the blitzed site at the corner of York and Donegall Streets, 'Belfast's brightest bit of the Saturday scene', as *Ireland's Saturday Night* proclaimed on 7 December 1957. There 'Hector the Hoarse' sold trinkets from the back of a van, a vegetable man offloaded quantities of sprouts from a cart and customers bargained with a man selling sheets and pieces of linen. There was a Glengormley plant man who grew double primroses in 'the right sort of peaty ground' in Northern Ireland, then exported them to Devon. It was 'an oasis in technicolour, a tonic in the Belfast Saturday morning scene'. Its days were numbered, however, because of development plans to site Belfast's College of Art and a 'public rest garden' there.[18]

Many of the war-damaged buildings were unstable and a particular hazard for children who turned them into playgrounds. In May 1948 the blitzed church in Clifton Street collapsed, killing one child and injuring others.[19] John Campbell, recalling his childhood in York Street, wrote of the Blitz turning his area into 'a giant adventure playground for us kids'. The waste grounds became improvised football pitches, the air-raid shelters dens where they could smoke cigarette ends picked up from pavements, while the 'husks of bombed-out houses' became ready-made hiding places. 'Pretending to be soldiers or pirates, we would climb like monkeys through the rafter beams,' wrote Campbell, hiding in any intact room, prising up the floorboards in search of buried treasure.[20]

The early rebuild on the Serpentine Road was unusual and may have been due to pressure from private builders.[21] But the criticism of the standards of inter-war private building for working people discussed earlier finds poignant testimony in air-warden Ambrose's account of clearing the blitzed houses from Whitewell: 'This work proceeded very rapidly and it was surprising how quickly the entire fabric of one of these "subsidy" houses could be turned over.'[22] Generally the housing situation remained dismal into the 1950s: 'We were acutely ashamed of our failure to foresee and prepare for the phenomenon known as "the homeless",' recalled John Oliver of this time at Stormont, 'the great exodus of Belfast people to the suburbs, the … huts and shacks on the main roads running out from the city.'[23] Decommissioned Nissen huts (used by the National Fire Service) were drafted into use. They were adapted to provide a family with a 'scullery', living room and three bedrooms, 'two of them small', at a rent of 8s. 6d. per week.[24] A camp of twenty-four such 'hutments' on the Whitewell Road was converted in 1947, and they continued to be sought after until the early 1950s, even as the ministry was trying to close the camp down and rehouse the inhabitants.[25] But even these were seen as a step up from worse accommodation in the area. Another step up was a 'prefab', a prefabricated aluminium bungalow, a 'tin atrocity' as the president of the newly formed Federation of Building Trade Employers in Northern Ireland described such buildings.[26] There were prefab sites on the Longlands, Whitewell and Shore Roads and in Whiteabbey. In conversation with me in 2015 one long-term resident was rhapsodic about growing up in a prefab on the Shore Road and, while his memories were clearly coloured by the rosy views we often have of our childhoods, his description of the decor, the modern kitchen and separate toilet and bathroom does reflect the care the authorities took in the 1940s to turn these into proper, if temporary, homes. They all had gardens back and front and he recalled people sharing plant-cuttings and, in the summer, preparing the vegetables outdoors. By 1962, however, long after they were supposed to have been decommissioned, the local NILP candidate denounced the Shore Road prefabs. Situated near a cesspool and between a busy road and a dangerous railway line, it was little wonder that four children under the age of three had been killed there in the preceding ten years.[27]

The opening up of new spaces did, however, have the salutary effect of creating a new vision of a more spacious Belfast. The Belfast Planning Commission Report of January 1945 was 'a bold effort at reconstruction now, when enemy action and the circumstances of war have given us opportunities that may never occur again'. There would be reduced density of houses in central areas, which would necessitate the building of low-rise flats and the relocation of some seventy-five thousand people, a third of the population. The unloading of coal and driving, marketing and slaughtering of cattle in the central city should be ceased. Trees should line a widened High Street as 'a symbol of the renewed vigour and progress of the City after its ordeal of war', and the spaces opened up by enemy action should never be built upon again. New ring roads and bypass roads would help sustain this perceived spaciousness. One would bring traffic direct from Glengormley through the Whitewell area into the city via York Street. Industries would be relocated to outlying towns, Carrickfergus and Whiteabbey among them. The outward growth of the city would be limited and a green belt established to protect the Holywood hills, the Lagan Valley and the Antrim hills from uncontrolled building developments immediately after the war. It was an uplifting vision and welcomed as such.[28] In the light of this vision it is surprising that the building of the White City, about to take place in one of these areas of natural beauty between the Cave Hill and the lough shore, attracted so little opposition. As the commission put it: 'Few cities of comparable size in the British Isles have so close at hand a natural feature as fine as the range of hills … heather-covered and unspoilt, from Collen through the Black Mountain to Cave Hill … [a] precious natural playground for Belfast.'[29] The Housing Trust's commitment to spacious, aesthetically pleasing housing estates was part of this post-war optimism.

In general, areas for building were first suggested by the Health and Local Government Ministry; the sites were investigated and approval was then sought from the local authority's planning officer. The fact that the Whitewell site was criss-crossed by the boundaries of three local authorities was to present problems until the new local authority of Newtownabbey was created in 1958. It was the only one of the trust's estates to so straddle authority boundaries at this time.[30]

Preliminary site visits assessed the topography, which 'should be level, dry and easy of access'.[31] The White City was none of these and the full costs of developing the site could not at first be estimated because of its overgrown state and bomb damage.[32] Even so, the site report thought the thirty-one acres identified and lying between the Antrim, Whitewell and Serpentine Roads 'well adapted for developing as a building estate for small villas and cheaper types of houses. They are mostly situated just outside the City boundary between the Antrim Road and Whitewell Road and are close to trains and buses … These lands are ripe for building as evidenced by speculative preparations made in 1939.'[33]

These referred to foundations partly excavated or laid for a handful of houses on the Serpentine Road side and a further two on the Whitewell Road. The most extensive were those of John Ross – what became almost half the land of the new estate – for he had already started to lay roads and sewers. But all these preparations had been interrupted by the outbreak of war. The trust surveyor found the road fronting the Whitewell Road bomb damaged and undermined by flood water and pronounced it 'unfit for use unless relaid'. At the time of inspection (April 1946) Ross's land was being used for grazing livestock. In court arbitration proceedings in March 1950, the trust's engineer gave evidence that the local authority was not going to approve Ross's road. It was poorly laid and had already developed potholes, while the sewer he declared useless – it had been taken up.[34] It seems that even without the Housing Trust, the area that became the White City would have been developed by private interests as part of Belfast Corporation's programme. But the findings of the 1926 *Enquiry into Belfast Corporation* revealed the kind of unsavoury practice for which the councils were very generally criticised. Alderman James Barron, with insider knowledge, had bought land cheaply between the Whitewell and Antrim Roads, with the idea of its 'very profitable' release for development to the corporation.[35] Flooding was caused on the White City site in 1947 as Barron's old sewer was disturbed by trust work.[36]

Green had thought it a weakness for the Scottish association not to have powers of compulsory purchase. This risked having to accept whatever land the local authorities offered, which was not usually attractive: 'Our experience in Northern Ireland with negotiations by agreement is that they are protracted and unsatisfactory. They also lay themselves open to corruption or at least to allegations of its existence.'[37] So the trust should make an offer if the land was in single ownership. If not, or if it was believed that the land would not be 'willingly given up by agreement', they should proceed straight away to compulsory purchase by vesting orders.[38] Because of 'the number and variety of interests' on the land designated for the Whitewell estate, this is exactly what the trust decided to do and the vesting-order papers have provided one of my most fertile information sources.

James Alexander Whitla (or Whitlaw) of Bournemouth held plots between Thorburn Road and where Navarra Place and the shops would be located, leased out to seven others. The Royal Victoria Hospital had lands at the other side, adjoining the Throne hospital, and the Belfast Water Commissioners had tiny plots. Local farmers William Creswell and Andrew Crow had grazing rights and in her semi-autobiographical novel *The Sound of Anthems*, Marjory Alyn describes the Whitewell Road covered in cow-clap, as the 'prize bovines' were driven from their byres up to the pastures.[39] Some residents still recall taking a pitcher to one of these farms to buy fresh milk from the cows. But the bulk of the land was part of the Shaftesbury estate – first granted to the Chichesters in the early seventeenth century – and was leased to eleven others.

The vesting order became operative on 5 February 1946 and the various interests were invited to make claims for compensation. Compulsory purchase of one's land is always a disturbing development. Early maps show a largely rural landscape, rising from the coast to the slopes of the Cave Hill and dotted with a number of detached villas. William Lawther, of Sunnyside, Antrim Road, held over ten acres from the Barron estate, 'situated on the Antrim Road and [with] an excellent outlook over Belfast Lough … eminently suitable for the erection of detached villas of a superior type similar to those adjoining'.[40] Frederick McKibbin, estate agent and valuer, acting for Lawther, claimed that 'good class detached villas – 3 to the acre' might have been built: 'There has always been a big demand for good class houses in this excellent situation, on the Antrim Road with the magnificent outlook over Belfast Lough,' and he cited high prices being paid for such in the 1930s. It was not an opinion shared by the Valuation Division in correspondence with the Housing Trust:

> At the time of the publication in 1935 of our First General Revaluation there was an outcry against the valuations because, inter alia, property in Northern Ireland (it was said) had been treated as though it were situated in wealthy England. The prices landowners are now asking for building sites make England appear a distressed area![41]

McKibbin also stated that Lawther would lose a right of way along two lanes to the Whitewell Road from two detached villas, 'Marathon' and 'Hillcrest', as well as two semi-detached villas in Mount Lydia. These were big houses by any standard: 'Marathon' had three reception rooms, seven bedrooms, a garage and two WCs, 'Hillcrest' five bedrooms, a large double drawing room, a dining room and a garage. The two semi-detached villas each had three reception rooms, five bedrooms, two toilets and a garage. The estate agent thought the prospect of 'the erection of small workers [sic] houses' would reduce the value of these houses by 25 per cent.[42] The Housing Trust disputed this and thought there would have been little chance of Lawther actually building these houses. There was no sign that the surrounding leaseholders would grant him the right of way to secure access, while the trust thought that the incline from the Antrim Road was probably too steep for any road-making.[43] Lawther's challenge went to arbitration, but was dismissed by the High Court on 27 February 1946.

'Throneview', as it is named today, is the large house overlooking the estate in a 1949 photograph. In the trust's vesting documents it is part of Lawther's portion and the land below it (where our row of houses was built) was the subject of the vesting order. As children we used to greet its horses over our back-garden fence. I do not recall any class resentment being expressed about it or the other very large houses overlooking the estate, but some of my interviewees did indeed express some in retrospect. Apart from greeting the horses and joining other children in taking the apples that overhung the Snaky Path, the only encounter I ever had with these neighbours above us was a rather dispiriting one around 1954. As very young children, the entrepreneurial ambitions of my brother and myself suffered a rude demise in this affluent hinterland. Our hobby, shared with many other children at the time, was making plaster-of-Paris models. It was a labour-intensive hobby, involving regular trips to the model store in Queen Street, the long wait for the liquid plaster to dry in the red moulds and successive applications of paint and varnish. With Christmas approaching, we thought we would try to sell the end products. We (or was it our parents?) seemed to think that we would have more success among the detached villas on the Antrim Road and adjacent Ben Madigan than on our own estate. 'Thronemount' was the biggest house at which we called. From all of my six-year-old stature I recall an enormous fairytale-like door and knocker and a hall and staircase of equal proportions, with great cracks in the high ceiling. It was a searing experience, as we were turned away from door after door, the December gloom and freezing sleet adding to our misery. We sold one leprechaun and toadstool that evening. Admittedly, they must have appeared rather tacky, much like the plaster geese that adorned the chimney-breast of many White City houses then. In hindsight, I can see this as a form of inverted snobbery on the part of my family and, of course, as we know now from decades of social surveys, the working classes are much more generous in these sort of situations. Nor did we know then the understandable resistance of these middle-class private owners to the building of such an estate and quite possibly their lingering resentment.

Many of the vesting cases rumbled on for years and levels of compensation were only finally decided in May 1950.[44] But the trust had gone ahead on land successfully acquired, and in its second annual report (1946–7) it reported roads well advanced, manufactured parts of the frames and walls for over a hundred houses ready at the Orlit factory, and building already started onsite.[45] This was just the kind of speed that the government wanted and a circular had been sent to the local authorities in January 1946 urging them to expedite their own housing programmes. Grant wrote with some satisfaction to the prime minister in September 1945 that he felt confident of achieving their target of three to four thousand building contracts within a year of the ending of the war. The Housing Trust in particular 'has put in an immense amount of valuable work and has amply justified its creation'.[46] But mumblings continued among those 'backward rural districts', which complained that the Housing Trust was doing too much for Belfast. In a memorandum to the cabinet, answering such criticisms, he explained that the trust was carrying out his ministry's instructions by providing houses for workers 'in areas where in the opinion of my Ministry the need for such accommodation is greatest. The Trust have carried out their work to my entire satisfaction and have made substantial progress with helping those authorities who are helping themselves' – though he admitted that perhaps the time had come to give such 'backward' districts some help.[47]

By March 1947 the Housing Trust had contracted for 4,054 houses on the outskirts of Belfast and neighbouring towns and 1,981 were under construction. But progress was impeded by an abnormally severe winter and post-war shortages of building materials. The trust's upbeat tone changed:

> The more the housing problem is probed the more distressing it is shown to be. Every week scores of men and women are interviewed whose health and happiness and that of their children are being destroyed by the miserable conditions in which they have to live. There are only a very few houses to be allocated where thousands are needed. The Trust pays tribute, with sincere respect, to the dignity and courage of the thousands who have to be told they must wait indefinitely.[48]

By now 201 White City houses were under construction, but none was finished.

Post-war Northern Ireland had a surfeit of unskilled workers, which was one of the reasons why the government was so supportive of non-traditional, factory-made houses like the Orlits. But skilled workers were scarce and were still needed on such sites. As a result of all these difficulties – and in order to retain rents at the trust's gold-standard of 14s. per week – certain economies had to be introduced and bathrooms henceforth would be located on ground floors. But these did not seem to affect contracts already out, including the White

City, and we retained our separate toilets and bathrooms adjacent to the bedrooms upstairs – a merciful 'luxury', given the lack of central heating and the coldness of these concrete houses.

With the cessation of new contracts for 1947–8, attention was focused on those sites where work had already begun. Enquiries were made all over Britain and Éire and further afield to get supplies to the contractors.[49] At Stormont the Ministry of Home Affairs had become impatient with those departments in charge of supplies. The ministry reminded them of the various reports that had shown the dire need for housing and of its determination not to build inferior houses to those in England. The ministry's chief architect proposed remedying the shortages by banning the use of timber in working-class houses: 'He dislikes wooden floors, and he dislikes wooden stairs, and the idea of wooden skirting makes him shudder!', wrote the exasperated permanent secretary Adrian Robinson to his opposite number in the Commerce Ministry. 'He takes the view that with the modern materials that are available there is very little necessity to use timber at all,' and he seemed to favour all concrete.[50] Thankfully the trust had its own architects and we did have wooden skirting boards, picture rails and stairs. But we were left with poor insulation and concrete floors, covered in black pitch and smelling of it, while the metal window-frames rusted and cracked. No wonder the houses were cold and damp, and the flat, felted roofs were quick to let in water.[51]

The trust's report for 1946–7 shows the Whitewell estate partially built by March 1947, though mostly without windows, doors and paths. In April Sir Lucius was informed of a very serious shortage of steel and timber, and that timber would only be made available to houses already well advanced, including Orlits at Magherafelt and Whitewell, each requiring two tons of steel.[52] By June, 70 of the White City houses had been roofed. By July amended plans for the top (north-western) portion of the estate had been submitted to the local councils. By October, 43 had been completed and tenants had started arriving. Construction picked up speed by early 1948, with 124 completed by the end of February, 164 by April, 200 by the end of June and 257 by the end of that year. The whole estate of 314 houses was completed in March 1949.[53]

Anna Pearson moved into the Whitewell Road end of the estate in November 1947. I knew that the building of the rest of the estate was still ongoing after the first tenants were moved in, but she had no memory of the kind of disruption that normally accompanies building. Perhaps one of the reasons was the Housing Trust's aesthetic vision – her row of four houses was purposely set back from the main road by an intervening green space and a new by-road. Perhaps, as the estate-building continued further up the hill, it was because the contractors were entering from the Antrim Road side – which also had the advantage of a bus route, whereas the Whitewell Road did not at that time. But the main reason was the nature of the Orlit houses, which were factory made, enabling fast construction onsite.

The trust was justly proud of its commitment to space and greenery on it estates. There are always sapling trees in its illustrations. It also wanted its estates to have distinctive street names, avoiding the conventional 'street' and 'road' of the past, or the confusing use of the same name: 'It has tried to find a common denominator for the convenience of the public which would link all the addresses on each site.' Hence Cregagh was to have its streets named after Northern Ireland rivers, Falls after mountains and Whitewell after loughs.[54] Thus we had the happy experience of having our street (Portmore Hill) named after a magical lough and wildlife habitat in south Antrim, though I never recall any real curiosity about the unusual name. The new fashions for street-naming captured the public mood, which disliked the old term 'street', even though one commentator in the press found such naming of new streets in the suburbs rather 'Happy-go-lucky' and creating difficulties for the postmen.[55]

Experts came from England to view the new developments. Eric Bird wrote of his and Frederic Osborn's visit to trust estates in 1949:

> One advantage possessed by the Northern Ireland Housing Trust is that most of their sites are set in superb scenery. Few of them are entirely flat and the majority have fully grown trees. These sites give the Trust architects a chance which has been well taken. All the site layouts … are both imaginative and technically sound. It is true that the irregular nature and small scale of the country often make difficult the obtaining of sites that are easy to develop, and the variety of levels

raises costs by requiring expenditure on underbuilding, but in the great majority of cases solid virtues have been drawn from these necessities.[56]

Charles Brett, too, was complimentary:

> … despite their comparatively small size and austerity, the Trust's houses (and estates) were exceptionally well laid out and designed, and introduced quite new standards to Ireland … Its provision of open spaces, careful retention of trees and hedgerows, and attention to landscaping and tenants' gardens, were quite without precedent …

The trust's estates, he continued, were 'still amongst the pleasantest in the province'.[57] Bird also observed that, apart from providing open spaces, planting trees and cutting the grass, the trust had not yet had much time or finance to develop the public spaces: 'The open spaces have to await the creation of a communal spirit among the tenants and the eventual building up of reserves by the Trust.'[58] This too was a Housing Trust ideal:

> It is now generally accepted that everything should be done to help large new Estates to grow into real communities, by providing space for such buildings as schools, shops, post offices, community buildings, or halls for meetings.[59]

So what did this new estate look like? Firstly, it was very spacious. I showed the final plan for the estate to a relative, an architect and town planner for Belfast City Council. 'You wouldn't have such space in today's estates,' he commented. In England the Tudor Walters Report of 1918 recommended that 'not more than twelve houses should be built to the acre, each standing in its own garden, in a well-planned estate', as well as the 'provision of ample open spaces for recreational purposes'.[60] At a time when twenty per acre was considered the ideal for new developments in Belfast (and when the actual density was sixty),[61] the White City at ten houses per acre was indeed privileged. Moreover, the trust had decided to leave the four acres of the Throne lands, adjacent to the estate, free from development, thus creating what amounted to unspoilt countryside on our doorstep: 'On its northern boundary is the Throne Hospital and between it and the houses is a four-acre belt of well-wooded land, which is being retained as an open space and recreation ground'.[62] The estate plan also shows a number of small to large green spaces within the estate. Every house has a front and back garden. For the most part the houses are in blocks of four, two and occasionally three, with some blocks of five to seven houses in the longer streets such as Thorburn Road and Garton Way. There is also a handful of low-level flats (two levels). 'For some reason the idea of flats had never caught on in Belfast,' wrote Emrys Jones in a series of articles in the *Belfast Telegraph*, and only a small number had been built recently, 'of a height modest enough not to obtrude on the landscape'.[63] This describes perfectly those flats at the top of Portmore Hill and at the end of Thorburn Road (see photograph on back cover), which are indistinguishable from the surrounding houses. The houses were all white, except for a couple at the bottom of Portmore Hill and a scattering elsewhere, which were pink (I have been unable to discover why). A block of shops as well as a Housing Trust estate office, with flats above, were added in 1952 at the south-east corner of the estate, near the existing shops on the Serpentine Road.[64] They were a long way from residents at the top corner of the estate, where we lived, but a welcome source of pocket money, as a neighbour would regularly call on me to make the trek for her cigarettes.

The photo on the back cover is of the completed estate in 1949. It shows the tell-tale signs of the aftermath of building in the undeveloped gardens, though note the sapling trees. Three established trees, which I recall on our street, have been ringed on the planning map, possibly to prevent their felling by those landholders subject to vesting orders, which indeed had been happening. The photo is taken from the lower end of Portmore Hill, looking towards the flats at the top, the large villa called 'Throneview', and upward to the Cave Hill. The houses to the left are the pink ones, the streets opening into Garton Way and Thorburn Road; those to the right are in blocks of four, facing each other, separated by a green space and with no through roads. The Housing Trust sought to make estates safe for children and staggered streets to prevent through traffic. Thus were created those perfectly safe cul-de-sacs and green spaces where crowds of children would form into teams for skipping, rounders and the many other games with which we whiled away our childhoods. The photograph in the picture section, showing the estate in the process of demolition in the early 1990s, is taken from the same point and the sapling trees are fully grown.

Planning experts of the day clearly regarded the Housing Trust as a breath of fresh air. John Oliver recalled how the trust estates became instantly recognisable and admired by the public.[65] Emrys Jones, too, though critical of the ever-expanding suburbia, was very complimentary about the good planning and signs of better a standard of living in the new estates. The houses were:

> … much more commodious than those of the by-laws. They are well-designed to meet the needs of a medium-size family, and have essential amenities like bathrooms … Each house has its garden and back or side access, and on the whole architects have been at pains to provide pleasing designs and have not been afraid of using bright colours … This landscape is not merely for the housing of many thousands of people. Rather it is meant to be the creation of pleasant surroundings in which to live, and the provision of social amenities which recognise the full range of human activities.[66]

By all accounts, then, those who were fortunate enough to secure the tenancy of a house in the White City were moving into some kind of new Arcadia, at least in contrast to what had gone before.

4

The First Residents

*Belfast ... is really ... a number of little village communities ...
which come to have a separate, self-contained life of their own,
through the common interests, activities and institutions of the people
who live there.*

Hugh Shearman, *Ulster*, 1949[1]

'My mother visited Bellevue before the White City was built. She looked around and said: "this is where I want to live". I was sad that she died before I could tell her I got a house there.' Anna Pearson was from a farming family just outside Donegal town, south of the border. Her husband had been in the British army during the war and was working for the post office in Belfast when the opportunity to be housed arose. She had two children by then and had returned to Donegal to look after her father when her mother died. Her journey by various buses to Belfast, with a baby and toddler, carrying numerous cases and bags, was no easier as she neared her new home. In 1947 there was no public transport on that last sharp ascent from Greencastle up the Whitewell Road and she wondered if they would ever arrive. But, like the other first residents I have spoken with, she had joyful memories of moving into a brand-new house in the White City in November 1947. She was one of the very earliest to do so. Everyone was young. The estate was full of children and there was genuine neighbourliness.[2] Anna's story is very typical of the people who lived in the White City in its early decades: 'I never wanted anyone else to have that house,' she declared. Nor did they. She remained until this factory-made estate was demolished and replaced in the 1990s, when she moved to a retirement bungalow.

Tenants for the new Housing Trust estates were chosen on a strict points system. Need was the overriding consideration. A married couple with two children under ten were deemed to need accommodation with two bedrooms; every two children over ten of the same sex were deemed to need an additional bedroom; and a family of six needed a 'living room' – although this could be a parlour, dining room or kitchen. Strangely the absence of bathrooms in their existing accommodation is not included as qualifying for points, even though this had been such a heated issue. But the absence of a toilet was included, as were deficient ventilation and lighting, excessive dampness and the absence of a water supply. Service in the armed forces earned additional points, as did bomb damage during the Blitz and tuberculosis in any member of the family.[3] The result was a large number of serving and former servicemen and women on the estate, Catholic and Protestant alike. Indeed, the local British Legion was well known to service Catholics and Protestants and during the later Troubles its name was changed to the Veterans' club. Just like Anna's husband, Edwin, there were others from the south who had served in the British forces. Early residents recalled the wide range of accents on the estate, with many residents also coming from the country areas of Northern Ireland. Flo Kelsey had a particular liking for those from Armagh, where her family came from and where she continued to visit.

The 1954 Field-Neill Survey found that 54 per cent of residents had been living with relatives prior to obtaining a tenancy on the new estate. A further 18 per cent had been living in furnished or unfurnished rooms. A total of 15 per cent had tenancies of other houses, 6 per cent of a rural cottage, 3 per cent of wooden or Nissen huts. Of the thirty-one White City families surveyed as part of the study, fifteen had previously resided in north Belfast, six in north-west Belfast, six in County Antrim and three in County Down and one in south Belfast. This was in line with the settlement of Housing Trust estates generally, tenants remaining near relatives and previous homes. Also 35 per cent of applicants on these estates had served in the forces.[4]

Potential tenants were those who had already applied to the local authority, which passed on their details to the Housing Trust. The Housing Trust then sent out its own questionnaire. The applicants would be checked for eligibility. They had to be resident in Northern

Ireland and be 'workers' on a weekly wage sufficient to pay the higher trust rents.[5] They would then be graded according to the points system outlined earlier. Then a Housing Trust manager would visit them to assess their need. Those with the highest number of points were visited first, and, if approved, housed as quickly as possible. Although the trust often denied that this was a consideration, its managers did take account of how housewives looked after their accommodation. Indeed, I have been told that it was not uncommon for a trust manager to run her fingers over surfaces to check for dust. Sir Lucius told a UUC deputation on 23 May 1950 that, while the points system was the main criterion, there was also an element of discretion in the choice of those who would make the best tenants and here the visit was the second most important element, 'to see what kind of housekeepers the women were. If they were not good housekeepers with clean houses this always counted against them.'[6]

Sheila Burns recalled the preliminary visit. She had had a very hard time since her marriage in 1944. In July 1945 Terry, her husband, was working on the American air base at Langford Lodge, today's international airport, and she was in hospital for the birth of the first child. When he did not turn up for work one day, his friend, US airman Irving Silverman, travelled into Belfast and found him unconscious, the bed soaked in blood. He spent the next eighteen months in Whiteabbey sanatorium being treated for tuberculosis. She, with a new baby, needed outdoor relief and was badly treated by her Catholic landlord in north Belfast, who disliked the baby crying. It was a terrible fall from grace for someone from a reasonably well-off family and she was aged ninety when she finally brought herself to tell me about it.

When Terry was discharged from the sanatorium, they were found a dilapidated country cottage by his relatives in County Down. From there he continued his treatment in Belfast, making the weekly mile-long walk to the bus stop. The cottage, 'Cassies', was by all accounts idyllic. Family photos show Terry in country-squire pose, and Sheila spoke warmly both of the elderly woman farmer from whom they rented and of their neighbour, Lord Bangor, who would stop and chat to her as she pushed a pram through his Castleward estate. But it was very remote and primitive, with no running water and no inside toilet or bathroom. The absence of such amenities in previous homes is a common factor in all accounts of the White City's first tenants. Terry did voluntary work for the organisation of ex-patients and there was told, by Flo Kelsey's sister Maureen, about the Housing Trust and the White City. And so a lifelong family friendship was formed with Flo, because Maureen had asked her to watch out for the young family when they arrived on the estate. A second child had arrived in 1948 and, when the Housing Trust manager visited, Sheila was in an adjacent field, washing nappies in a great tin tub. 'If I'd known she was coming I would have tidied the house,' she told me, and she was to do that consistently before the weekly visits of the housing manager in the White City. She must have kept a clean house, despite the difficulties, for they were given the tenancy to a house there in 1949.

Shane and Anne McAteer were teenagers when they moved into Thorburn Road in 1949, with their schoolteacher mother and train-driver father – a mixed marriage, Shane joked, as regards class. Anne had been at the Holy Family primary school in nearby Newington before the Blitz destroyed their Cavehill Road home, and she never returned. They became Blitz refugees in Randalstown and she recalls severe overcrowding – both in the accommodation, where there were often four to five to a bed – and in the various schools. They moved accommodation frequently and her schooling suffered terribly. Shane and Anne recalled Rita Ward, a local councillor from the Newington area and the daughter of a Catholic publican in Greencastle, alerting the family to the existence of the new estate. Along with Sheila, she thought the Greencastle parish priest may also have had some influence. But it was their mother who filled in the Housing Trust forms.

Flo had been working in London, where she had met her husband, Fred. But she found Londoners very cold and hard, so she and her husband returned to Belfast to have their first child in 1947. They lived with her mother and father and her siblings in North Queen Street. Her husband joined the Belfast Harbour Police that year. She moved into a ground-floor flat in the White City in 1949, 'while they were still building'.

Eileen Gordon's grandfather was a Dubliner who had moved to Belfast in 1922. Her family came from Sandy Row. Living conditions were bad, with no inside toilet or bathroom. Brian Dunn, too, recalled lots of relatives visiting to have a bath when they first moved into the White City. Given the terrible housing conditions described earlier, families were moved in as and when houses became available. Brian's parents moved in within a week of signing the tenancy agreement. With unforeseen delays, parts of the estate remained a building site longer than they should have done. Eileen Gordon and Gerry Mulholland were just children when their families moved. Both remembered continued building, with site huts, big ditches and mounds of earth, where children made see-saws from planks of wood.

Gerry's family had been living in very crowded conditions in an old house with no electricity in Greencastle village. Their house became something of a rescue post where other bombed-out locals were accommodated. 'Our house was often full of total strangers,' he told me. 'An old railing, balanced between the sides of a big hole in the house wall' was the improvised cooker, stoked by wood gathered from outside debris. They moved into the White City to an end house in Bresk Hill in 1948. Though a corner plot appears on the planning map, Gerry's father, another keen gardener, negotiated with the construction team to have it incorporated into their garden.

House numbers changed as more were completed. Despite frequent requests from the Housing Trust to Belfast Corporation, which was responsible for the various utilities, the provision of lighting on its Falls and Whitewell estates was only finally approved in January 1949. Even then there was a sense of living in the country, for the lighting on the Antrim Road was reduced to half that within the city boundary and none at all when it was switched off during the six weeks before and the six weeks after midsummer.[7] The Housing Trust was anxious that Belfast Corporation should coordinate lighting plans with it, because 'a great deal of care has been expended in planning the layout of the estate' and it wanted lamps 'to harmonise with the general design'. It also feared that installation might interfere with the pavements already laid. The trust recommended electric lighting, but the corporation chose gas.[8] And so the gas-lamplighter became part of the early story of the White City (until 1958, when electricity finally arrived on the streets), a strange throwback in an otherwise very modern estate.[9] But the iron prongs that protruded from the metal lamp-posts to assist the lamplighter were perfectly adapted to our home-made swings, on which we could play well past sunset, bathed in the watery light given off by the gas mantle.[10]

The trust's tenancy agreement read as follows:

> At the start of a new tenancy the prospective tenant and the guarantor should be present as well as the wife, or member of the family, with whom the Housing Manager will normally be dealing, when the conditions of tenancy are read. The husband is usually the tenant because he is usually the wage earner and it is upon him that the legal responsibility rests.[11]

Technically this allowed the trust to sue the guarantor for recovery of rent, although the guarantee expired after three years of the tenancy and it seems that an alternative to a guarantor was a £10 deposit. The existence of the guarantor gave the trust a lever for the recalcitrant tenant, who usually paid up rather than face the shame of a relative being informed. The guarantor system was abolished for existing tenants in 1957 but retained for new ones. The tenant also had to pay stamp duty of around 10s. (varying with the rent) until 1963, when it too was abolished.[12]

The agreement – in addition to all the normal clauses about keeping the premises clean and in good repair – contains a clause forbidding the keeping of 'pigs poultry pigeons rabbits or other livestock'. This might seem rather superfluous to us today, except that pigeon-keeping was very prevalent in working-class areas and Belfast was trying to restrict the presence of livestock in the city centre and pigmen collecting food scraps door to door, which continued well into the 1950s. Indeed, I recall one of our neighbours, a jolly man with equally friendly children, parking his truck full of such scraps and tin buckets at the end of the street. And, while one domestic pet was permitted per household and none whatsoever in flats, both regulations were often broken. In line with the trust's commitment to green spaces, incoming tenants were forbidden from erecting sheds or huts and from cutting down any trees, bushes or shrubs. An additional clause was inserted extending this to the tenant's children:

> The tenant shall be responsible for seeing that his or her
> children behave properly on all parts of the Trust's estate …
> so as not to cause a nuisance or annoyance to other tenants
> or to the public, and that his or her children do not spoil
> or damage any buildings, walls, fences, gates, trees, shrubs,
> plants, turf or anything on the property of and belonging
> to the Trust.[13]

Trust houses had no external fixtures for holding flags, as there
had been in older public housing. I would like to think that this
was because of its politico-religious neutrality, but I have found no
evidence for this. It is more likely that it was in line with the general
policy of deterring any damage to the exterior of the houses, and
new clauses were introduced to this effect when TV aerials started to
appear.[14]

Then it was time to move in. 'Working class tenants find these
houses palatial compared with the very poor accommodation to which
many of them have been accustomed,' wrote Eric Bird, after his and
Frederic Osborn's visit to Housing Trust developments in 1949. 'Most
tenants come from poor and overcrowded dwellings and have never
before had a home of their own.'[15] All of those I spoke with recall the
sense of space, brightness and newness of their allotted houses. Anne
remembers the excitement at opening the cupboards and doors to
find yet more space, and above all the sheer relief at having 'a room at
last', after so many years of sharing with relatives. Anna wondered how
they were going to furnish it, since the rooms seemed so big. Another
recalled a relative remarking acidly that she would have no excuse for
a dirty house now!

The Orlit house was the biggest of the factory-made houses used
by the trust. The three-bedroom ones, the majority in the White City,
had a bathroom and separate toilet, both on the top floor near the
bedrooms. There was plenty of storage, the two largest bedrooms
having built-in wardrobes, large enough for the children to play hide-
and-seek and the parents to hide the Christmas presents. Downstairs,
one entered directly into an ample hall, off which a combined dining
room and living room stretched from back to front, with windows on
both sides, and an open fire, which also heated the water. Emrys Jones

despaired of the attendant smoke pollution, for he thought it negated the environmental advantage of factories being absent from the new estates:

> This will not mean that residential areas will be smokeless now, for, unfortunately every house is fitted with the standard coal-burning grate. This means that, although we may be on the eve of legislation for smoke abatement, we are, in our house design, ensuring a continuance of that pollution for half a century.[16]

The kitchen – or 'scullery' as it is called in trust reports – had a built-in larder, a floor-to-ceiling cupboard, which also housed the electricity meter, a sink with two draining boards and a gas cooker. This led onto a covered alleyway, designed to allow coal deliveries, since there was no open access to the back.[17] In fact, it became part of the house, a place to keep pets, a covered play area and somewhere for sewing on a Singer treadle sewing machine. The flats were also spacious, with two bedrooms, a kitchen and sitting room. External doors were painted every four years, with 'top-quality materials'.[18]

However, the interiors did leave a lot to be desired and were certainly inferior to some other trust estates, such as Cregagh in east Belfast, which was built in traditional brick and had wooden floors and terazzo in the bathrooms. In an angry letter to the evaluator about charging White City tenants the same rates as Cregagh, J.D. Calvert, deputy manager of the trust, explained:

> When the Cregagh Estate was being considered by your division, due regard was given to the surrounding district, the tone of which was classed high. I think you will agree that the Whitewell neighbourhood and the approach to the Trust's estate there do not come up to the Cregagh standard. Indeed adjacent houses on the Serpentine Road are not nearly so good as those on the Cregagh Road.

Calvert had to admit that the gardens were larger in the White City and so the rates remained slightly higher.[19]

Furnishing the houses was a challenge. The 1953–4 survey by Field and Neill commented:

> Removal to a spacious new house from one room or a small overcrowded kitchen house is almost invariably accompanied by the necessity for buying new furniture [beds a main issue] … The light and space in a new house accentuates the grime and shabbiness of old furniture which served its purpose in small dark rooms. New houses have large windows which must be curtained against the curious eyes of neighbours and passers-by.[20]

The Housing Trust had sought powers to supply furniture, as had been the case in Scotland. This would have made it easier to acquire and cheaper, but it was prevented from doing so because of representations from the furniture companies.[21] They had suffered considerably from wartime austerity and Eileen Gordon's father had lost his job in the Glenarm furniture factory as a result. They also resisted the idea of utility furniture, and its introduction only came in October 1944, eighteen months later than in Britain generally. Utility furniture was considered better than that produced during the war, for 'a sound standard of workmanship had been introduced and enforced on all manufacturers'.[22] Certainly I recall the typical sturdy utility furniture from my childhood home. Residents told me that they bought furniture on hire-purchase and in charity shops. 'But the beds were new. We would never have bought a charity bed.' The Field-Neill survey of 1953–4 found residents paying an average of 10–15s. per week on hire-purchase, at a time when most applicants to the Housing Trust were earning less than £8 10s. (ie 170s.) per week, and unskilled workers less than 133s.[23] No case was found of a TV set on hire-purchase and only 9 families from the sample 363 had one.

There were few negative comments by those interviewed for the survey, but a key criticism was of the coldness, dampness and draughtiness of the houses. There was another open fireplace in the largest bedroom. I do not recall it being used in our house; indeed, it added to the draughtiness. But it did produce the sense of a separate living space and this is where my mother's younger sister resided during her training as a nurse, before she emigrated to America. I was told that in another house it became the private space of one tenant when her two sons married and brought their wives to live in the now very overcrowded house. Paraffin heaters were ubiquitous, causing mould and excessive condensation. The Housing Trust calculated that one gallon of paraffin produced an equal volume of water.[24] 'We were so glad to get a place,' Flo told me, 'but the houses were rotten. They were like fridges.' Anna agreed and she never did get a wooden floor. A central-heating installation programme began in the 1980s, only to be stopped on the discovery of 'irreversible structural defects' in the Orlit design.[25]

Tenants were responsible for internal decor and I recall a very colourful home. Brighter colours in her new communities had been one of Octavia Hill's ideals and was a feature of manufacturing as rationing and wartime drabness receded.[26] The exterior doors were painted every four years – red, yellow and bright green, as I recall for the years we lived there. Their painting carried an equally colourful history, as Brendan Behan was part of one of the painting teams. 'I wanted to take the door with me!' chuckled Flo as she told me of her move from the flat to a house on the estate after the birth of another child. With two doors on the frontage of every house, this was a lot of colour against the white houses. At one stage I recall both outside (the front doors) and inside (the hall/staircase) being decorated in bright yellow, the latter with embossed wallpaper, which was very difficult to hang for the novice. The living/dining room was slightly quieter in tone, with fawn and maroon embossed wallpaper (matching the maroon suite, one of the standard pieces of utility furniture).[27] Colour exploded again in the kitchen, the washable wallpaper covered with brightly coloured pictures of vegetables and cooking utensils and the Formica table and kitchen chairs again coloured yellow.

'It has been suggested that the Trust always tends to have the better tenants and that the local authorities are left with the less satisfactory tenants,' claimed the Cameron Commission in 1969. That, indeed, was the common perception. 'There is no doubt that Housing Trust tenants felt themselves to be a cut above the rest,' recalled Charles Brett. 'Indeed, many of its ex-tenants still do.'[28] The Field-Neill Survey found that 59.7 per cent of male householders of Housing

Trust estates were 'workers', or class III, 'skilled manual' in the registrar general's classification; 4.6 per cent were 'clerical', also class III, with smaller numbers in classes IV –'semi-skilled manual', 8.6 per cent – and V, 'unskilled manual', 18.6 per cent.[29] In the grant of tenancies, the term 'worker' was very loosely defined. They also found 8.6 per cent in classes I–II, 'professional' and 'commercial'. A snapshot of male employment in the White City in the years 1949–50 reveals a largely similar breakdown. Portmore Hill, the last street to be completed, has a larger number of what the registrar general classified as classes I–II ('professional', 'commercial'), possibly because of the large number of two-storey, two-bedroom flat units – twenty-four of a total fifty-nine dwellings – that went to one-child families. Thus we had five clerks or civil servants, a shipwright, a 'salesman', a 'traveller', a commercial artist, a member of the 'air ministry', several in the armed forces (one 'admiralty police', one soldier, one Merchant Navy, one Royal Navy).[30] Otherwise the social mix was much the same as elsewhere on the estate. There was a sprinkling of policemen. The general blend remained fairly stable into the mid-1950s.

In those days before widespread car ownership, carrying toolboxes to and from work was part of the daily timetable for men. Brian Dunn recalled an unusual method of timekeeping in their neighbour George Hamilton, a tug pilot, who could see Belfast Lough from his home. Whenever he saw a boat coming in, he knew that it was time to leave for work. Norah Van Puten, too, remembered neighbours saying that they set their clocks by her father's 6.30 a.m. departure for work as a fitter, then supervisor at the air-force construction site near the docks.

By 1959 there were fewer in the class I–III social categories, possibly reflecting the better housing circumstances by then, or a greater ability to purchase. These figures confirm the very high employment situation reflected in the 1953–4 survey, with only 3.9 per cent of males unemployed and a further 30 per cent of females working full or part time. Although the decline in the heavy industries had already started, and there were big payoffs at Harland and Wolff in 1952 and at Shorts in 1958 and 1959, there was a shortage of both skilled males and female workers generally, notwithstanding the 1951–2 textile slump. Also it was the government's policy to site new factories on the outskirts of Belfast, and a number were opened at

Larne, Carrickfergus, Monkstown and Carnmoney in the late 1950s.[31]

My own recollection (supported by that of others) is of a higher proportion of women in the workforce than reflected in the Field-Neill Survey. Women were employed in the mills and factories of the area and the Throne hospital; they also worked as waitresses, shop assistants, 'home helps', secretaries, civil servants and occasionally teachers. 'Lots of the women worked,' Flo told me. 'There was plenty of work.' Nor did the survey reveal levels of 'domestic industry'.[32] In this age of continuing austerity, everyone has recollections of dressmakers and knitters on the estate. I recall many visits to a very talented and industrious dressmaker (and with rather less affection the range of tartan skirts and pinafores that she made, in which our mother insisted on dressing both my sister, who was five years younger than me, and myself). This was Annie Johnson in Garton Way and she figures prominently in estate memory. 'She was a wee dote,' commented Lizzy's daughter May Doherty. 'She baked me a second tier of my wedding cake free of charge because her husband had omitted to watch the oven and the first tier had overcooked.' Flo also told me that the warehouses delivered bundles of handkerchiefs for hand-stitching at home.

Some of this may help explain why the standardised questions about shopping posed by the 1953–4 university researchers were confusing to the interviewees, for many shopped randomly on the way home from work or from visiting relatives. Also, people did not always shop in the sense of actually going to shops. Rather the shops came to them in the form of mobile outlets.[33] I recall a mobile grocery, two different bread vans (with huge wooden drawers pulled from the back to reveal the array of buns to insistent children) and a neighbour who worked in a home bakery taking orders for boxes of weekend pastries. Such was the demand for cakes and biscuits, reported the main Belfast bakery, Inglis, in 1956, that it had outstripped capacity and it was opening a new factory to meet the demand.[34] Lorries also brought soft drinks, manufactured by local mineral businesses Ross's and Cantrell & Cochrane. Such regular delivery men became part of the community. Big, jolly, ginger-haired and moustached bread man Mr (Billy) Major was a particular favourite of ours and Gerry Mulholland remembered him intervening with the long pole he used to pull out the bread-van drawers to stop one child being bullied. People always seemed to be calling on the houses for payments and to take orders in this pre-car age: insurance-company representatives, Betterware men selling brushes and hardware, the 'Co' representative, who took the weekly grocery order, the gas-meter man, who emptied the electric meter and refunded a certain percentage, the rag-and-bone man, who exchanged cups for old rags. Gerry was a part-time delivery boy for Herron's greengrocer's on the Serpentine Road and remembers the big heavy bicycle from which he delivered orders all round the area.

Most residents, it seems, ate fish on Fridays. Moira Morrow recalled the fish van going round the estate on Fridays, the vendor shouting, 'Herrings today!' Back then I always thought Friday fish-eating some kind of Catholic penance. I was disappointed to find the state school in Glengormley where I sat my eleven-plus exam also serving fish that Friday – denying me the one chance I had of closet dissidence. We had no fridge at home and we still had none when we left in 1963, although we had had a TV set and a car for nearly a decade by then. There were no shops on the estate until 1953,[35] but a range of small local ones supplemented the above: there were a grocer/greengrocer, a butcher and a chemist on the Serpentine Road and general stores on the Whitewell Road and Longlands. There were also hole-in-the-wall stores or 'parlour shops',[36] 'almost run from a front sitting room' as Moira recalled, which would serve at all hours of the day.

There always seemed to be a good supply of fresh vegetables – too good and not varied enough for us children. Just as the Housing Trust had hoped, there was a number of enthusiastic gardeners on the estate, including my father. The Field-Neill Survey showed healthy diets on the estates, though also a high meat intake. Fruit was not in great supply, except local and seasonal apples, pears, plums, and, as I recall, eternal jam-making. Bananas and oranges were treats that appeared in Christmas stockings and we had the additional treat of a box of mandarins sent each Christmas from New York by our father's aunts. Yet it was the ready supply of bananas and other foods that struck an English visitor in September 1951, as well as the more positive shopping experiences: 'the lively people in the smaller shops are delighted to see you; it is often otherwise in queue-weary England'.[37]

The estate shops opened in Navarra Place, at the Whitewell/

Serpentine Road end of the estate, in 1953. These consisted of the Housing Trust estate office, a greengrocer and fruiterer, a bakery, a newsagent and confectioner, a drapery, a hairdresser, a dry cleaner and, the following year, the chippy, or Whitewell Supper Saloon. Finally, here was some amusement for the teenagers on the estate and the chippy became a magnet for them. Gerry recalled the owner bribing him and his friends with a free bag of chips to congregate away from the entrance. Above the shops were eight new flats let out to a labourer, a driver, an electrician, a 'private detective', a woman, possibly widowed, and a male hairdresser, who had moved from one of the Thorburn Road flats.[38]

The Housing Trust was extremely proud of its new estates, and not just structurally. It sought to run them as 'communities', the Health and Local Government Ministry's Ronald Green wrote in 1951: 'The present Trust have always shown themselves quite as keenly interested in management as in building.'[39] The Housing Trust cared about its tenants. It fought hard to keep rents down: 'It is no real kindness to give a family a house if they are unable to afford the rent.'[40] There was also an understanding of how difficult things might prove in the early days of acquiring an unfurnished tenancy:

> It must be remembered that the better houses now being built involve extra household expenditure in addition to the rents and rates. Most of the families moving in have never had a house but have been existing in one or two rooms. Furniture has generally to be bought, and, in a number of ways the family moves on to a better standard of living. For instance, anyone passing through a Trust estate will notice the bright clean curtains on the windows and an occasional glimpse of the interior suggests a degree of comfort and personal taste not possible in the cramped quarters from which the family has come. All this ... vindicates the Trust's faith that most families, if only given the opportunity to make pleasant homes, will do so. But it costs money. The money could not be better spent and will reflect itself in health and happiness, but this expenditure must be taken into account and reinforces the need to keep down rents.[41]

These early reports by the Housing Trust board read like a sculptor or artist standing back and admiring the finished product. But would their handpicked tenants look after that product? Enter the housing managers, trained in the Octavia Hill system. As Herbert Bryson, the trust's final chairman, told the Cameron Commission in 1969:

> The Trust has from the very start adopted a very sophisticated form of house management as opposed to rent collection. We have highly trained, mostly women housing managers one of whose functions is to collect the rent and for that purpose calls [sic] fortnightly [weekly until 1959] at every house. The other main function that she has is to do a sort of welfare job with the tenants, see that our standards are maintained, that the gardens are kept neat and tidy, the hedges trimmed, the estate looking nice and as far as possible encourage the tenants to take a pride in the estate. She also talks to the wives about their housekeeping if there are any difficulties of a financial nature, and she also helps them with house appliances that have been installed ... We also have spent a lot of money in planting trees and shrubs and cutting the grass to make the estates look nice ... and we try to encourage the tenants to appreciate them.[42]

The Housing Trust manual gives some idea of the minutiae overseen by the managers. These range from detailed instructions about how the property should be looked after to warnings about cleaning products: Johnston's Glo-Coat, Sposs or Poliphalt should be used to polish the mastic asphalt floors, rather than the ubiquitous Mansion floor polish, and the toilet cleaner Harpic is never to be used on baths.[43] Tenants should report necessary repairs, but the manager should keep 'a vigilant eye' during her weekly visits. Under the heading 'Marital Difficulty', the manager is exhorted to be vigilant for the husband who has, or is about to desert his wife, and is trying to terminate the contract. He should be told that if his family remains, he will still be made liable for the rent.[44] Other issues highlighted are resolution of 'squabbles between neighbours' and 'difficult or poor rent paying tenants interviewed and cajoled into co-operation'.[45] However, notices to quit were infrequent and 'nuisance' or 'annoyance' tended to be the cause as often as non-payment of rent; and the tenant was given generous time to make good.[46] Nowadays most people would find this weekly check on the tenants and their lifestyles intrusive. However, these were different, less informed and less questioning times and, for the kind of tenant sought by the Housing Trust, the system probably worked well. Sheila Burns recalled the manager Miss Dunlop as being a very nice person, as did others. Gerry Mulholland remembered her commissioning his mother to bake for an event she was organising and paying generously. In practical terms it also meant that faults and necessary repairs could be reported and dealt with quickly.

I spoke with two former female housing managers. Both recalled the Housing Trust as being very solicitous towards its employees and they were very well aware of the career opportunity opened up to them. Both from working-class backgrounds, their parents could not have sacrificed their earning potential while they went to university. Rather, they were able to acquire their qualifications while working for the trust through distance learning and day release. They also recall a rather militaristic organisation, run by formidable tweed-dressed women, who were sticklers for rules and procedures.

Although the Housing Trust acquired a second-hand Morris Minor car, which could be pre-booked, the housing managers generally chose to walk and take the bus. Little wonder most people's recollections are of their sensible shoes and clothing. They went door to door with their leather Gilbert rent bag. This, the former managers with whom I spoke explained in some detail to me, was very well ordered, and they clearly retained an admiration for its simplicity. In the Gilbert system, the internal folder contained three copies of a rent sheet for each street. Each tenant's rent-book was aligned with the address, date and amount and initialled, so that exactly the same entry appeared on the rent-book and in the manager's record. Three different colours of pens identified payment of rent, arrears or 'void' (house unoccupied). The housing managers did not find the bag cumbersome, but did recall difficulty in keeping the sheets dry if they were kept at the door. It was more normal, however, to be invited in, given tea and scones, lunch and even sherry on a bad day. Necessary repairs were noted in a book. The manager would then commission the work and return to inspect it before the invoice was paid. They also listened to a range of problems, including noise issues. An area that would have been very beneficial for tenants was advice on 'matters of a welfare nature … families requiring skilled specialist advice are referred to welfare officers or organizations'. And the managers maintained close contact with both voluntary and official bodies.[47] In an era when no one on the estate, to my knowledge, had a telephone – the one public telephone box was located near the shops, while post offices were long walks away on the Antrim Road and at Greencastle – this was a valuable service. There was certainly a very high uptake of the services available to mothers with babies and infants in the area, with mothers very keen to avail of advice on the care of infants as well as the food from the clinics.[48]

Although dealing specifically with slum clearance, the papers delivered by the Housing Trust managers to a conference in November 1957 provide a good insight into tenant–housing manager relations. They clearly grew quite close to these tenants and do seem to have provided the 'sort of welfare job' described by Bryson. Tenants were talked through the extra expense of moving into a new house 'and the dangers of becoming too involved in hire-purchase'. But it was also the tough love of Octavia Hill, with her emphasis on 'the regular payment of rent', cleanliness and tidiness and resistance to anything like a dependency culture, by helping tenants to help themselves.[49] Most, even from slum-clearance schemes, became 'model tenants', though 'it is difficult to foster friendly relations' with those who needed constant reminding about 'arrears of rent or a dirty house'.[50]

In talking with former and existing residents, I have not encountered as much resentment about such apparent condescension as I had expected, and where I have it is usually from males, who would have had less contact with them. Also the criticisms come from the 1960s, and the fact that Miss Dunlop's successor, I was told, lived in one of the big houses looking down on the estate and 'followed the hounds' may have been a factor in this. Former head of the Northern Ireland civil service, Sir Ken Bloomfield, recalled the Housing Trust as an 'admirable' though 'somewhat elitist body whose lady housing managers in many cases evinced the zeal of a Florence Nightingale'.[51] Certainly on another Belfast estate by the 1960s a tenants' association spoke of the 'Housing Managers of whom the women were afraid and the men were in terror'.[52] However, given that the arrears of rent and repairs in 1951–2, on *all* trust estates, were £78 against £275,000 rents collected and £273 6s. 6d. against £1,200,000 collected in 1957–8, the system seems to have worked well.[53]

There is some sense in the 1957 conference papers that the tenants did not always share the trust's vision and pride:

> The Trust takes a great interest in the welfare of its Tenants, but I regret to have to say that most of the tenants, especially in clearance areas, take little interest in the Trust, as such! I have often attempted to explain the 'set-up' to them, but they just listen with polite indifference.[54]

It has been said also of Octavia Hill that her ideal was not always that of the tenants: 'she somewhat erred in sympathy by urging them to attain her standards for them instead of their own for themselves'.[55] In the final analysis, as Brett comments, this 'formidable body of women, a source of great strength to the Trust, was regarded by tenants with mingled awe and respect; indeed some of them were dragons, even if they were also in fact both competent and humane'.[56]

Both Octavia Hill and her Housing Trust followers spoke frequently about building a real 'sense of community' on their estates. What exactly they meant by that is unclear, though in trust documents it is usually related to the provision of amenities. The trust did not permit public houses on its estates, and although there had been talk of a community centre and a playground in the White City, neither arrived until 2009–10. In fairness, such centres and playgrounds were the responsibility of the local and education authorities and the trust was still complaining of their inactivity in its final reports.[57] Ultimately it was so frustrated at the lack of progress that it started to supply such centres itself on the larger estates, though not on ours. By then it refers to a new source of finance coming from the Ministry of Community Relations.

We never missed such facilities, although they might have provided a means for the mothers to socialise, which otherwise was arranged through church halls. As it was, there were so many children of the same age that a group very quickly formed when any were seen playing outside. Street play ranged very widely indeed, depending on the weather and numbers involved: making dens in the covered alleyways; playing hopscotch on the flagged streets; pretending to be Stirling Moss with a discarded pram wheel or home-made 'guiders' (motorless go-karts) made from similar pram and Tan-Sad wheels – for which the White City, with its many hills, was a natural racecourse. Hours would be spent bouncing tennis balls off walls, sometimes as many as three or four at a time, advanced levels of expertise commanding considerable respect from other children. Marbles were played by girls and boys alike, the brightly coloured 'bulldozers' the desirable prize. The large space at the top of Portmore Hill lent itself to more organised play – rounders, Pussy-in-the-Four-Corners and skipping, with the older girls able to manipulate two hefty ropes simultaneously and queues of children lining up to jump in while chanting the many colourful skipping rhymes.

The first residents had been selected by the Housing Trust from 'the thousands of respectable and deserving families living in miserable conditions'.[58] They were also the early beneficiaries of new thinking about workers' housing, which saw a sharp move away from the endless, gardenless terraces of the past and the beginnings of constructive thinking about developing neighbourhoods and real communities.[59] Whether or not such a sense had developed in the White City would become evident in a series of highly unusual events in the early 1950s.

5

The Dramas of
Not-So-Everyday Lives

Once we begin calling every week for the rent, we find out all manner of strange things … people have most interesting, and even lurid, life histories to tell.

Northern Ireland Housing Trust, *Annual Report*, 1957–8[1]

There was something very creepy running through my early memories of the White City. On reflection, this is surprising, since it was such a safe place, where we were allowed to wander freely and to play outdoors far beyond lamplighting time. I always thought it was those life-size fairytale characters that my artist father had painted on the new house's bare plaster in my bedroom, which frightened me so much that he had to cover them with run-of-the-mill wallpaper. I still feel guilty about that. Then there was the death of my grandfather way down in Kerry, necessitating the disappearance of my mother, and the coat that hung on my bedroom door, which assumed his shape during the night. Did others recall similar feelings? A few from my own age group did, though among the earliest residents 'politeness' prevailed, even in their memories, and they were reluctant to comment on anything unsavoury. There seems to have been an extra layer of knowledge among postmen's, milkmen's and police officers' families and I was told of a 'bawdy house', where fashion models lived; of rumoured paedophilia at the Throne school; of the alcoholic husbands who abused their wives and of admiration for those wives who held their families together nevertheless; and in my memories there certainly were men who smelt too much of drink and whom we children included in our 'dirty old men' category – people to be avoided. But it was only when I researched this book that I started to recall bigger things causing a frisson throughout the estate.

The lord chief justice reported 'a great post-war tidal wave of crime' in spring 1948, which the newspapers attributed to the return to civilian life of so many ex-servicemen. He warned residents not to leave pound notes out in bottles for the milkman and to ensure that their properties were secured when vacant. The *Irish News* advised leaving phones off the hook when away, advice which would have affected very few in the White City, but which endured and was repeated by my mother long after I had moved away from Belfast.[2] Then there were the murders. It may be hard to imagine in post-Troubles days, but they were sufficiently rare then to have been sensational. Between 1922 and 1955 there had been eleven executions for murder in Northern Ireland.[3] Even so, two murders happened uncomfortably close in place and time to my childhood. One was in the Newington area, where we had relatives and where we all went to school. I recall my father and others saying that it was Robert 'the Painter' Taylor who killed fifty-two-year-old Minnie McGowan in Ponsonby Avenue. Why do I have any memory at all of this, since it happened in 1949, when I was too young to remember? Perhaps in characteristic ghoulish childhood fascination I had heard the adults talking about how horrific the murder was, for the poor woman had staggered outside after being strangled, bludgeoned and stabbed multiple times.[4] Or was it because she was a Catholic and he was a Protestant who played on sectarian loyalties and, against all the evidence, was acquitted on retrial? Or was it because the initial guilty verdict had been handed down by Judge Curran, a local unionist bigwig from nearby Whiteabbey?

They also talked about (John) Christie, one of Britain's most notorious serial murderers and 10 Rillington Place in London, the scene of the crimes. Christie's neighbour was wrongly executed in 1950. Christie himself was eventually brought to justice in spring 1953 and executed that July, media reports in Northern Ireland coinciding with continued unease about the near-contemporary murder that happened not far from my childhood home. Shortly after Christie's execution my aunt Mamie took me to stay in London, possibly to help my parents after my sister Geraldine was born. I am still surprised that she was allowed to take me, at the age of five, into the Chamber

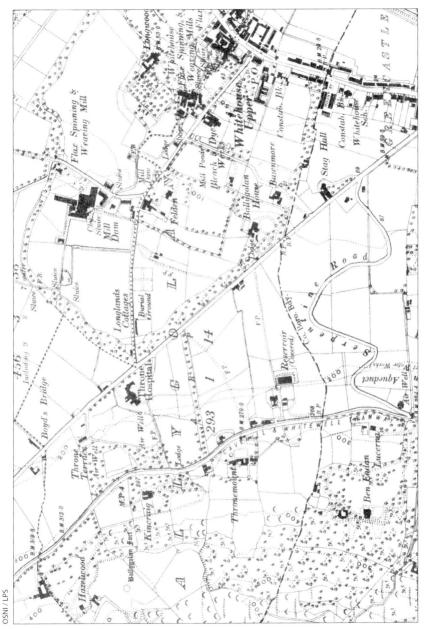

A 1901 map of the Ballygolan area with the Throne hospital
and Whitewell Road clearly visible.

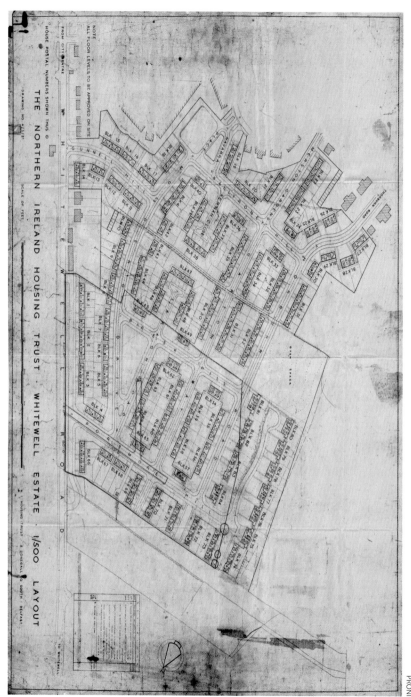

The Housing Trust's plan for the Whitewell estate, 1946.

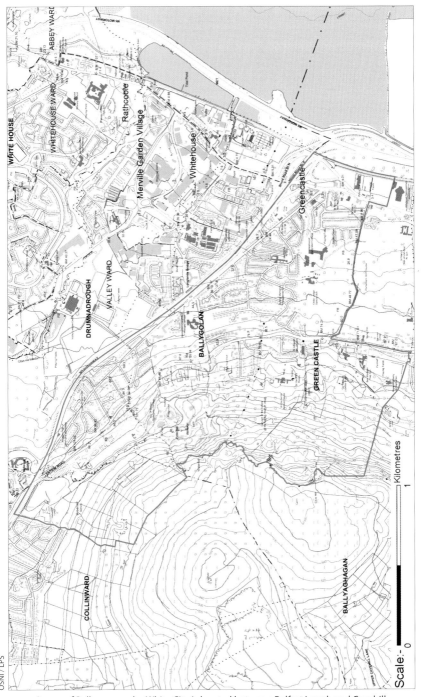

OSNI / LPS

A map of Bellevue ward – White City is located between Belfast Lough and Cavehill.

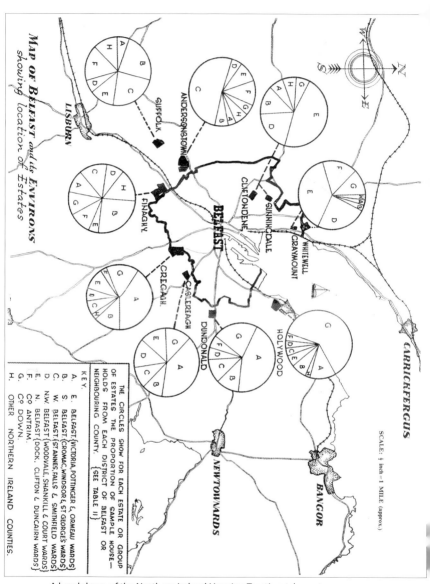

A breakdown of the Northern Ireland Housing Trust's catchment areas.

My parents, Terry and Sheila, at Belfast Castle, *c.*1950.

With my siblings, 1960. I am on the left, holding baby Eleanor,
with my brother Terry and sister Geraldine.

A street party on the estate to celebrate the Coronation, 1953.

The White City, 1949, nestled at the foot of Cave Hill.
Visible in the background is Throneview.

My father, Terry (right), with his American friends,
Royal Avenue, Belfast, *c*. 1945.

Gerry Mulholland and Michael Gillen – two members of the Brothers showband – on the White City estate, June 1963.

of Horrors in Madame Tussaud's wax museum. It was here that I was confronted by the lifelike Christie and the kitchen scene in Rillington Place where the bodies were found. I still remember the chilling layout details and the bottle of red tomato ketchup on the table was just too much. I gather that I screamed the place down. But the murder scandal that hit the headlines at the end of 1952 happened in the hinterland of the White City and has become part of its folklore.

The Curran family of 'The Glen', Whiteabbey was part of the unionist establishment. The father, Lancelot Curran, was a prominent Orangeman, unionist MP, attorney general (1947–9) and High Court judge. As such, he was to preside over some of Northern Ireland's most famous trials, including those of Robert 'the Painter' Taylor and Robert McGladdery, the last person to be executed in the province in 1961. With his wife, Doris, and three children, Curran lived on a ten-acre estate in one of those mansions where the mill-owning aristocracy of the previous century had resided. His sons, Desmond and Michael, were following him into the legal profession. The daughter, Patricia, was a spirited girl, keen on sport and definitely challenging the staid role of females in her position in the 1950s. In November 1952 she was a first-year student at Queen's University, studying social sciences. The evening of 12 November 1952 was one of those dark, drizzly evenings that I recall so well from travelling back to that part of the city from Queen's nearly two decades later. Patricia was last seen heading from the bus stop towards the heavily wooded and unlit grounds of her home. And that is where her body was found by members of her family in the early hours of the following morning. She had been attacked with enormous brutality, sustaining thirty-seven knife-wounds. And yet there was little blood at the scene, whilst her university books and bag were in such a neat pile as to give rise to popular belief that the location of the body was not actually the place of the murder. Nor was there a proper examination of the scene, as the young policeman called to attend found her father, brother and family solicitor loading Patricia's body into a car to take it to the local doctor.

A young airman from Scotland, Iain Hay Gordon, then based at the nearby Edenmore RAF camp, was subsequently convicted, but declared insane. He was confined to Holywell mental institution in

Antrim and released in 1960. However, the process by which the verdict had been reached was so flawed that it was overturned in 2000. Gordon was only twenty when the murder happened and considered a bit slow. He had become acquainted with Desmond Curran through Whiteabbey Presbyterian Church, whose minister, the Rev. S.J. Wylie, was also chaplain to Edenmore camp. Desmond Curran had sought to recruit Gordon to the Moral Re-Armament group (the same group to which Mary Whitehouse belonged), and had invited him into the Curran home – much to both his mother's and brother's annoyance. Indeed, Gordon thought Patricia 'the only normal one there'.[5] There were suggestions that Gordon was homosexual and he was certainly intimidated by such suggestions when, after several days of interrogation, without the presence of his own counsel, a confession was dictated to him and he signed it. Claims that a homosexual ring operated in Whiteabbey only added to the frisson, as 'thousands, mostly women', turned up for Gordon's remand hearing at a special court convened in Whiteabbey's British Legion hall.[6]

The identity of Patricia Curran's murderer has remained the subject of local speculation. There can be no doubt that the Curran family members were protected because of their status. They were never called as witnesses to the trial and police waited several days before searching the house. Mark Langhammer – longstanding Labour councillor for the area – later got to know the young policeman called out in the middle of the night. He told Langhammer that he had indeed objected to the removal of the body from the crime scene, but was told his career would suffer if he said anything. The Unionist Party rallied round. Even Gordon's defence lawyer made it a condition of his agreement to take the case that he would not have to interview Judge Curran. The brother, father and mother were accused in turn in local lore. Another rumour was that Patricia was murdered in the house, then brought outside. Flo Kelsey thought the father did it. She worked with an older woman who knew the housekeeper and visited the house. 'She saw the big stain inside. But people like him ruled the roost and could cover up. The same with people in the banks – [they] treated our kind [working people] with contempt.' Others accused the brother, attributing his conversion to Catholicism and service as a priest in the townships of South Africa to remorse. Then there was the mother. 'Both father and mother were heavy drinkers,' Mark Langhammer told me. 'The father was also a gambler. The daughter was very liberal for the era. Drove a van for the builders MacMillan's, which the mother disapproved of.' However, none of this was ever proved and wanting to avoid scandal is not the same as guilt. Even a feature-writer from the *People* newspaper – contacted by Gordon's mother and claiming to prove that Patricia had been attacked in her bedroom – did not entertain the idea that it was a family murder. Rather he concluded that it was done by an intruder and that the body was then carried outside.[7] The Curran murder has remained among the most notorious unsolved crimes of modern times, giving rise to successive lurid reports in the British tabloids, a number of television reconstructions and fictional creations, including Eoin McNamee's Booker-prize nominated *The Blue Tango*.[8] As Flo concluded, 'They made an awful lot of that murder.'

As the Curran murder and the fate of Iain Gordon still occupied the press, it was overtaken by reports of a number of travel disasters. The crash of a passenger plane at Northern Ireland's civilian airport, Nutt's Corner, on 5 January 1953 left twenty-seven dead out of the thirty-five passengers and crew, including a number of students returning to Queen's University after the Christmas break.[9] The 1950s witnessed a number of air crashes. But it was the cancellation of flights out of London because of gale warnings on 30–1 January 1953 that caused Northern Ireland deputy prime minister and finance minister, Major J. Maynard Sinclair, as well as the unionist MP for North Down, Sir Walter Smiles, to travel by sea on the Stranraer–Larne ferry. The mode of transport was out of character, since Sinclair's dislike of a sea crossing was well known.[10] Many other passengers had likewise been obliged to change their travel plans. Major Sinclair had been in London discussing the imperial contribution and various impediments to Northern Ireland's economic progress with the British government, and they were returning on the early morning British Railways-operated ferry, *Princess Victoria*. Just 35 minutes out of Stranraer, the ship was hit by raging seas and a 120-mile-per-hour gale.[11] Shortly after 10 a.m. the waves smashed through the car-deck doors and the radio officer David Proudfoot tapped out in Morse the first of his fifty-eight SOS calls that day. As the ship was blown off course in the storm – and by now the snow – the rescue vessels could not find it.

At 1.15 p.m., just off the Copeland Islands and, normally, within sight of Belfast Lough, the order was given to abandon ship. Women and children had already been gathered in what seemed the safest place, sheltered by a deckhouse from the gale. But as the ship listed, recalled James Carlin (a former officer with RAF Coastal Command during the war), his wife and sister-in-law, who were among the group, slipped into the sea. Other efforts to secure the women and children also proved fatal, for most were boarded onto one of the earlier lifeboats, only to be dashed against the sinking ship by the gale. Women and children formed the highest percentage of those lost in the tragedy. None survived.[12] Alas, survivors were few in number – only 44 of the 177 crew and passengers who had boarded that morning. Most of them were rescued by the Donaghadee lifeboat.[13]

It was a particular tragedy for Larne, where many of the crew came from, and as news started to spread – courtesy of short-wave radio in this seafaring town – people crowded to the docks, then left for Donaghadee, where they were told survivors had been brought. There were grim scenes also at Pollock Dock in Belfast the following evening as bodies were stretchered ashore. Mortuaries were set up at the Royal, City and Lagan hospitals.[14] Other bodies were brought into Donaghadee and taken to the Ards and Bangor hospitals. Over the coming weeks more bodies of the drowned were washed up along the coast, including that of a female with £900 in Scottish notes pinned to her clothing, which she had clung to desperately, telling those trying to help her that it constituted all the money she had in the world.[15]

In this era of limited modes of communication and no adequate passenger lists, family and relatives had no way of knowing whether or not their loved ones were alive, until the list of survivors was published on 2 February.[16] There are harrowing stories of relatives going from mortuary to mortuary, while emergency enquiry bureaux were set up in Stranraer, in Belfast and at Euston station in London.[17] There were a number of victims from the Longlands, Whitewell, Greencastle and Antrim Road areas.[18] But James Kerr, from the Serpentine Road and Shane and Anne McAteer's brother Donal were among the survivors. Donal had been working in England as an electrician employed at the

Swan Hunter shipyard, Newcastle upon Tyne. But his brother Shane told me that he had not been happy in England and came home regularly to the White City. He helped rescue some passengers trapped in the dining room as the ship was sinking, and was rescued by the naval destroyer *Contest* from a lifeboat. At the inquiry he told of how he had been seasick in the third-class lounge and how others even less able were helped to the deck.[19] Captain James Kerr, master of the coal-boat *Ballygilbert*, was returning home on leave. He told the press:

> In all my time at sea, I have never seen anything like it. It was just pure hell … The vessel burst her ramp doors after she had come out of Loch Ryan … and from that on until she sank off the Copelands the slow drift down the Irish Sea with passengers and crew helpless, was one of unadulterated horror … During the ship's last moments terror-stricken passengers jumped onto rafts but the heavy, pounding seas smashed the rafts to match-wood.[20]

It was the first big disaster that Gerry Mulholland, then aged eleven, remembered. People from Greencastle, where his family had lived for generations, had perished. 'It was like the *Titanic*,' he told me. The *Belfast Telegraph* broke the story of the *Princess Victoria* that night and crowds gathered outside its building looking for news. One reporter, Malcolm Brodie, recalled making his way to the house of the wife of a seafaring captain to listen to events unfold on a short-wave radio and realised the 'magnitude' of what was happening. The next day the *Telegraph* printed a special edition on the tragedy.[21] A full inquiry sat for three weeks at Crumlin Road Courthouse and found the British Transport Authority guilty for allowing an unseaworthy ship to operate. Although the *Princess Victoria* had been one of the pioneer roll-on-roll-off car ferries when it was built in 1947, there had been a number of serious incidents involving the stern doors, which had not been strengthened. Irish taoiseach Éamon de Valera wrote to Lord Brookeborough expressing sympathy, particularly at the loss of his colleague, Major Sinclair. It had been thought that Sinclair would succeed Brookeborough as premier. The head of the Catholic Church in Ireland, Cardinal D'Alton, issued a press statement paying particular tribute to Major Sinclair, whom he had met the previous year.[22] This was a shared tragedy.

The storm that took so many lives had swept through northern Europe, causing Holland's dykes to burst and flooding coastal areas in Britain, killing three hundred and rendering twenty-one thousand homeless. For people in the White City and elsewhere, the day the *Princess Victoria* went down was a point of reference for life stories, much as the 'Big Wind' of 1839 had been for people in the nineteenth century. It was one of those epic disasters that grip the imagination of peoples and the whole of Ireland was stunned by it. My mother told me that she and my father were supposed to meet my aunt and myself (aged four) off the Dublin train that day; but there was no transport, all the lines were down and chaos prevailed in Belfast.

With uncanny regularity a third incident unfolded the following year. In 1954 Garton Way was one of those longer central arteries of the estate, bounded by Ballyroney and Portmore Hills and intersected by Bresk Hill, in the good Housing Trust tradition of promoting intimacy and a communal atmosphere. Its social profile had remained stable, residents showing the same mix as noted in the last chapter, with the unusual exception of engine inspector R.J. Reid, awarded an MBE in the New Year Honours and made a JP also that year. Number 32 was one of a block of four houses near the Portmore Hill side of Garton Way, giving its family easy access to the new bus route on the Whitewell Road. It was one of a handful of houses in the White City that changed tenants often and was 'vacant' for the 1953 street directory, but 'occupied' the following year. The new tenants were Ernest McGeehan, a fifty-one-year-old Belfast Corporation labourer and his thirty-nine-year-old wife, Barbara (*née* McElroy). They had two children, four-year-old Bernadette (Bernie) and eighteen-year-old Ernest Junior, who was employed by Harland and Wolff as a catch-boy (one in a line of workers keeping the riveters supplied with red-hot rivets from the furnace).[23] The two children of different sexes, one a teenager, would have contributed points towards a three-bedroom house, as did the conditions in which they were living beforehand. Since 1947 they had been occupying one room at 29 Lonsdale Street, near the Carlisle Circus end of the Crumlin Road on the north side of the city centre. It was a classic overcrowded tenement, into which people had poured after the Blitz. There were even larger families than the McGeehans occupying only one room there – perfect conditions for the spread of tuberculosis. The plight of such families in Lonsdale Street was taken up with the relevant authorities by the Belfast and District Trades Union Council and the Young Christian Workers organisation in 1952–3.[24]

The McGeehans were a handsome family, always neatly turned out in photographs. Barbara was from County Carlow and had had a tough childhood. Her parents died when she was young and she was brought up by an aunt. She was treated differently from her aunt's two girls and ran away at the age of sixteen, coming to the attention of the police on a number of occasions between 1936 and 1939.[25] She and Ernest were married in August 1939. Barbara seems to have suffered a number of miscarriages. She later claimed that she had been given Bernie in 1950 by Ellen Brown, also of 29 Lonsdale Street, who wanted rid of the baby. She said Ellen was a singer and was being pursued by the police for carrying the baby around with her. She was 'keeping company' with Patrick McDonagh, who had 'a stick leg'. There was some truth in this, for Dubliner Patrick McDonagh and Ellen, though clearly unmarried, had been together for many years and had three sons, aged eighteen, sixteen and nine when they lived in Lonsdale Street. He described himself as a 'street singer' and Ellen sometimes accompanied him, along with Nicholas, their nine-year-old. Ellen died in hospital in June 1953. Bernie was christened on 24 December 1950 in St Patrick's Catholic Church, Donegall Street, Mary O'Connor of neighbouring Fleetwood Street acting as godmother.[26]

On 18 December 1954 Barbara came home with another baby, a boy. But things were not as they appeared, for Barbara, having apparently given birth to a stillborn baby – a claim later discounted by the consultant gynaecologist who had conducted a hysterectomy on her in 1953 – had travelled to Dublin and taken baby Patrick Berrigan from a pram in Henry Street. His mother, seeing a teddy in a shop window, had dashed in to buy it. Only days before Christmas, the stolen baby was a huge human-interest story and the press in Ireland and Britain carried full details. Louise Doherty – a publican's wife originally from Castlebar in Mayo, then returning to her home in north Belfast – got into conversation on the train with Barbara McGeehan. For someone who had just stolen a baby, Barbara was surprisingly open, telling Doherty about the lack of milk and clothing for the baby and of her own residence in the White City. She then made her way by bus to the Whitewell Road terminus, a short walk from her home.

Louise Doherty read about the stolen baby in the *Sunday Independent* and recognised it. On 22 December five tenders carrying fifty police arrived at the White City amidst pouring rain and began door-to-door searches. 'They were looking for a tall, dark-haired woman,' recalled Flo Kelsey as her own house in Thorburn Road and that of a friend – both matching the description – were searched. In Garton Way, 'a street of small white dwellings', one of the residents told the constable of having heard a baby crying that Saturday night in number 32, and that is where they found baby Patrick asleep downstairs in a cot. The press carried detailed descriptions of the home, decorated for Christmas, 'Happy Christmas' written in white across the mirror above the fireplace, an illuminated tree in the window. Barbara McGeehan admitted immediately: 'this is a terrible thing I have done', but asked to be allowed to defer their departure until it was dark. A young policewoman was brought in and the baby was taken to Musgrave Street police station, where a Christmas party was in full swing. A crowd had gathered outside the house in Garton Way and it was reported that Barbara McGeehan was booed as she was escorted out by two uniformed police and a detective. However, in the memories of long-term residents I have found nothing but sympathy for Barbara McGeehan and the booing was almost certainly directed against the police. At the police station her statement was taken:

> About six or seven weeks ago I gave birth to a still-born baby at 111 North Road. It is the home of a friend of mine … About a fortnight later I returned home. I told my husband that they were keeping the baby in hospital to build up its strength. I did not want to tell him it was still-born, as he would have been disappointed.[27]

Baby Patrick was reunited with his parents on 23 December.

They had travelled to Belfast the previous evening after Mr Berrigan, a porter, had finished his shift. Given the huge publicity, their journey back to Dublin had the appearance of a presidential visit. The Belfast 'orphans' at their Christmas party in the City hospital were leaning out the windows, cheering, as the Berrigans left. There were also cheering crowds at Newry, where they stopped for lunch, and again in Dublin when they arrived. The newspapers north and south carried photos of them in Belfast and of their extended family listening to the news on the radio. A meeting of the taoiseach, the minister of justice and senior gardaí in Government Buildings in Dublin sent a formal telegram of thanks to the RUC.

The case prompted investigations into other missing Dublin babies. Gardaí came to Belfast to investigate the case of Pauline Ashmore, stolen from her pram in Camden Street Lower, Dublin, on 19 October 1954. Then there was Elizabeth Browne, taken from her pram in identical circumstances to Patrick Berrigan and from the same street in Dublin in November 1950. In pursuit of this case the police returned to Garton Way on 23 December and removed Bernie to the nearby Bawnmore children's home. A sympathetic reporter visited a devastated Ernest McGeehan. He found him surrounded by Bernie's toys – a toy duck, dolls, a money-box – as well as her cot. He had brought them downstairs to remind him of her. Holding his head in his hands and sobbing, he said, 'She is everything I have got. When the police told me she was not my child my world collapsed.' On Christmas Eve he went by taxi to Bawnmore children's home with a teddy bear and other gifts. He asked the waiting reporters whether they thought he might be allowed to see her. He was not. The term 'bewildered child' was used in the reports to describe the little girl and that is just how she appears in contemporary photographs – as, indeed, does Ernest McGeehan. He recounted receiving a telegram from the nursing home where his wife was giving birth in 1950 to say that mother and baby were doing well. Barbara stayed there about eight weeks. In fact she had spent some time at the Legion of Mary hostel in North Brunswick Street, Dublin. She had arrived late at night on 21 November 1950, saying she was separated from her husband and hoping to find work in Dublin. Later she asked for the money for her fare back to Belfast and left on the twenty-third.[28]

Bernie was identified as Elizabeth Browne, daughter of John and Julia Browne of Blackditch Road, Ballyfermot in Dublin. They already had four other children, ranging from seventeen to seven years old when Elizabeth was found. On the day she disappeared, Julia Browne had been obliged to bring Elizabeth with her to work at the newspaper stand on Henry Street as her husband was on relief work with Dublin Corporation and there was no one at home to look after the baby. In the photographs the Brownes appear older and less well dressed than the McGeehans, but they argued that they were in relatively secure circumstances, with a weekly income of £10 and two of the eldest children also in employment.[29] Just after midday on 20 January the Brownes arrived at Bawnmore children's home and asked to be allowed to take Elizabeth away. The matron brought the child to them but called the city welfare officer, Keith Magee, who came immediately and explained that they could not take her because the legal position had not yet been resolved and that had been explained to them in court.[30] They accepted that and left. The High Court was anxious to resolve the case quickly and had blood tests sent to England to prove Elizabeth's parenthood. But there were clearly worries, as she was moved to a children's home in Larne. The Brownes were back in Belfast on 5 February, hoping to get the child. Elizabeth was finally returned to them at Belfast City Hall, after a hearing in the High Court, on Saturday, 7 February 1955. Ernest McGeehan also turned up for a final glimpse of the child. The press did not take sides in this sad case and there are heartbreaking descriptions of the child being driven away crying and clutching the teddy, Ernest's Christmas present to her.[31]

By all accounts the McGeehans had been loving parents. At her trial Barbara took great exception to Louise Doherty's suggestion that she was not looking after baby Patrick properly. Head Constable Marion McMillen and a voluntary social worker both confirmed that the 'house was well kept and that the children were well looked after', adding that 'both children were well-mannered'. (Good manners was certainly something cultivated by our parents back then.) 'Mrs McGeehan was spoken of as being of a kindly nature towards her neighbours, and there was a strong bond of affection within the family.'[32]

That is how Barbara McGeehan is remembered by those I have spoken with about the scandal. Gerry Mulholland, then a teenager living close by in Bresk Hill, told me in 2016 that the women of the estate had made a chain in front of the house to stop the police. They were 'a lovely family', he recalled, and they continued to be so viewed, even after the scandal. Lizzy Welshman, who had been a neighbour in Garton Way, also recalled her as 'a lovely woman. Mrs McGeehan was a lady … She was clean. She had the house spotless,' and Ernie 'was a wee gentleman … an innocent cratur'. She re-emphasised that Barbara McGeehan was 'dead clean', what good parents they were and how happy the children were, and spoke sympathetically of her time in prison and how difficult it must have been: 'If she hadn't gone back to Dublin for that second baby no one would have known.'

It is the tragedy of the situation that has lingered. 'I did not fully comprehend the awfulness of stolen children until I heard about such a case when I was visiting in the US,' Flo Kelsey told me. 'They were lovely children. I felt sorry for her.' This is confirmed in trial proceedings. She was spoken of as a kind person, with a strong bond of affection towards the children. Judge Curran – for Lancelot Curran was indeed the trial judge – stated in his summing-up that the children 'have been kept clean, healthy and good mannered', and he passed a lighter sentence in consequence. She was sentenced to two years in Armagh's women's prison. But she was allowed to return home on parole for Christmas 1955 and was released early the following February.

The missing babies remained a major interest story even after Barbara McGeehan's release. A *Belfast Telegraph* reporter went to see Elizabeth Browne in her Ballyfermot home in Dublin. He reported that she was becoming more affectionate towards her parents. She had two dolls, one of which she called Bernadette, her old name, which her parents wanted her to forget.[33] Why then did they agree to let the McGeehans visit Ballyfermot in May 1956, or for Bernie, her two sisters and her brother Christopher to visit Belfast, and all again in the glare of the press?[34] Indeed, Barbara McGeehan told a reporter that the Brownes had agreed to let Bernadette remain with her until the age of fourteen – a claim which the Brownes denied, though they said they had agreed to three months. She would call on them to resolve the issue in July, when she also claimed she was returning to Dublin to adopt a baby boy.

There was clearly some psychological problem affecting Barbara McGeehan, including an ability to invent and believe certain stories. Her behaviour matches known patterns of baby-stealing. There was a lack of affection and petty delinquency in her youth, a preoccupation and desire to have children and real or imaginary miscarriages.[35] Barbara McGeehan was understandably watched and was back in the news in May 1957 for looking after a child for payment without giving notice to the welfare authorities. A case of 'commercial baby farming' was how the prosecution described it. It actually looks like a case of informal fostering, Barbara McGeehan telling the court that because of her past she knew that she would not be allowed formally to adopt a baby.[36] Elizabeth Browne went on to have three children of her own but died of cancer at the young age of thirty-eight.[37] The McGeehans remained in Garton Way, still listed in 1977, but in Barbara's name after 1974. Lizzy Welshman recalled neighbourly concerns for Barbara's state of mind after Ernest's death. One day she was seen sitting dangerously on the upstairs window-sill of her house and neighbours came to talk her down. Notable among the caring neighbours were Mary Kelly and Annie Johnson, whose names surface regularly in my interviews as genuinely neighbourly people.

I was almost the same age as Elizabeth Browne and recall a sudden and very noticeable rise in anxiety about children's safety at the time. In my memory it is entangled with the childhood trauma of having a favourite doll stolen from outside our home and with the usual warnings about not accepting sweets from strangers. There was a real identification with the little girl. The photos – down to the haircut and the mandatory floppy ribbon bow – looked like dozens of us at that time. Every newspaper carried front-page coverage. Photographers were outside the house in Garton Way taking 'dozens of pictures' on the first night, as baby Patrick Berrigan was brought out by WPC Jean Bleakley.[38] The RUC and garda officers, the witnesses and the natural parents all became minor celebrities. Court appearances drew more crowds and many had to be refused admission, while police struggled to hold back the hundred or so women outside the City Hall when Elizabeth Browne was handed over to her Dublin parents. In the south, too, public interest drew crowds to the Brownes' Ballyfermot home, trampling the gardens of neighbours to get a view of the little girl.

These dramatic events of 1952–4 had a cumulative effect on my early place memory and they merged into those fearful dark winter nights that formed their backdrop. Latterly, and perhaps perversely, they all contributed to the inward-looking comfort zone of this small and contained neighbourhood. The Curran murder – admittedly worryingly close geographically – was nevertheless a 'society' affair. In the *Princess Victoria* disaster 'our boy' had survived and acted bravely to boot. As for the stolen babies scandal, more than any of the others it reveals how small communities can often rally around their own against the outside world, whatever they have done.

6

Having It So Good, Belfast Style

World War II in Europe ended … that Sunday in May… The spring of 1945 was a time of optimism for most people in Greencastle; a time of solidarity. Victory was imminent and people joined clubs, coteries and cliques for the greater good of humanity. Aunt Madge volunteered to become a nurse's helper … Uncle Dan assumed the captaincy of the hurley team and spent Saturdays and Sundays, as Grandmother put it, 'running the guts out of lads subsisting on nothing but Spam and margarine rations.' Grandmother said Spam was a great equaliser … Things were more personal then; we visited each other often for mutual entertainment and enlightenment, the sources of which were gossip, yarns, the wireless, and the newspapers – in that order.

Marjory Alyn, *The Sound of Anthems*[1]

In January 1950 *Irish Times* diarist 'Quidnunc' spent two days 'meandering' around Belfast and wrote reflecting on the changes brought about by the war. Éire had been neutral during the war, so had not experienced all its deprivations. In dress, he found that Belfast men had moved away from old conservatism. Where beforehand dark suits and bowler hats had been the norm, now their wardrobes were brighter and more varied, though clothes were obviously bought 'with an eye to long wear'. 'Belfast girls dress with less exuberance' than those in Dublin, he thought, but 'with better taste, and with a more artistic sense of *ensemble* effect'. And, whilst make-up was as abundant as in Dublin, in Belfast it is more 'enhancement of what is already there', than trying to look like 'Hollywood's latest fancy'. Though the city looked 'drab and depressing' in the January fogs, there was no sign of slump. Goods in the shops were as cheap as in Dublin, although limited in range and quality. People ate out more than formerly, and the city was full of milk bars, with a 'remarkable variety of snacks

… at astonishingly low cost', though high prices in normal bars had reduced the drinks trade to 'a mere trickle of its wartime flood'. There was huge working-class interest in sport: 'Proletarian Belfast still flocks to greyhound racing, boxing, the cinema, and above all, to soccer matches.' For the 'higher brows' there were good choral and orchestral concerts, a film society and two repertory theatres, 'roughly' comparable to the Gate and the Abbey in Dublin. Thus did an outside observer catch a city resolutely coming out of the grimness of war, still with an eye to frugality, but otherwise enjoying to the full the leisure opportunities on offer.[2]

As noted earlier, the Department of Social Studies at Queen's University conducted a survey in 1953–4 of the new Housing Trust estates in Belfast. The White City was one of them. Published in 1957, it has its limitations, not least a questionnaire largely based on English surveys, which the fieldworkers found unworkable at times. Also, since they were university staff and second-year students, there was inevitably a class issue, for although there had been an increase in scholarships at the university after the 1947 Education Act, there were still only ninety available in 1952 and the surge of grammar-school products was yet to come.[3] Interviewees were chosen randomly from files on tenants supplied by the housing managers, a sample of one in ten. The housing manager effected the introduction and explained the nature of the survey to the housewife, for it was she who was interviewed, though she was 'given the opportunity to consult her husband'. They found the size of the households on these trust estates slightly larger than the Belfast average (4.86 residents against a Belfast norm of 3.97), confirming the youthfulness of their residents. Indeed, they noted that the proportion of under-fourteens on the estates was almost twice that of the general population and predicted problems when they became adolescents – for these estates had a lower turnover of tenancies than elsewhere.[4] Like Anna Pearson, most stayed. She was still there in 1986, when a report found that the average length of tenancy on the estate was 20.8 years.[5] Some of my interviewees have lived in the White City for fifty to sixty years.

In economic terms, the survey found almost full male employment (96 per cent) and a lower proportion of unskilled workers than in the general population, most being skilled manual and clerical.

'The apparently disproportionate number of workers in Public Administration and Defence' was probably due to the fact that ex-servicemen were given preference in both housing and employment in public bodies. Tables show only 3.9 per cent male unemployment on these Housing Trust estates, but 12 per cent below human-needs standards, based on Rowntree's human-needs standard of 1950, which Field-Neill used as a benchmark. This was the result of larger families, the family allowance of 8s. for a second child and 10s. for subsequent ones (after 1956), being 'only about half the cost of feeding and clothing alone'. It was at this stage that families would find the higher rents and rates on the trust estates burdensome.[6]

The average weekly income on the estates, from a sample of 319 families, was £10 6s. 4d. This was considerably higher than the Belfast average of £5–7, though it excluded a tiny number who were not in employment and the majority, 65.2 per cent, earned between £6 and £10.[7] As the researchers admitted, however, people were reluctant to discuss income, so these figures will only be approximate. Also, the assessed number of married women in employment, 17.4 per cent, is lower than my recollection.[8]

Average rents were 14s. 6d., rates (including water rates) 8s. 3d., together accounting for 11.9 per cent of income on average. Rents, therefore, had remained the same since 1947, a significant achievement for the Housing Trust. Because of rising interest rates (affecting the trust's loan payments) it felt obliged to raise rents in 1955 and again in 1957.[9] But rents for new lettings were higher, resulting in a disparity of rent between new and sitting tenants for the same type of house or flat. This issue was addressed in 1965. By then there was a much more vociferous body of tenants and there were many protests. They contacted all fifty-two MPs at Stormont and twelve at Westminster, calling for an investigation into the Housing Trust. The Ministry of Development pointed out that there had been no rent increase since 1957: 'People were now receiving higher wages and were prepared to pay higher prices for goods, but they seemed to think their rents should stay the same for ever.'[10]

Predictably, the 1950s survey found a large portion of each tenant's income going on fuel – 9.3 per cent (higher for the lower incomes), which was a third higher than Rowntree's human-needs standard. At

May 1954 prices it represented a weekly consumption of about 1.5 hundredweight of grade-three coal. Families usually purchased a bag of slack as well, as a way of economising and prolonging the fire.[11] The wet coal-dust and granules of slack formed a kind of skin over the coal fire, which eventually turned into a long-lasting glow – though not before its wetness had filled the room with fumes. In line with the perception of a better standard of tenant on the trust estates, the Field-Neill Survey found no case of children entitled to free school meals, almost double the average number of children staying on at school beyond the school-leaving age, and 91 per cent with insurance policies, mostly funeral insurance and endowments on the children. I recall the insurance man from the Pru calling each week at our house and those special birthdays when an endowment policy on one of the children reached full term.

Of those questioned in the survey, 83 per cent were 'very', 'quite' or 'fairly satisfied' and, although many felt fortunate that they had been granted a house, there was little sense of obligation towards the Housing Trust. Almost none had any awareness that their rents were subsidised. A small number expressed a desire for a parlour or equivalent, largely for privacy, as people outside could look straight into the living room. A preference for more privacy was also the finding of sociological studies on English estates, but one largely ignored by the planners.[12] When asked about possible improvements, the major topic on all the Belfast estates was the desire for fencing, hedging or railings around the front gardens. The trust's policy forbade such enclosures. A low wall of fifteen to eighteen inches or railings was stipulated and any hedge grown was to be no more than two feet in height. Nor was there a gate to the path leading to the front door, although the back gardens were safe for small children: 'The appearance of the estates is the sole reason for this policy as the Trust feel that "open" gardens are more pleasant than high concrete posts and wire fences round small gardens.' The trust's enthusiasm for external neatness extended to garden competitions, eighteen thousand gardens being visited by forty-six judges in 1958, and only twelve estates showing little interest.[13] Various reasons were given by the tenants for their desire for a fence, mostly the lack of respect for privacy and plant life shown by other people's children and dogs or the difficulty of keeping small children off the road. The report suggested that 'an enclosed front garden, such as is customary in middle class housing, might also have been valued for its own sake as a symbol of status'.[14]

For the housewife, the large numbers of children on the estates offered opportunities for easy social relationships and high levels of neighbourliness. This indeed is my recollection – the women calling regularly, borrowing the proverbial cup of sugar, helping mothers with new babies and looking after sick children when mothers had to go to work. Thorburn Road's Mary Kelly was mentioned by several of my informants as lending a christening gown for newborn babies or a shroud when there was a death in family. Gerry Mulholland's mother was a music teacher, so there were always people in and out of the house. He also recalled pushing their family piano to a neighbour's for a wedding, as well as Catholic friends lending black ties to neighbours, only to see them later being worn in Orange parades. He chuckled in recollection of such apparent incongruities.

But respondents found the question about 'friends' – 'Amongst what people have you made your closest friends?', taken from an English survey – baffling and required a lot of prompting, as they did also for the idea of 'visiting' such 'friends'. It seems that such formal concepts of 'friends' and 'visiting' were reserved for relatives, with whom visiting was very frequent, or for people in the old neighbourhood from which they had come. Brian Dunn's mother travelled back to the Crumlin Road area every day (sometimes twice a day, with the infant Brian in tow) to visit her mother and usually also carried her shopping back from there. I too remember frequent visiting with my father's family in north and west Belfast, as well as around Strangford and Downpatrick. A significant number on the estate were from the Greencastle area, so in effect had only moved up the hill. Perhaps surprisingly, church and social organisations were far down the list of where friends were made. Again, taking their lead from English surveys, which had classified residents of estates as 'superior, respectable, ordinary, and rough', Field-Neill found neighbourliness and 'mutual help' less likely 'at either extreme of the economic scale'. Kinship rather than neighbourhood was the real decider of 'friendship', and given that over 60 per cent of tenants in the White City, and the smaller Graymount estate nearby, came from north and north-west

Belfast, this represents a very significant continued identification with the north of the city.[15]

It is just as well that neighbourliness was so common, for a large proportion of these housewives (40 per cent) rarely went out of their home except on errands or to visit relatives, or very occasionally to go to the cinema. There was of course a practical reason for this – childcare and levels of income – and men and young unmarried adults are largely invisible in this study. Certainly I recall that going to the cinema was either with other children or with our father. He too had a much better social life outside the home and it was his friends that 'visited', in the sense of staying to eat. Overall, though, I think the survey deficient in this area, for many women on the estate worked part time, which brought some level of extra sociability. Also, although it recognises leisure outlets offered by the Women's Guild, Women's Institute and Mothers' Union, some 16 per cent attending events run by these and other 'political, social or religious organisations', it gives very little detail and specifically excludes church-based activities, while the wide range of social activities noted by the *Irish Times* journalist is largely absent. The social activities arranged by the Whitewell Road Wolfe Tone GAA club also figure in people's memories, Protestants and Catholics alike telling me that they went to Irish dancing there.

In the decade after the war there was a real hunger for entertainment. Belfast came alive with the return of shop and cinema lights. In April 1949, after ten years of darkness, restrictions were finally lifted on lighting shop windows and there was an immediate rush to acquire neon lighting, though in 1951 the ban on their usage for advertising was reimposed. There was a very large number of cinemas in Belfast and five within easy reach of the White City. Even with the restrictions of childcare, the Field-Neill Survey found that, for those housewives who did go out, 'cinema-going was by far the most important activity'.[16] The closest cinema, the Lido on the Shore Road – the forty-fifth cinema in Belfast – opened to quite a fanfare in March 1955. It was the first cinema in Belfast to accommodate a new wide screen. All 1,050 seats were taken for its opening on Saturday, 26 March and many more people lined the back and the sides. The film was a comedy western, *Take the Stage*, with Vincent Price, and there was also a variety show featuring Belfast comedian Frank Carson.

The cinema had another new feature, a large café. As the press report proclaimed: 'altogether, the Lido scheme has given this rather drab stretch of road an almost Continental aspect'.[17] Such were the levels of 'going to the cinema' that it began to appear as a new evil in some Catholic bishops' pastoral letters, read at Sunday masses. The 'present unnatural desire for constant amusement ... the picture-house, the dance-hall, the dogs, the tavern, or the club', proclaimed Derry's bishop, Dr Neil Farren, had made homes no more than places to eat and sleep.[18] Teachers, too, complained of children skipping school and going to as many as six 'picture shows' a week.[19]

The White City was full of young people. My own parents were only in their twenties when they moved in and were as enamoured of contemporary music and screen stars as young people always are. There was always singing in our house, as our next-door neighbour recalled when speaking with me in 2012. From my mother came the sweet, rather soppy ballads of Thomas Moore, picked up from her own father in Kerry, as well as snippets from opera, for she was the classical-music person in the family and had the radio on constantly. Songs by Mario Lanza and *The Student Prince*, screened in 1954, were my father's particular favourites, and as a young child I knew all the words. Our record collection was a strange mix of opera, American crooners, John McCormack, Mario Lanza, various Irish balladeers, film scores, Connie Francis, local girl Ruby Murray, Helen Shapiro and then the early Beatles for my older brother, while both he and I tuned in regularly to Radio Luxembourg for contemporary rock music. Listening to the many radio broadcasts today featuring songs from old Hollywood musicals, I am struck by how many I know, words and all. Indeed, I recall my family as being rather star-crazy. My father, a very active amateur-drama actor, kept a scrapbook of his theatrical experiences, and two my schoolfriends and I kept scrapbooks of our favourite pop and film stars, swapping duplicate images much as boys swap football cards.

The American influences may have been due to my father working on the American air base at Langford Lodge towards the end of the war and meeting the 'stars' who came to entertain the forces. With up to three hundred thousand Americans billeted in Northern Ireland by 1944, there can be no doubting the modernising effect of this proximity to American culture. The *Irish Times*'s 'Quidnunc' found Belfast women speaking with 'a faint American overtone' in 1950, possibly from the films, but more likely, he thought, from experience in the war years.[20] 'Your father did not need glasses,' my mother told me, 'but he saw the Americans wearing them and did the same.' Indeed, early pictures show him with fashionable rimless spectacles.

Flo Kelsey spoke very warmly of the American servicemen: 'The Americans were terrific. They'd blow their horns and wave at you on your bicycle,' but 'so many didn't come back' from the war. She shook her head sadly. Often, she said, 'I was shaking hands with corpses.' They were mostly from the southern states. They told her how they came from poor backgrounds and of how the forces had transformed their lives. But she did not like the way they kept 'the coloureds' apart in certain towns. She danced in the Floral Hall. 'The local men were awful. They stood at the side reading the newspapers. Then the GIs came. They had lovely uniforms and tans. The girls all went for them, and the local men had to up their game. Females weren't treated well in Northern Ireland then … the Americans changed that. They did wonders for this country. Our men had to stop and take a look at themselves. They changed our men's habits. They smartened up. The girls dressed better for them.' Romie Lambkin, a young Dublin Catholic girl who travelled north to enlist in 1941, had similar good memories of the American forces and of the excitement they brought to Belfast. She too was critical of their treatment of their black compatriots, telling of efforts by other Americans to ban black servicemen from the dance-halls and of the Irish girls pointedly dancing with them to show their distaste for such prejudice.[21]

A number of stars visited Belfast in these years, attracting crowds outside their hotels. The crowds were repaid their trouble when in 1953 American singer Frankie Laine, the biggest music star of the 1950s, sang to them from his hotel window. Huge crowds would also gather when personalities came for commercial promotions. In March 1954 the royal dressmaker was mobbed when he visited Robb's department store at Castle Junction. In 1958 several thousand again besieged Robb's when Diana Dors, Britain's answer to Marilyn Monroe, came to open its hairdressing salon and had to be smuggled through the back door.[22]

I recall, too, the arrival of skiffle among the teenagers on the estate. Our lovely next-door neighbours were very musical and I have a very early memory of Mrs Brooks playing what we called a 'mallojan' – a melodeon or miniature accordion – by the fireside. The children were older than us and into Teddy Boy gear and loud music. One group would play guitars and skiffle in the field at the other side of the Snaky Path. Gerry Mulholland would join them for sessions before he and his brothers went on to form the very successful Brothers showband. As a fourteen-year-old in full Teddy boy gear he must have passed our house regularly. Self-mockingly, he told of himself and friends disappearing into the GAA hall to avoid a policeman chasing them from waste ground. 'Just imagine us in our sparkly coats, sponge soles, black shirts and bootlace ties' invading an Irish-dance class with lots of 'wee lads in short pants'. It was not long after this that the same sparkly coat suffered the ignominy of being cut into pieces and piled on the kitchen table by his disapproving father.

Many local marriages came out of social occasions in the GAA hut, as they did from encounters in that other teenagers' pleasure palace, Pootsies American Soda Bar at the bottom of the Whitewell Road. Fond memories of Pootsies crossed communal and generational boundaries. Unusually for Belfast, it was open on Sunday mornings, and people would congregate there after services in the adjacent Catholic and Protestant churches. Gerry Mulholland recalled Pootsies and its proprietor, Billy Poots, in admiring terms: 'There was never any trouble, even outside,' and Billy, 'a Protestant, did a lot of work during the Troubles to bring people together'. In December 1957 *Ireland's Saturday Night* reported on the 'extraordinary' growth of the milk-bar trend in Belfast, along with that of skiffle groups and boys with 'Tony Curtis' haircuts – that recognisable 'ducktail' style that broke so decisively with the previous generations.[23]

In fact, Belfast was buzzing in these years, much as Britain generally was, with all manner of halls, past pupils' associations, choirs and other groups staging festivals and musicals, in addition to the array of cinemas. There were over 112 dance-halls servicing the mid-1950s dance craze and large numbers attending dance classes.[24] There was a lively amateur-theatre culture, where many of those who later became stars of television and film began their careers. My father acted with a number of these. His theatrical career added a new dimension to Hallowe'en for us children, as stage make-up was commissioned for the annual dressing-up ritual and tour round the neighbours' doors. Amateur theatre took up a lot of his time, particularly when the company went on tour, which must have been difficult for my mother, with three children under the age of eight by 1953. It may have been this that prevented him taking up an invitation from the BBC to audition in London, though my mother later told me it was because of rumours of rampant homosexuality in the industry and expectations that the new recruits would sleep with the directors. Whether true or not, this would have been in tune with the general Irish Catholic belief that England was a place of loose morals.

Whilst the Field-Neill Survey found few of the housewives going to libraries, my memory is quite the opposite. There was a mobile library that serviced the estate, and we made regular visits to the Central Library in Belfast and another in Glengormley, as well as visits to the second-hand book stalls in Smithfield. Like many residents, we took the *Reader's Digest*, the occasional newspaper and various comics and magazines. My father had a fascination for true-crime magazines and classic detective stories, again, both largely American. We all read books. Certainly, the statistics for books borrowed from Belfast's libraries show a steady increase in these years – assisted by the repair of the Blitz-damaged Central Library between 1956 and 1958. A total of 1,635,153 books were borrowed in 1949 and 2,373,979 in 1958. In addition, figures from Antrim County Council, which accounted for part of the White City area, were 625,357 and 1,200,000 for the same years.[25]

There was a large number of recreation halls in the area, as the assessor for war damage reported in 1948: the Catholic Star of the Sea hall at 29 Whitewell Road, a 'church hall used as a church' at number 21, the North Belfast Mission hall at number 70, the Orange hall at 72, Greencastle Methodist Church hall opposite and a British Legion hall at 4 Railway Road. There were also the GAA playing fields and Wolfe Tone clubhouse on the Whitewell Road. The assessor was surprised at 'this social and recreational boom in the area', which was much greater than elsewhere in Belfast. He thought this might have been due to expectations created by the new estates: 'The district is far from the city centre and has no cinema or other public halls. Therefore churches and other bodies were probably under pressure to provide recreational facilities.'[26] The parish magazine for St Ninian's Church of Ireland on the Whitewell Road reveals a very active social organisation and many references to the increasing population of the area. Most activities had a militaristic flavour, with numerous 'parades' and 'drills', Boys' Brigade, Life Boys, the Church Lads' Brigade, a football club, a badminton club, Brownies, Girl Guides, a Mothers' Union, a Flower Guild and a choir (which had an annual outing). With various fairs and pantomimes also organised, parishioners hardly wanted for entertainment.

This of course raises the question of whether such church-based leisure was divisive. I cannot give a conclusive answer, but am told by interviewees that they did attend social activities in the premises of what we would think of as the 'other' community: Protestant neighbours played hurley and attended Irish dancing in the Whitewell Road GAA hall; a Catholic woman accompanied her friend to dances at the mainly Protestant Crusaders football club; a Catholic girl told me of attending Girls' Brigade events at Dunlop Memorial Presbyterian Church on the Serpentine Road. 'That's the way things were before the flags came,' concluded Gerry Mulholland in our May 2016 conversation.

The coronation of Queen Elizabeth II in 1953 also throws some light on popular pastimes, notably the sudden arrival of television. It occasioned the rushed installation of a temporary BBC television mast on Glencairn Hill, the signal coming in from Scotland and across the Irish Sea, with predictably poor results to the 900 or so owners of TV aerials in the province. Even though there was an upsurge in the acquisition of television sets thereafter, few could have afforded outright ownership at sixty-two guineas for the tiny twelve-inch screen and seventy-eight guineas for the seventeen-inch.[27] Thousands travelled by train from Dublin to view the public screenings in the Belfast cinemas. The *Irish Times* also reported 'a rush order of TV masts' in the republic, the Irish national airline Aer Lingus transporting a special delivery of aerials from Cardiff a few days before the coronation. Since Irish television, RTÉ, was not introduced until 1961, these were to pick up BBC signals. Commentators noted the excessively tall aerials required to do this.[28] One of the public screenings was in the Floral Hall in Bellevue and people had been arriving with picnic baskets from early morning for a day of open-air entertainment.[29] In the White City there were street-parties and a fancy-dress competition for the children. The picture taken on Thorburn Road after the judging reflects the kind of children's play outfits common at the time – the girls in nurse uniforms, the boys in cowboy and Irish Guards ones. I have been told that there was a cross-community element in the estate's celebrations.

The centre of Belfast itself was a space for communal celebration. Older residents recalled travelling to the city centre for VE Day celebrations in May 1945, which continued through the night before the formal declaration of the end of the war on 9 May. Trams were immobilised in Donegall Place and Royal Avenue as singing and dancing crowds moved between them. After years of blackout the skies were lit with bonfires, fireworks above the City Hall and the cinemas igniting their flashing signs, despite the fact that there was still a ban on full lighting.[30] Over the next few years the newspapers reflect this tradition of crowding into the city for public celebrations of major events: the fall of Japan (August 1945), the Freedom of the City celebrations for General Eisenhower (August 1945) and Field Marshal Montgomery (September 1945), the very large number of parades of returning servicemen and women, the many royal visits and the celebrations for local heroes.[31] Well into the 1950s, particularly with new conflicts like the Korean War and threatened hostilities with Russia, there was quite a militaristic aspect to formal city celebrations.[32]

There was also cross-community pride in Belfast heroes like seaman George Magennis, the only person from Northern Ireland to be awarded the Victoria Cross, and world flyweight champion Rinty Monaghan, both Catholics. Magennis later fell on hard times and his name became part of the Catholic victim story, as Belfast City Council did not accord him the Freedom of the City. However, his bravery also discomfited nationalist Belfast. Gerry Oates, who had been a nine-year-old at Magennis's old school on the Falls Road, summed this up well. The master told his pupils that Magennis was certainly brave, but 'he didn't do it for Ireland'. Of a visit from Magennis in December

1945, Oates recalled 'a shy, handsome young man' being brought into the classroom:

> Nobody rose … I remember feeling proud that I was Irish and that I hadn't honoured king and country by standing up, but there lingered an uneasy feeling inside me that I had hurt the poor, young lad Magennis in some way, and for years afterwards I could still see his kind, smiling face and his elderly mother by his side as we sat stubbornly in our seats.[33]

However, the wider Belfast population celebrated their new hero and a public subscription had raised £3,016 18s. 2d. for him – a very large sum indeed for the 1940s. Belfast's lord mayor, Sir Crawford McCullagh, had come into the City Hall especially early – and this on his seventy-seventh birthday, reported the *Irish News* approvingly – to head the crowds awaiting Magennis at York Road railway station.[34] The press carried pictures of him and his family at Buckingham Palace receiving his medal and his home street in the largely Protestant Donegall Road area was decked with union flags and bunting to welcome him home. The official tribute to him took place in the grounds of the City Hall on 19 January 1946, timed to allow shipyard, aircraft and other workers to attend.[35]

I would often hear Rinty Monaghan being talked about. In March 1948 Monaghan fought the world-title fight at the King's Hall. The press reported an eerie silence in Belfast as 'almost every household radio was tuned-in for the broadcast. The temporary quiet quickly gave way to scenes of unrestrained enthusiasm' when the result was announced. In many parts of the city, and particularly around his home in Little Corporation Street, huge crowds came onto the streets, celebrating with bonfires and songs.[36] The pictures in the press are joyous, particularly of the champion and his father singing popular songs for the crowds from the roof of a taxi. Immediately after the fight the new champion was presented with a mattress and pillows by the local firm Robert Dunn and Co. – none of the usual fripperies of flowers and champagne for this champion of a more utilitarian age. Indeed, I was struck, in my reading of contemporary newspapers, by the spontaneity of popular street celebrations in central Belfast in those days, which the progressive reconstruction of the city and move out to the suburbs would soon make more difficult.

I remember also being taken into the city centre by my parents for student rag days and the Lord Mayor's Show (from 1956, when it first started). Pride of the 1958 show, and taking first prize, was the float of British Thomson-Houston's turbine factory, recently attracted to Larne. It captured the new space-age excitement after the launch of the Russian satellite *Sputnik 1* the previous year. Moira Morrow recalled *Sputnik* as one of her most memorable childhood experiences, as the Pearson family would track its flashing light and bleeping sounds in the night sky. The float, with a forty-foot-long red rocket, a model of *Sputnik* mounted on its nose, surrounded by whirling planets and giving off the satellite's 'familiar double bleep', was the most popular, particularly with the children who 'cheered wildly' and 'swarmed' through the crash barriers near the City Hall. The army's float had 'a swivel hipped guitarist … aping Elvis Presley' and a skiffle group played on another float.[37]

My mother told me that she did take us to the Orange parades in town, and I heard the same from other Catholics, thereby confirming what I had thought an urban myth. It cannot have lasted long, however, as I have no recollection of it. Nor do I remember that other regular communal activity in Northern Ireland, the making and burning of the bonfire for the Twelfth, the highlight of the Orange Order's year. I was told that there were no bonfires until the late 1950s, which may explain why I have so little memory of them, for by then car-ownership meant July holidays with my Kerry grandmother. But my younger sister, Geraldine, remembered all the boys collecting wood from the fields for the bonfire and she thought they were Catholic as well as Protestant. Others from her age group said much the same. The older Protestant residents, recalling a shared past, were reluctant to talk about bonfire night – or indeed anything else that suggested there might not always have been constant good neighbourliness. 'It happened in the big open field off Thorburn Road,' away from the houses, they told me, and was cleared away quickly. Others said that there was a bonfire at the end of every street, and that must have happened on some occasions, as I have very vague memories of being rather terrified as flames seemed very close to our windows.

I don't remember seeing anyone wearing Orange sashes, though I have been told that a number of the men belonged to lodges. There was an Orange hall at the Greencastle end of the Whitewell Road, serving Temperance Loyal Orange Lodge. Edwin Pearson was in the Sons of Donegal Lodge in Sandy Row. Like many Donegal Protestants, he was dismayed at being caught on the wrong side of the border after partition, much as border Catholics in the north also were. But his wife, Anna, was very firm in not wanting him to wear his regalia back into the estate. There were marches along the Shore Road to St John's Church of Ireland Parish Church at Whitehouse for Orange services, which would regularly attract numbers in excess of four hundred – two or three times those of the normal Sunday services. There seems to have been a falling off of numbers in the 1960s, as reported by the *Belfast Telegraph*, and less interest among the young.[38]

Then there was the shopping. In this pre-refrigerator world, shopping was a daily activity. It cannot have been easy for mothers with very young children to travel far afield. Field-Neill recognised this – that a woman's freedom of movement was restricted to the distance she could push a pram, and prams were big in those days. You certainly would not have been able to take them up the steep Snaky Path to the Antrim Road bus stop. Buses were not routed up the Whitewell Road until 1953, six years after the first residents had arrived, and they were infrequent, for it was not an arterial route like the Antrim Road. My mother told me of her struggle, carrying a baby up the path every day to meet the other children off the bus from school. Even so, I recall regular trips to the impressive array of department stores in downtown Belfast, and there was local pride in the older department stores such as the Bank Buildings, Anderson-McAuley's and Robinson and Cleaver's. Sinclair's in Royal Avenue, with its clock tower and Art-Deco facade, was where we went for haberdashery and the matching gloves and hats so essential in those days. I recall the women of the estate dressing very fashionably. After all, that was a feature of Sunday observance for all faiths. It took the churches a long time to recognise the competitive vanity, to say nothing of the distraction, involved in the compulsory female hat-wearing.

Slowly the stores bombed during the Blitz reappeared. Things were expensive. Even in the sales a pair of man's shoes or a good woollen blanket could cost a fifth of the average weekly wage for male Housing Trust tenants.[39] The highlight of the 1950s would have been the small cultural revolution brought about by the arrival of the reasonably priced Dutch fashion store, C&A, in September 1954. The police were overwhelmed by the crowd of three thousand who jostled to enter in the first hour, when the store had a capacity of only fifteen hundred to two thousand.[40] The Trades Union Council was worried about the progressive replacement of local shops by such incoming chains as British Home Stores and Marks and Spencer.[41] But for the estate resident they marked an end to the drab utility of post-war fashion, as well as facilitating the explosion of youth culture in the 1960s. A trip to the big Co-op at the York Street end of central Belfast was a regular event, usually associated with the collection of the 'divvi' – a dividend, much like a modern loyalty card, only more generous. It ensured that 'the Co' was our main provider of food, milk, coal, clothes and much else.[42] The visits to the Co's offices would be the occasion for tea or lemonade and chocolate teacakes or lunch on special days in the Orpheus café. This was also one of Belfast's leading ballrooms, its spaciousness, bandstand and special lighting adding an air of mystery over and above the normal café. Sadly, I never experienced it from the other side as, by the time I was old enough to go to dances, the Orpheus had a reputation for being staid and strictly for the older dancer. Now it has disappeared forever, demolished in 2016, despite a public campaign to save it.

The Belfast newspapers of the 1950s lend credence to Peter Hennessy's assertion that this period saw the beginnings of the consumer society. The word enters the Belfast and District Trades Union Council annual reports in 1959, which offers, for the first time, advice on 'consumer goods'.[43] The arrival of commercial television with UTV in 1959 accelerated the new consumerism. Whereas the precarious existence of the working class before the arrival of the welfare state involved regular resort to the pawnbroker, pawnbrokers were in sharp decline by 1960. They were replaced by hire-purchase agreements, despite government efforts to restrict their growth before 1954. This was particularly important for the rise of standards required by the acquisition of a Housing Trust house, as Field-Neill commented. They noted keeping up with the neighbours as one of the reasons for hire-purchase and the debt incurred was 'often out of all proportion to the weekly income'. Some 44 per cent of their sample group in 1954 purchased furniture or a domestic appliance on hire-purchase, accounting for some 8 to 9 per cent of weekly income.[44] Our father worked for one of the hire-purchase firms, Bannon's of North Street in central Belfast. First opened in 1951, it was still a family firm when it finally closed at Christmas 2015.[45] Shane McAteer and another neighbour also worked there. Being a 'tick man' was a perfect job for someone as sociable as my father. My mother used to blame his love of talking and storytelling for his lateness home from work on Fridays, the day he collected payments. And, although Bannon's was a Catholic firm, it also served the needs of Protestant working-class customers, as I later found out from workmates when I started student Saturday jobs in the Belfast chain stores.

In 1954 the Belfast Co-op returned profits of 7.5 per cent, higher than Co-ops anywhere else in the UK. It was also early to take the lead in the new media of television, having extended its York Street store to include 'a complete up-to-date workshop' for the maintenance and after-sales service of radio and television sets. We acquired a TV set some time during that decade. It was the first in our street and my parents seemed happy enough to allow our living room to become a mini-cinema for our friends. Watching TV in neighbours' houses was also the experience of several of my interviewees. We would be lulled to fuzzy security by *Watch with Mother* in the afternoon, and in the evening frightened out of our wits by the *Quatermass* serials, particularly the final series of December 1958–January 1959, with endless American westerns and sitcoms, such as *I Love Lucy* and *The Phil Silvers Show*, in between. I definitely watched more television than was good for me. Although with only thirty-five hours of programming per week permitted by the postmaster general – expanded when UTV arrived in 1959 – this would not have been difficult.

Children were starting to notice if neighbours had televisions but they did not. Moira Morrow recalled looking longingly through their neighbour's door at the black-and-white box and then, on the day when they were to acquire a television, walking home from school and looking to see which kind of aerial had appeared. Two were needed to access both the BBC and UTV and with them the neat symmetry of the boxy estate, as well as the unimpeded views to the sea, was gone.[46] She remembered *The Lone Ranger* as the children's favourite. Her mother became an early and lifelong fan of *Coronation Street*. UTV was the first regional channel to buy the Manchester soap from Granada, recognising its working-class appeal. Colour television arrived in 1967, though few could have afforded the £300 price tag. It was not until 1969 that colour televisions were made more widely available, just in time to further dramatise the unfolding of the Troubles.[47]

Our first family car also materialised in the mid-1950s – a big black Austin with old-fashioned running boards. It was the first time my father had driven a car and he was only able to stop it at the top of Portmore Hill by driving against the kerb. Licences could be got without driving tests at that time and Flo Kelsey told me that she and a number of the women on the estate applied for them before the test became compulsory. Local-authority planners started to recognise the consequences of the increase in car ownership – which had tripled between 1938 and 1956 – as well as the escalating accident figures, and 1956 saw the introduction of driving tests and the thirty-mile-an-hour speed limit.[48] A car opened up new opportunities and the gloom of a normal Northern Ireland Sunday started to lift. Even before then my family had taken annual holidays to nearby Bangor, Groomsport and Newcastle. Once the car arrived, the long journey to my grandmother's in Kerry was an annual event. The car also enabled my father to pursue his interest in fishing, which all the family embraced. However, until we could afford a brand-new car, which was very much later, we had to make do with old cars that were not very reliable, and I recall being caned by a dragon primary-school headmistress who would not accept a broken-down car as a reason for lateness.

Yet, as I prepared to start grammar school in the autumn of 1959, one brother preceding me to a fully funded grammar-school place and two sisters to follow, I do recall my parents' joy about the opportunities we were given that had never been open to them, while TV and the car had also opened up new horizons. Indeed, a new sense of rightful access to leisure time and facilities informed the changing nature of trade-union demands in the early 1960s. With paid holidays and a five-day week having expanded leisure time, the cultural and recreational needs of working people had started to figure in the press and in the literature of various campaigning organisations.[49] Undoubtedly, however, it was the dramatic post-war reforms in health and welfare provision as well as education that had the greatest impact on working-class lives in Belfast.

7

The Impact of the Welfare State on Everyday Lives

The 1950s brought vast improvements in social conditions. Everyone benefited from the welfare state, rationing came to an end, employment figures increased and the standard of living rose.

Eric Gallagher, Belfast Central Mission[1]

This period in British history is considered a golden age, with an end to austerity, the introduction of the welfare state, full employment, free education and the arrival of the idea of leisure. Certainly that is also how residents of the White City remember it and many remembered hardship before they arrived there. Their lives in the new estate coincided with the introduction of the National Health Service (NHS), the closure of the workhouses and the transformation of educational opportunities.

At the very outset the Housing Trust was in communication with the Ministry of Education about 'the provision of schools, nursery schools, community centres and youth welfare facilities' for its new estates. However, at a time when it was otherwise forging ahead of all the other authorities, it was held back from providing the amenities it considered essential to building new communities by the other agencies it had to deal with. Even the Health and Local Government Ministry was uncertain how far it could assist the trust without going through other public bodies. The education minister also was critical of the education and the local authorities who were responsible for arranging facilities for youth and community centres in housing estates, but had 'done very little in exercise of their powers under existing legislation and … the youth and community service had to rely … on the efforts of voluntary agencies'. He therefore thought it pointless discussing such provision on the new estates with them: 'In the present circumstances the initiation of youth centres and community centres should be left to the spontaneous effort on the part of the inhabitants of the estates.'[2] They were still being called for on the eve of the Troubles in 1969.

Schools provision was an even more urgent concern, because of the Blitz, past neglect and legislation extending the age of compulsory education. Even the smaller trust estate of Graymount – contracted for 114 two-bedroom houses and completed in 1946 – was creating overcrowding in the schools of the area, and the trust warned that the situation would become much worse when the nearby Whitewell (White City) estate was completed.[3] The Housing Trust appears to have been the first authority to automatically provide the Education Ministry with building plans and to regularly update them. The plans by 1948 were to close Whitehouse primary school on the Shore Road, then with 271 pupils, and to replace it with a larger school for 490 pupils on the Serpentine Road. A nursery school was also to be built, but with lower priority. Then there was the additional issue of separate Catholic schools, a right won by the Catholic Church in the nineteenth century and still jealously guarded today.

On the surface it is clear that the Catholic Church had little reason to trust a state that exuded anti-Catholicism. However, as with so much in Northern Ireland, once you get below the admittedly high-octane public wranglings, the reality was often rather different. In fact, the Northern Ireland government's record on education was as good as it could have been in such a divided society, and successive education ministers (aside from the virulently anti-papist Harry Midgley, education minister in 1950–7) acted with pragmatism and fairness, as did the Belfast Education Authority. In the 1940s working-class children would have struggled to move beyond elementary education, for the equivalent of today's primary schools were overcrowded and inadequately accommodated. There they would stay until the age of fourteen, for there was no secondary education as we now know it. Grammar schools were fee paying and offered only a handful of scholarships to those on low incomes. University entrance was even more restricted, with only fourteen scholarships to Queen's University available in 1947.[4] The 1947 Education Act

(Northern Ireland) – belatedly following Britain's 1944 Butler Act – established the principle of free education at all levels (though a means test for grammar schools persisted until 1951) and extended compulsory education to the age of fifteen. In the south, children were condemned to remain under the old system until 1967. The Northern Ireland act also introduced another tier of secondary education with the secondary intermediate schools, to service an anticipated 80 per cent of the post-primary age group. The other 20 per cent gained entrance to selective grammar schools by means of a 'qualifying' exam taken in the child's eleventh year, leaving the bulk of ten- to eleven-year-olds sensing that somehow they were not good enough.[5]

By 1950, therefore, the County Borough of the Belfast Education Committee was being challenged by a host of new needs, in addition to the Blitz-damage repairs of schools and the consequences of long neglect, and it would not be until the 1960s that the full impact of the 1947 act would be felt. The 1947 act and post-war reconstruction created a sense of urgency and a flurry of activity in these years. Finding sites for entirely new intermediate schools with playing fields was a real problem, given similar difficulties being experienced by the housing authorities.[6] Certainly, throughout the 1950s the press is full of pictures of big new intermediate schools being opened. And there was considerable excitement at what they had to offer. I was chastised by my primary-school teacher for saying I did not really want to go to the grammar school because the uniform of the new intermediate was far more attractive. In the event, it was a fat envelope that arrived through our letterbox that indicated that grammar school was my destination, though by then educational experts were already challenging the justice of deciding a child's future at the age of eleven and calling for the introduction of a comprehensive system into Northern Ireland. The teachers' union had been arguing as much even as the Education Bill was going through. My own recollections endorse the educational findings of the inappropriateness of selection at such an early age. For of those of my year from the estate who went to grammar school, I estimate that only 20 per cent continued beyond the statutory leaving age.

And the elitism of the grammar schools continued for some time after the introduction of scholarships. Several from the estate, including myself, remember latent snobbery towards the influx of working-class scholarship pupils. Norah Van Puten had to take two buses to her grammar school on the east side of the city, because the Protestant grammar schools in north Belfast were still fee paying when she passed her eleven-plus in 1958. At her first assembly the headmaster referred to the new intake as 'Belfast guttersnipes' that the school's mission was to pull up. The parents' evenings were full of well-off middle-class people and the kind of events mounted for public and parents, such as light-opera performances, would also have been offputting for working people. Reflecting back, she marvels that her father was able to afford to keep her there into sixth form and eventually to a scholarship at Queen's University. Grammar schools, with strict uniform regulations and many other calls on parental income, were expensive. There were three boys from the Mulholland family simultaneously at the north-Belfast Catholic boys' grammar, St Malachy's, but Gerry's parents could not afford to maintain them into the sixth form. All four of the Burns family went to north-Belfast grammar schools. It must have been a struggle for our parents.

The trust consulted the managers of Catholic schools and, in the case of the Falls and Cregagh estates, agreement was reached with Catholic Church authorities to site new schools there.[7] There was already a Catholic primary school in the Whitewell area – St Mary's Star of the Sea at Greencastle – but some children were travelling as far as St Mary's in Glengormley, the Holy Family in Newington and the Convent of Mercy on the Crumlin Road, reflecting an identification with the old areas where their parents had come from. There were two state primary schools in Greencastle and Whitehouse, but some Protestant White City children were also travelling to Glengormley. The 1953–4 Field-Neill Survey found the White City (with Dundonald) unusual in that its children generally had to take the bus to school. The tenants of the estate had sent a memorial to Belfast Rural District Council in September 1949, complaining of the lack of educational facilities and asking that a new school be sited near the estate.[8] Flo Kelsey recalls collecting signatures for it. The trust already had plans to do so and two were finally opened in 1955.

The Belfast Education Committee had stressed the need for primary schools to be located near children's homes. But it would be many years before White City families had this luxury and, at a time when few had cars, the journey to school was hazardous. There was no bus from Whitewell to Glengormley, nor from Whitewell into Belfast until 1953. Trolley-buses ran the Antrim Road route at the top of the estate from 1949,[9] but even from the last houses it was an arduous climb up the Snaky Path and a treacherous one in bad weather or in the dark, for it was unlit. Once on the Antrim Road, blind corners and excessive speeds added to the danger. Children's safety seems not to have exercised the authorities very much, for there were no dedicated crossings on the road. In 1961 the local council was still calling for a footpath at the dangerous corner between the Throne hospital path and Hazelwood, but it never materialised.[10] High speeds by inexperienced drivers added to the dangers and the casualty figures on Northern Ireland's roads in these years are quite staggering.[11] In May 1951 joiner Robert Boyd of 13 Laragh Road, White City, gave evidence in a tragic case when four seven-year-old girls were killed by a speeding driver who mounted the pavement in nearby Whitehouse.[12] An English visitor to Belfast in September 1951 commented: 'Motorists travel at a speed which at first strikes terror into the hearts of those who expect a thirty-mile speed limit in built-up areas.'[13] In 1947 the RUC and Belfast City Council had resisted suggestions of a speed limit for the area, on the grounds that no one had been killed in the previous year and it would be difficult to enforce. But given the explosion in the numbers of vehicles on the roads (private car registrations trebling in the period 1952–5) and the growing publicity, speed limits and driving tests were finally introduced in 1956 – though on that section of the Antrim Road where estate residents crossed, only in 1959.[14] Since my school bus stop was located on this very corner and there were no lights or crossings, I wonder how we all survived.

Two state (Protestant) primary schools were finally built near the estate in 1955 – Ballygolan on the Serpentine Road and the Throne, between the Snaky Path side of the estate and the Throne hospital. The Housing Trust had been anxious about the absence of such amenities and had sold the necessary land to Antrim County Education Committee in 1951–2.[15] I have been told that there were some Catholic pupils at the Throne school and the Catholic primary school in Greencastle was within walking distance, at least from the lower part of the estate. However, many Catholic children of my generation continued to make the trek by public transport into north Belfast. Catholic and Protestant grammar and new intermediate schools were also located there. Some boys also attended Carrickfergus Tech, a long bus ride from the Shore Road.

Graymount, the nearby girls' state intermediate school, was one of the first in Northern Ireland, opened in April 1949 on the lower Whitewell Road. Most of my friends went to Graymount. The principals of both Graymount and the new boys' intermediate school, Dunlambert, seem to have been progressive. Helen Graham of Graymount was a Dubliner who came north after partition in 1921 and was said by the *Belfast Telegraph* still to speak with 'a pleasant Southern brogue'.[16] At a meeting of the Young Ulster Society on 13 January 1959, chaired by Samuel Lynn, headmaster of Dunlambert, and addressed by Queen's University professor of Irish history, J.C. Beckett, on 'The Study of Irish History', she asked him about the Ulster flag. All heads of state schools in the Belfast Education Authority area had been sent an Ulster flag, along with a union flag, and instructed to display them prominently. He responded that the Ulster flag was 'just someone's invention' and, as far as he knew, had not been recognised by the official body, the College of Arms. Flags were much less noticeable in those days than today. There were only fifteen days designated officially for flying flags, though of course they were more prevalent around the Twelfth.[17] Professor Beckett lamented the lack of knowledge of Irish history among children. But, he continued, Irish history was now on the school curriculum and the situation was improving, and, 'like it or not', Irish history was so long bound up with British that you could not divorce them. Mr Lynn also said that when he first started teaching he found children very ignorant of Irish and local history and when he tried to remedy this he found there were no textbooks (Professor Beckett's own history of Ireland was above the level of secondary-school children).[18]

Dunlambert's headmaster was referring to Jim Beckett's *A Short History of Ireland* (1952). That he thought it too difficult for his students speaks volumes of the lack of background knowledge on Irish and Ulster history, as he acknowledged, for Beckett was a gifted synthesiser of his own mastery of the discipline. I was privileged to have been taught by him at university and to have become a friend in his later days. He had been a schoolteacher himself for a decade after graduation from Queen's, at Belfast Royal Academy, the state grammar school nearest the White City. Today that school is so mixed that it is over-subscribed by Catholics. By the time of the 1959 Young Ulster Society debate, Beckett was a university professor, one of the most prominent historians in Ireland and a noted progressive thinker. Along with a handful of other such luminaries, he was invited onto Northern Ireland's first current-affairs radio show, *Your Questions*, in 1953 and was a regular thereafter, leading on such issues as the teaching of history in schools and flags – which was undoubtedly why he was posed those questions at the 1959 meeting.[19]

The progress of the building of Dunlambert attracted much press coverage because of the interesting history of the site. It was an ancient fort, where King William was said to have stopped in 1690 and the Protestant patriot Volunteers had staged a mock battle in 1781. The large estate house was demolished to build the school and it is striking at this time how many old buildings were being torn down and replaced with new, boxy structures.[20] But they were bright. The *Belfast News Letter* was struck by the spaciousness and colourfulness of the interior of Ballygolan primary. The main walls of the stairways were deep red, contrasting with light hallways. Each classroom was painted a different colour, again with contrasting walls. The medical-inspection waiting room was 'gaily-decorated' to avoid medical overtones. There were separate toilets for the younger children and a play enclosure with a sandpit and paddling pond. The dining room could seat 360 and also had a spacious, white-tiled kitchen.[21]

It was little wonder that I was so impressed by the facilities and airiness of the state primary school where I sat my 'qualifying' exam in 1959, when my ancient, though educationally excellent, Catholic primary school had bare floorboards, outside toilets, no dining facilities and no separate medical room. The physical accommodation of my (equally educationally excellent) Catholic grammar school was similarly deficient, an old Nissen hut serving as assembly hall, a place to eat our sandwiches, a gynasium and a drama hall. The post-war school-building and improvement programme finally arrived with the opening of a new wing in 1953 and another in the mid-1960s.

The outcome was a state-of-the-art gynasium – alas, too late for the discovery that I actually had some athletic ability, for I had spent most of my time in both my schools bored by what passed for PE, with too many activities organised around the throwing of beanbags and the one team sport, netball. At least my parents were spared the additional expense of the sports equipment required by the better facilities in the state schools, much as Norah Van Puten remembered.

There was a reason why my schools were so deficient in modern facilities. Catholic schools did not receive the same capital funding as state schools – though still far too much for ultra-Protestant demagogues – as Catholic clergy endlessly reminded their parishioners. While the state schools such as Dunlambert were opened by leading unionist politicians (in this case the prime minister himself, Lord Brookeborough), nearby Catholic school buildings were opened by Catholic bishops, usually with speeches claiming that they received no building grants from the state and urging communal giving.

In fact this was only partially true. Even if, on the eve of partition, the Catholic Church had good cause to be suspicious, it was slow to change its views and some clergy have never done so. The history of education in Ireland is a fraught topic, with sectarianism and heated religious and political disputes at its heart. The attempt by Britain to introduce free non-denominational schooling in the 1830s foundered on the anti-popery and proselytising activities of evangelical Protestantism. The outcome was to be a resistance to interdenominational education on the part of the Catholic Church and fierce protectiveness of separate Catholic education. The storm caused by the enlightened proposals for post-1944 educational reform reprised all the bitter arguments of a century earlier. Protestant campaigners mobilised to retain compulsory Bible-teaching in state schools and to resist concessions to Catholics. The liberal unionist MP for Clifton and minister of education, Samuel Hall-Thompson, suffered particular vilification for such concessions. He was forced out of office in 1949 and lost the seat he had held since 1929 in the 1953 election.[22] The proposals were also attacked by the Catholic Church as smacking of state interference and a danger to Catholic social teaching.[23] In my Catholic home, educational achievement was highly valued, particularly by our mother. Although I have written extensively about the Catholic Church's resistance to state interference in educational and medical matters, when researching this book I was nevertheless taken aback by its hostility to these reforms, which were to make such a difference to its community, known disproportionately to occupy the lower social levels. Even if Belfast Catholics did not read the *Irish News* – which saw the legislation as creeping state control, and that state was agnostic England – they would have been a captive audience at Mass on Sunday, 8 February 1948, when the Lenten Pastoral of the bishop of Down and Connor, the Rev. Dr Mageean, denounced the 'aggression of the state' inherent in the new legislation.[24]

The actual situation was this: before partition schooling was largely paid for by central government, though in effect it had become denominational. In the 1920s in Northern Ireland an attempt to resurrect the non-denominational ideal of the nineteenth-century national schools foundered on the opposition of both Protestant and Catholic clerics. The 1940s legislation required the addition of two representatives of the education authorities to the management committees of voluntary schools. While the Catholic Church had little reason to trust local educational authorities, it did have a reasonable working relationship with central government and the Ministry of Education – even unionist prime minister Basil Brooke (Brookeborough after 1952) stood up against the ultras in his own party who resisted concessions to Catholic schools. The church's refusal to accept education-authority representatives on their schools' management committees resulted in Catholic schools securing only 65 per cent in capital grants until 1968. The burden imposed on the Catholic community by the need to find 35 per cent of all building costs delayed the construction of new Catholic schools and improvements to the old, as envisaged in the 1947 legislation, and condemned my generation to substandard conditions and reduced opportunities. It was a disadvantage that only finally started to shift in the 1960s, particularly with the return to more even-handed policies at the Ministry of Education under Midgley's successor, William Morrison 'Morris' May.[25]

The surge in such schooling as a result of the 1947 act produced a true kaleidoscope of different school uniforms on the estate, symbolising a religious as well as an educational divide, on the backs of children who otherwise lived side by side and socialised together. In practice, however, I found that it did not undermine existing friendships. These uniforms were expensive and children changed as soon as they came home. Then we were all the same again. Despite the attention that was and continues to be paid to the high-level disputes over separate religious schools in Northern Ireland, I am struck by how normally things seem to have worked among the education authorities and the high levels of cooperation between the state and voluntary sectors.[26] And there is no doubt that the reforms altered working-class lives for the better. Figures for the school-building programme of these years are impressive: three new grammar schools, fifteen state and six Catholic intermediate schools and a technical college were built, on the post-primary side alone. All of this 'continuous effort', as the chronicler of the Belfast Education Authority for the years 1947–60 describes it, extended to a new emphasis on the acquisition of land for playing fields for the new schools: nine acres for Dunlambert, eighteen for the model schools at Ballysillan, nine for the Shore Road, twenty-seven and a half for Whitewell. There was also a state special school built in the 1950s at Mount Vernon and Catholic equivalents at Whiteabbey and on the Somerton Road.[27]

Concern and provision for youth welfare and recreation was something relatively new. The 1938 Physical Training and Recreation Act (Northern Ireland) had prepared the way for various recreational and sporting schemes. This was shelved because of the war, but the war also created a growing interest in youth work. A committee of investigation under the Ministry of Education led to the 1944 and 1947 Youth Welfare Acts, the establishment of a special committee and the provision of funding for various aspects of youth recreation and sports.[28] The outcome was the establishment of a number of youth clubs in the area. Although the ministry appears to have been even-handed in its grants, the clubs were largely under the churches' supervision, even if they might still be mixed religion.[29]

If the new schooling system organised the routines of children as never before, it was the sea-change in health treatment that transformed the lives of people in the White City and beyond, and it was again William Grant's new Ministry of Health and Local Government that oversaw the changes. Britain's Beveridge Report of 1942, recognised as the originator of the modern welfare state, had already laid the ground. 'It is hard to realise today what an impact that monumental piece of work had on social thought,' recalled John Oliver, one of the key civil servants in Grant's new department, 'and how comprehensively and effectively it shaped the plans of governments.'[30]

The scourge of tuberculosis was the first serious health issue to exercise the Northern Ireland authorities after the war. At 9.3 per cent in all ages at the beginning of the 1940s, deaths from TB were higher in Northern Ireland than elsewhere in Britain, though similar to Éire. Indeed, Belfast had the highest incidence of TB-related deaths in Britain – 50 per cent of deaths among 15- to 24-year-olds, according to a damning report by the Belfast Health Services in late 1941.[31] Predictably, then, survivors of the Whiteabbey sanatorium – the main centre for TB treatment – figured prominently among the young families of the White City, as they did among my family's wider friendship group. Most from that generation recalled visiting friends and relatives in Whiteabbey and continued fears informed my early childhood.

Until 1941 the treatment of TB had been the responsibility of Belfast Corporation, but an inquiry of that year exposed corruption and neglect in the management of Whiteabbey sanatorium and led to a further inquiry into corporation corruption. This, and the horrifying statistics revealed by the 1941 report, resulted in a total transformation of treatment and the establishment of the Northern Ireland Tuberculosis Authority in 1946, two years before the NHS arrived. With its mass radiography and vaccination programme, the Northern Ireland Tuberculosis Authority was so successful in tackling the TB crisis that in 1959 it was dissolved and its staff and duties were merged into the General Health Authority. The eradication of TB was 'the greatest success story of public health in the Province since the war', pronounced the *Belfast Telegraph* in a feature article, 'the product of better housing, plentiful fresh food, an educated public opinion … alongside new drugs and surgical techniques'.[32] But our parents remained vigilant, the chesty coughs that plagued many childhoods producing overreaction by today's standards. TB revisited the area amid the worst winter Northern Ireland had ever experienced, in January 1963. A teacher and five pupils at Whiteabbey primary school were admitted to hospital and four hundred pupils were tested. A mass radiography unit was sent out, the affected classroom was disinfected and books were either treated or destroyed.[33]

The war years, following the poverty of the 1930s, had also highlighted the poor health and hygiene of children, particularly from Belfast. Infant-mortality rates in urban areas were high – seventy-nine per thousand in 1945 – though lower in rural areas.[34] By the time the first residents moved into the White City, maternity and child-welfare clinics were operating at Whitehouse, and attendance was reported as being very good.[35] Baby foods were supplied at cost price and I remember walking to the Mill Road clinic with my mother in the 1950s, with our coupon-book for free orange juice, cod-liver oil and baby formula. The orange juice was thick, the cod-liver oil awful, served up with a spoon of sugar.

The NHS was introduced on 5 July 1948. It transformed the lives of families such as ours. Suddenly everything we could not afford beforehand was free and, as a newspaper survey reported, there was a 'Public Rush Effect'.[36] The rush mainly affected dental treatment and spectacles and over-prescribing of the now-free drugs. Already by January 1949 – when there were 370,000 free prescriptions issued in that month alone – there were worries about the high costs of the new health service.[37] Although a charge of one shilling was introduced in 1952, the rise of this 'vast army of drug takers' was declared 'relentless' through the 1950s.[38] There are anecdotal stories of people getting dentures who did not really need them. There also appear to have been an awful lot of unnecessary fillings and tooth extractions – although the over-indulgence in sweets after rations were removed in 1949 and the failure of adults to recognise the harm, may also have contributed.[39] The chief medical officer wrote despairingly in his 1957 report:

> I am still seeking a way of getting children of all ages to realise that it is no more strange to clean their teeth and mouths than it is to wash their faces and hands. It does seem strange to see children (and countless adults) who are particular about being tidy of dress and having well cleaned exposed skin surfaces but who have teeth 'natural' or

'unnatural' in a filthy state with stagnated food stuff. There is no class distinction in this matter.[40]

Unfortunately, prioritising children's needs produced the horrors of the dental clinics – blighting my generation's first encounters with dentists – and the degrading school health visits, with their hair examinations for 'nits' (head-lice) in front of the rest of the class – at least in my primary school, which lacked the facilities of the new state schools. Children were deemed not to need privacy. Such was the rush and pressure on resources in the early years, however, that charges were reimposed for spectacles and dentures in 1951.[41]

The idea of preventative medicine might not yet have arrived in dental care, but it had in other fields. Childhood diseases such as mumps, whooping cough, scarlet fever and measles were regular visitors to the Whitewell area, necessitating long treks by parents to Purdysburn, the fever hospital at the other side of Belfast, and generally to the one public telephone box at the south-west corner of the estate. But vaccination against whooping cough, introduced in 1952, had produced 'a remarkable drop' in cases by 1957.[42] It was polio, however, that was prioritised. There had been a major epidemic in Northern Ireland in 1947 – the worst ever recorded – moving west from England and Scotland and coinciding with an unusually warm summer. Some 65 per cent of those infected were paralysed and 9 per cent died. By 1959, however, 80 per cent of children had been immunised.[43] I recall our family doctor coming to our home and immunising the children in the family. In typically selective childhood memory, I also recall him sharpening his needle on his matchbox in our living room – hardly likely to appease our fears. Even so he was a kindly, elderly man, who held his surgery in his Antrim Road home, the most welcoming medical environment that I have ever encountered.

Unfortunately the Health Services Act (Northern Ireland) of 1948 did not mirror the British act in one important aspect. It did not include that clause permitting hospitals with religious links to maintain their ethos within the health service. So the Catholic-run Mater hospital on the Crumlin Road, which served the needs of the largely working-class community of all creeds in north Belfast, was excluded from state funding, after a nasty debacle in which both the unionist government and the Catholic Church dug their heels in, though in the early stages talks had been constructive.[44] Once again it was about retaining a Catholic ethos and transfer of property – there was a consecrated chapel at the heart of the hospital and a convent of the nursing sisters in the grounds – and the Mater was the only Northern Ireland hospital not included in the new scheme. My own recollections are of my family using all the hospitals in Belfast, irrespective of ethos, though making a voluntary donation when it was the Mater. The exclusion of the Mater was, however, something of an aberration, for the NHS was popular with both communities, its establishment generally lacking the sectarian controversy surrounding education.[45]

Overall, everyone in Northern Ireland benefited from the government's policy of parity with Great Britain. I recall the regular family allowance as another welcome source of income, paid directly to the mother and involving ritual, though pleasurable walks to collect it at the old post office below Belfast Castle on the Antrim Road. Family allowances began in August 1946 at 5s. per week after the first child. This was increased to 8s. in 1956 for a second child and 10s. for any further children.[46] Initially the bill had proposed limiting the increases to the third child. Nationalists claimed discrimination. But, as even many unionists pointed out, large families were not confined to Catholics and such a proposal would have marked a real departure from policies of parity with Great Britain.[47] By now the new welfare state in Northern Ireland and Britain was a trump card in the unionist propaganda battle over how bad things were in the south, particularly since recent controversies there over efforts to introduce free health care had foundered on the opposition of the Catholic hierarchy, as well as the doctors.[48] Free milk for children at schools and subsidised milk for expectant mothers was also seen by the 1950s Field-Neill Survey as a major contribution to the new sense of well-being.[49]

'The most remarkable of the post-war years' is how the *Belfast Telegraph* summed up 1948. 'A great deal of history has been made.'[50] And so, indeed, it had. Incomes more than doubled between 1938 and 1951 and continued to rise into the 1960s.[51] My own parents had come a long way since the tough life they had had in the war years, and as the 1960s got under way they had saved enough to obtain a mortgage and to buy their own home. The Housing Trust estate had been good to them, but moving up from being tenants to owner-occupiers was valued as giving them a new status.

Yet it was TV that increasingly filled our leisure time and the cinemas and theatres, so abundant until now, progressively shut. There were worrying undercurrents that were not immediately evident to us at the time. In hindsight too little was done to anchor the many good things that had been happening since the war. Assessing the foregoing decade at the end of 1959, the *Belfast Telegraph* saw causes for optimism in the political sphere, a new confidence and signs that Northern Ireland 'had come of age'. Despite a continuing IRA border campaign, 'Ulster went calmly about its business without communal strife,' that year's general election being marked by 'moderation'. Economically, however, the report was less upbeat. There were, of course, plenty of signs of better living standards in the acquisition of cars, TV sets, 'home aids' and increased spending in the shops. However, the paper thought that Ulster had not shared fully in Britain's economic expansion and a number of nettles had not been grasped.[52] As F.S.L. Lyons pointed out in one of the BBC's radio lectures in 1957, 'A new generation is growing up which will take for granted elaborate health services, the chance of state-aided education, and a high standard of housing,' and it was unlikely that they would think the same as those who had grown up in 'the old Ulster' that had gone before.[53]

8

Arcadia Undone

The trembling vibrant community has gone … The houses that were homes to thousands of people have been bulldozed from the skyline to be replaced by an ugly ribbon that cut through the heart of a district that has now become nothing more than a state of mind.

John Campbell, *Memories of York Street*[1]

Today the White City continues in name and location. However, it is only partially the estate of which I have been writing. It has been totally rebuilt. The houses are much better than the originals and it has finally acquired a community centre and playground. Yet in almost every other way it is diminished from what it once was. Undoubtedly some of this was inevitable in an estate raised in a hurry to meet the immediate post-war housing crisis. However, since at least the 1980s there has been a sense of being at the mercy of uncaring planners, officials and politicians and, in retrospect, a nostalgia for the Housing Trust and its accessibility through the female managers.

Flo Kelsey told me that there was a sense in the White City of belonging to no one. Her own road was a tangible example of this, falling within three different local authorities, with those houses inside the city boundary subject to higher rates. There were no bus shelters where White City people would wait for buses, though they appeared elsewhere, because none of the many authorities for the area would accept responsibility for their absence.[2] And unthinking and competing bureaucracy played havoc with children's early school experience, as they were separated from friends or moved from one of the estate's primary schools to the other when boundary changes happened (as in both Norah Van Puten's and May Doherty's experience). Experts at the time and subsequent commentators recognised the problem of such antiquated local-authority structures and in particular their inability to deal with the housing problems of 'bulging' Belfast. Indeed, it became the 'theme song' of the 1959 Local Government Conference held at Portrush.[3] Even the city planners were unsure where Belfast stopped. All agreed that 'Belfast as an economic and social entity covers a very much wider area than the actual city'.[4] But with the suburban creep of post-war building there was little space left to rehouse families who faced losing their homes in the overdue slum clearance about to get under way in Belfast city. A special report in the *Irish Times* in February 1959 asked where the occupants of the eighteen thousand houses to be demolished in Belfast were to go. There were an estimated sixty to seventy thousand people among them, more than the whole population of Fermanagh. The option of continuing to build on the outskirts was no longer possible, as post-war developments had already seen housing devour much of the surrounding green belt.[5] Some 50,535 Belfast people had migrated to 'the new housing estates which fringe the city', wrote Emrys Jones in a series of articles in the *Belfast Telegraph* in July 1956. He was complimentary of post-war ambitions to give working people more space in which to live. However, it had led to 'the town disintegrating into an amorphous sprawl which is slowly destroying the countryside'. How far, he asked, could such expansion continue before authorities called a halt?[6]

One option was to extend the city boundaries. But this was controversial and held no promise of appropriate housing developments, given Belfast Corporation's continued dilatoriness and poor relations with central planning authorities.[7] But something had to be done, for it was the local authority that had responsibility for rehousing its people. The answer was to create new areas with new authorities. So a sprawling area extending from Carnmoney to Jordanstown and Whitewell was transferred to the unimaginatively named new district of Newtownabbey. Such a suggestion had been criticised by the 1945 planning report as 'too close to the City', simply extending its built-up area.[8]

The new name caused consternation. A public meeting was arranged on the evening of 2 January 1957. Admission was restricted to those eligible to vote in local elections and proof would be required.

Only eighty-four votes were registered at the meeting, hardly reflecting the thirty-three thousand ratepayers, as one councillor pointed out, and he had yet to meet a single one who approved. It was claimed that there had been an inadequate response from the public to a press call for suggestions and in the end the Belfast Rural District Council just chose the name from those submitted after the first call early in 1956 and transformed itself into the new town's first council.[9] Even though I was only a child at the time, I recall annoyance in the White City and a degree of confusion over postal addresses.

Tuesday, 1 April 1958 was inauguration day. At 9 a.m. H. Robinson OBE, JP – a Belfast businessman and former chairman of Belfast Rural District Council – was elected chairman at the Town Hall in Whitehouse. The minister of health and local government, John Andrews, bestowed the chains of office and they left in a fleet of hired cars to unveil the first boundary sign on the Shore Road at Greencastle. The *Larne Times* reported the extra policemen on duty for the occasion looking 'conspicuously out of place among the remarkably few spectators'. A special song, 'A Town Is Born', written by Larne housewife F.R.S. Hall, was sung by blind singer Gerry Brereton. Three and a half thousand local children had a special holiday and many firms gave their employees a day off. There were inauguration services in the local churches, Protestant and Catholic alike, entertainment in the Alpha cinema in Rathcoole and a Carnival Ball in the Floral Hall. The carnival was to continue until 12 April, involving a bonny-baby contest, a beauty contest to find 'Miss Newtownabbey', a parade with floats and the award of a new pram, cot and clothes to the first baby born in Newtownabbey. There were immediate complications here as many, including those from the White City, continued to be born in Belfast hospitals.[10] Indeed, the original strong links and identity with Belfast, and particularly north Belfast, while recognised and facilitated by the Housing Trust, were always a problem with the town planners.

Much was said about building a community in the new district. It would be 'a kindly place, a homely place', where people would dwell together as 'good neighbours', 'the apparent dispersed character' of the area notwithstanding.[11] Among the gains from this new urban council would be an extension of the licensing hours of the ten licensed premises in the area, though only by an hour, from nine o'clock to ten o'clock in the evening. Another would be the development of the lough shore from Jordanstown to Whitehouse, turning Hazelbank into 'a Riviera on the doorstep of Belfast'.[12] This took place, a concrete walk eating further into the remaining unspoilt shoreline. However, it was balanced by a promise to retain Carnmoney Hill as one of the larger open spaces. The authority also looked forward to a day when residents would say, 'I come from Newtownabbey.'[13] Few did and before long those wards that encompassed much of the White City were petitioning to be taken out of Newtownabbey and returned to Belfast: 'We are Belfast people and the only thing left to do is to make it legal.'[14] In effect the White City has continued to be considered as part of north Belfast, even though the local administrative structures do not reflect that.

Emrys Jones – in a talk he gave at Queen's University in December 1958 – was critical of the creation of Newtownabbey. It was unique in having a cemetery as its centre. Creating satellite towns so near to Belfast merely gave rise to new problems. He found the decision not to extend Belfast's boundary incomprehensible, given that Belfast had half the industry and a third the population of the entire province. New towns should be at least twenty miles away from Belfast.[15] This was a jaundiced view, perhaps, but one built on his own recognised expertise and endorsed by others since. 'There is no evidence today,' wrote former divisional planning officer for Belfast Bill Morrison (in 2006) of the creation of Newtownabbey, 'that sound principles of town planning, by now well established in Britain, were seriously applied to what became Northern Ireland's first "new town" since the Plantation.'[16]

It was only with the Matthew Report regional plan, published in 1964 with an interim report in 1961, that the problems of 'bulging Belfast' and boundary demarcations left over from the grand plans of 1944–5 were finally addressed.[17] Matthew's answer to anxieties about Belfast's urban sprawl was to declare a 'stop-line' beyond which Belfast should not spread, though, ironically, Newtownabbey was considered within it. Instead he put forward plans for the development of other towns in its hinterland (Antrim, Ballymena, Bangor, Carrickfergus, Downpatrick, Larne and Newtownards) and the creation of a new one in County Armagh. This made sense, given the preference of new industries to be near Belfast, with all the transport facilities it offered. However, Downpatrick aside, they were all majority unionist areas, while two-thirds of the jobs were designated for Ballymena and what became Craigavon. Among the geopolitical sensitivities of Northern Ireland, the outcome proved explosive. Matthew also was a bit baffled by Newtownabbey. The area had seen an 87 per cent increase in population between 1951 and 1961 (20,215 to 37,440), but lacked 'a well-defined town centre' or ' recognisable focus'. Locating its centre at Whitewell had been discussed, as well as a new regional sports centre on the 165 acres acquired by the council there. However, he thought it 'too close to Belfast to have established a separate identity and regional functions ... Newtownabbey is in fact a suburb of the City and must be considered an integral part of the Belfast Urban Area.'[18]

The government-commissioned Matthew Inquiry was the outcome of perennial disputes between Stormont and Belfast Corporation. John Oliver, a longstanding and much-respected civil servant dealing with planning, recalled the endless and bitter disputes with the corporation in these years. 'It was in this negative period that we suffered some of our most unhappy relations with Belfast Corporation.' In retrospect, he was more understanding:

> Here we had the juxtaposition of a city of some considerable standing that dated from the seventeenth century and enjoyed a royal charter, with a parvenu parliament and a government dating only from 1921. Relations had never been easy. The city clearly resented interference by government. They resented even more any attempt to equate them with other local authorities ... [to whom] they felt superior ... They were convinced that the country members of parliament conspired to depress the city's position.[19]

What particularly rankled with the corporation was that its wish to extend the city boundary was rejected by that very parliament rather than by the government. That had been City Hall's excuse for not building more houses. Despite the early success of the Housing Trust in acting as a spur to dilatory local councils, the post-war plans for redevelopment had not been fulfilled, and Belfast was falling behind British housing and planning standards. Then one day, Oliver recalled, a Belfast Corporation deputation, 'in an unguarded moment', conceded that they might build a few houses outside the boundary, provided an independent advisor was appointed. The ministry 'seized' on the suggestion and immediately contacted Sir Robert Matthew in Edinburgh to draw up a Belfast regional plan.[20]

Matthew was 'a wake-up call, rediscovering the wartime visions for town planning' in Northern Ireland, wrote Bill Morrison, an overdue response to Belfast Corporation's failure 'to deal effectively with urban renewal, housing, industrial overspill and traffic problems in the post-war years'.[21] There was a sense of rush in the early 1960s as Matthew was implemented. Oliver recalled act of parliament following 'hard on the heels' of act of parliament, commission following commission, plan following plan, all under a new ministry – carved out of the old Health and Local Government Ministry in July 1964 – the Ministry of Development. Even Belfast Corporation seemed invigorated, appointing consultants and its first ever city-planning officer in 1967 and finally cooperating with the new ministry to produce a plan for the whole urban area. This came rather too late, unfortunately, because it ran into the Troubles and the reorganisation of local government, which saw housing taken out of the hands of the councils altogether.[22]

Oliver found the road planners of the new ministry the most difficult, almost 'building roads for their own sake' instead of integrating them with general planning strategy. 'Those virile men in roads, I had the impression at first, took a poor view of the old women on the planning side, concerned as it seemed with pretty scenery and scandalised at the sight of … concrete post-fencing.'[23] The White City residents, particularly the children and teenagers, would have endorsed Oliver's criticisms. The estate was barely finished before plans were afoot to further alter the surrounding landscape. The increasing number of cars on the roads and escalating accident figures led the Ministry of Commerce to approve plans in 1954 for a number of fast approach roads to the city. The north approach road, which tore up the White City's sea-facing perimeter, was designed to take 'progressively denser' traffic from the built-up area of the Antrim Road. The road would 'run across open country, roughly parallel to the Whitewell Road'.[24]

The map accompanying the report in the *Northern Whig* envisages the demolition of sixty to seventy houses at the top and bottom of the Whitewell Road, the diversion of the Longlands Road and its rerouting under the Antrim Road near the zoo, as well as an almost complete takeover of the centre of Greencastle village.[25]

Thus did the lower part of the White City lose its sense of country idyll. 'They took away our field,' Gerry Mulholland recalled of the football ground and GAA playing fields at the opposite side of the Whitewell Road. This was a serious loss of recreational facilities, just as the children of the White City were becoming teenagers. Moira Morrow recalled the mounds of earth as their vista became a building site, her father bringing back soil for the garden in his wheelbarrow and losing his wedding ring in the mud. The road became part of the larger M2 project in 1966 and the once-proud mill village of Greencastle was largely obliterated. One woman recalled returning from Belgium in the 1960s to find her mother and grandmother very distressed that their home was to be demolished to make way for the motorway. Their family had lived in Greencastle for generations. Bill Morrison, again, was critical:

> The Matthew Plan may have represented a high point in the history of regional planning, but regrettably it was not the result of enlightened thinking in the highest levels of government – it was largely devised to defuse a power struggle between Belfast Corporation and regional government. It was based on a range of assumptions that subsequently proved false. It was cavalier in the way it dealt with people forced to move to the new regional centres ... Wholesale clearance of areas awaiting long-promised redevelopment left the inner city looking like a barren wasteland. Town planning as such was held to blame for the destruction of entire communities.[26]

It was largely to address the problems of slum clearance – only properly confronted in the 1956 Housing Act – that the Matthew Report was commissioned. Before the war little had been done to deal with the problem and an English visitor to Belfast in 1951 was appalled: 'The Victorian ugliness of Belfast's slums was something of a shock … the Corporation in its impressive City Hall are not doing all they could.'[27] The Housing Trust said much the same: 'in respect of slum clearance … the Trust is prepared to help in so far as it can, but the powers and responsibility rest primarily with the local authority'.[28] The 1960s strategy for the redevelopment of slum areas took Matthew as its guide. But the land required for such redevelopment would leave none for recreational space, and need for this was part of Matthew's report. According to the 1961 census, 41.4 per cent of housing in Belfast was without a hot-water tap, 49.1 per cent was without a fixed bath and population density was 135 people per acre. There was still a real shortage of public housing, 56.2 per cent being rented from private landlords. An estimated sixty-one thousand new homes were needed – thirty-one thousand of these as a result of the inner ring road – of which only twenty thousand could be built within the city.

By 1963 it was estimated that housing for as many as seventy-four thousand people would be needed over the next twenty years, twenty-five thousand from slum clearance.[29] Some of these might be built on undeveloped portions of existing Housing Trust and corporation sites. There were some reservations about whether 'the type of person' being rehoused from slum areas would meet the trust's criteria for selection of tenants.[30] The trust itself seems not to have shared this view. Its members told a conference on slum clearance in November 1957 that slum-dwellers were no different from tenants elsewhere. They lived there because generations of their families had and they valued the friendship and neighbourly comradeship. Admittedly, paying the higher rents of Housing Trust houses might pose a problem, but there is also a suggestion that by this stage the trust could not be as selective of its tenants as it was in the early days. Then, the housing manager had had 'large numbers of applicants and a smaller number of dwellings'. She was able to select tenants who, in addition to need, would be 'appreciative of better housing conditions'. The situation was different now: 'This no longer applies! She has little or no applications and enough dwellings to go round.'[31] There was certainly an abundance of Housing Trust provision in the Newtownabbey area by the end of the 1950s. Beside Rathcoole's 366 acres and ongoing building of a planned 2,968 houses, earlier estates such as the White City's 31 acres and 322 houses looked like niche enterprises.[32] It was thought that the cleared sites in the city would only accommodate 40–50 per cent of the people displaced and, 'as those residing in slum areas are of the lowest income group', adding travel costs if they were sent out of the city was quite an issue.[33] The trust had made an agreement with Belfast Corporation to rehouse slum-clearance families as re-lets on their existing estates and a further twelve houses were built on the White City estate in 1964, on an undeveloped site identified on the Whitewell Road.[34] The whole area was being redeveloped by the mid-1960s, with council estates under construction on the lower Whitewell Road, Mill Road and Bawnmore.[35]

The breakup of old neighbourhoods and communities by this redevelopment scheme was deeply unpopular. This was 'the compulsory removal of people from Belfast', admitted Belfast Corporation, and Charles Brett believed that it contributed to the sectarian violence of the Troubles. He saw 'the old sectarian boundary-lines' that had been established the previous century largely holding good for central Belfast until now, quite unlike the mixed-religion post-war suburbs.[36] Redevelopment now spread the old into the new. Although, as the Housing Trust reported, such families could not have afforded the new council or trust houses on pre-war incomes, 'the increases in wages and the improvements in the social services ... in recent years' meant that this was no longer the case. Even so, there was one group presenting more than a simple housing problem – 'families with a bad domestic standard unsuitable for immediate transfer to a new estate among tenants who take a pride in their houses and surroundings'.[37] Whatever their background, a different kind of tenant did start to arrive in the White City around this time. I was told that they had come from exclusively loyalist areas where bunting and flags would have been the norm. Then 'there was a certain amount of intimidation when they knocked on doors and asked where your flag was. Most people didn't want that and Miss Dunlop called a meeting to have it stopped.'[38] On the other hand, 'I can understand how people from the Shankill, suddenly finding themselves living next to Catholics, might have felt uncomfortable and frightened,' a long-term Catholic resident of a neighbouring area said to me in 2016. But affected Catholics did move out, as did some Protestants: 'It wasn't the White City people put the Catholics out, but the newcomers,' I was told.

As the Troubles began to highlight such developments, the newly created Community Relations Commission (CRC) made the same connection. It described the White City as 'a densely-populated Housing Trust Estate of 350 houses and flats with no sport and recreational facilities'. Indeed, it considered the loss of recreational green space in the area a real factor threatening the traditionally good communal relations and considered the way it found itself on 'the periphery' of different local jurisdictions as part of the reason for such 'neglect'. Then there were 'the problems relating to redevelopment', the lack of integration between the old and 'new residents from "Belfast"' and 'the tension that the "new" have brought with them from the various areas of Belfast'.[39]

By now the estate was beginning to disintegrate, literally. Although normally very positive about the Housing Trust, the Housing Executive's third chairman, Charles Brett, is less so about its legacy in estates such as the White City:

> It must be said, however, that not all the Housing Trust's legacies to its successors have been equally happy. The technical advances of wartime had, by 1945, brought about an unfortunate over-confidence in the miraculous potentialities of new methods and materials … a mistaken belief, contrary to all experience of Ulster's climate, that flat roofs could now be relied upon to keep out the rain for as long, and as reliably, as pitched roofs.[40]

More seriously, the actual material used to construct Orlit houses – ensuring speed of construction to resolve the post-war housing crisis – was progressively corroding the structural beams. By the 1960s the trust had recognised the defects of Orlit houses and had stopped building them, though it continued to build other, non-traditional forms.[41] All over the UK Orlit houses were now causing the same problem, and in England a programme of demolition was started.[42]

The White City was the biggest and earliest Orlit estate in Northern Ireland. But, as stated by the 1986 report commissioned by the North Belfast Community Resource Centre, the defects of 'dampness, water penetration, disintegration and cracking of external cladding, window-frames and gable ends have been a common characteristic for many years. The houses are structurally unfit and will have to be demolished, there is no other solution.'[43] The defects had finally been brought to light when the Housing Executive started to rewire them in the course of installing central heating in the 1980s. Although the demolition of the White City was decided by the Housing Executive in December 1984, it took a long time to get under way and even longer to complete. The rebuilding programme seemed endless. The Housing Executive delivered a news-sheet to residents in 1994 proclaiming: 'The flat roofs and concrete blocks are gone. The old White City is no more!'[44] However, as the *Belfast Telegraph* reported on 6 September 1994, 'puzzled residents' looking out of their windows still saw seven of the old blocks remaining, as the picture accompanying the story confirms. By then the derelict homes were being used as drinking dens by teenagers and were infested with vermin. My mother and I had returned to our old street two years previously. There were still a few houses occupied, including our old one. But most were empty, the hedges were unkempt and rubbish was starting to accumulate in the gardens. The tenants' association had highlighted this problem in 1986. Several were interviewed for the BBC Northern Ireland Community Archive in February 1986. As their homes were prepared for demolition, they were moved from one house to another of those still standing. These were often in a very poor condition and here they were expected to live for five to ten years. 'We were living amidst dust,' Linda Taylor told me. She had to resort to steel wool to remove the grime, even from the windows. The houses that were boarded up were being broken into and boilers and other equipment stolen. Rats became a problem; dogs were trailing out rubbish and children were playing in it. Others said their houses were flooding.[45] The 1986 community report, *WhiteCity: Crumbling Orlits*, shows desolate, boarded-up houses, overgrown gardens and toothless fencing.

Residents were critical of the new, larger authority, the Housing Executive, which had replaced the Housing Trust in 1971. The Housing Executive seemed unconcerned about the uncertainties and worries caused by 'this sudden announcement' and the financial and physical hardships to be endured, particularly since rebuilding was progressively delayed. Frustration leaps off the pages of the 1986 report. The Housing Executive had failed to keep the residents informed, their meetings recording 'a series of broken and empty promises':

> The patronising 'we know best' syndrome needs to stop. As the people living here, no-one [sic] knows better than us what we want and need. We will still be living here after re-development, unlike the ever changing Executive officials who briefly descend on the estate.[46]

Older residents recalled the Housing Trust with some nostalgia and, while the rent-collection function of the housing manager was remembered less positively, it had given them the chance to air grievances. In contrast, the Housing Executive was 'impersonal', poor at carrying out repairs, which were shoddy and unchecked, and generally negligent of the green areas and open spaces. It must be remembered that the Housing Executive's remit was considerably larger than that of the Housing Trust. 'There was intense debate on what we should do with the Orlits,' former Housing Executive officer Séan McKenna told me, and even the Housing Executive was becoming 'frustrated with the technical people'.

The report shows a remarkable continuity of residence, the average length of tenancy being 20.8 years and many tenancies being a lot longer. Unsurprisingly, in that time children had moved away and tenants had grown older: 46.6 per cent of households were of 2 or fewer; 34 per cent were classified as old-age pensioners; 26 per cent wanted to move: 'Many of these are elderly tenants who find themselves in accommodation too large for them and inconveniently situated at the top of steep hills with no amenities in the area.' The remainder, however, expressed an 'overwhelming' desire to stay and to keep the same neighbours. 'The Whitecity is a long established and traditional community ... and residents are concerned that despite redevelopment it should remain so.'[47]

Crumbling Orlits, while critical of the inferior quality of the original houses, shows that the original pride of place and neighbourhood had persisted. While the houses were being demolished, residents asked the Housing Executive to do everything necessary to prevent the White City becoming blighted, while Belfast City Council should maintain the cleanliness of the streets and green spaces. Indeed, they asked for more green space, even though there was already more than the average Housing Executive standard. They also wanted the estate's existing layout and character retained. They got some of what they wanted, and today's houses are a considerable improvement on the originals. So why was there lingering resentment against the Housing Executive? I found out when I returned in the mid-2000s. The estate seemed smaller and I could not find my old street.

'Where is Portmore Hill?' I enquired of two women walking by.

'You're standing on it,' one responded, pointing to the broken rubble under my feet. 'It doesn't exist any more.'

The new estate represented only two-thirds of the old. Gone were Bresk Hill, Laragh Road, Portmore Hill (the longest street on the original estate, accounting for seventy-five households), part of Thorburn Road and the shops and flats in Navarra Place.[48] All the points at which one could access the estate from the Snaky Path had been closed off, reflecting the role played by security in estate design during the Troubles. In a conversation with me in 2014, Brian Dunn described the replacement White City as a 'shrunken community'. The Housing Executive had not rebuilt 150 units, so some people could not move back – 'a lesson on how not to let your community disappear', he concluded.

By the time of the 1986 report the White City had become an area of high unemployment, with only 27.5 per cent working and 60.7 per cent on housing benefit.[49] This was a long remove from the Housing Trust tenants of earlier decades, ability to pay the higher rents on trust estates being a prerequisite for tenancy. The greater availability of housing mentioned earlier and the trust's inability to be quite so selective was one factor, the ageing of the original population another, the securing of a mortgage to become property owners in their own right (a very well-publicised aspiration in the 1960s) yet another. But for quite some time the economic situation in Northern Ireland had not been quite as rosy as government cared to admit. Even the pro-unionist *Belfast Telegraph* commented that membership of the UK was not bringing the kind of material benefits that one might expect.[50]

Certainly the industries that had given full employment to the White City in earlier decades were now in steep decline. In the 1950s there was an upbeat, optimistic tone to press and official statements about the economy, and a major economic survey of 1955–7, which pointed to Northern Ireland's poor productivity when compared to the rest of the UK, was considered much too gloomy.[51] The editor of the *Belfast Telegraph*, Jack Sayers, ran a series of articles early in 1956 that were full of confidence about the 'brightening hopes' for Northern Ireland over the next ten years. The proposed redevelopment programme was one part of this, the attraction of new industries another. He was, however, very critical of the linen industry as having exercised a 'crippling and dispiriting' influence on Ulster's economy for far too long.[52]

The flax mills and associated dams and bleaching works had been a defining element of the Whitewell, Whitehouse and Whiteabbey area since the early nineteenth century, all the post-war press and official publications reflecting the status of linen production as Northern Ireland's key staple industry. By the 1950s the 'Miss Irish Linen' contests were a regular feature of the local news, usually organised by the Whiteabbey Weaving Company.[53] In 1949 figures gathered by the Housing Trust showed that linen and related industries provided employment for 2,350 people in the Whitewell, Whitehouse, Whiteabbey and Mossley areas, 1,507 of these female.[54] By the 1950s, however, the industry was in trouble. Because of the 'serious employment position', a deputation from Belfast Rural District Council sought a meeting with the Ministry of Labour in September 1956 to press for more employment in the area. The Whiteabbey Weaving Company alone was down to less than a third its normal workforce and it looked as if it was about to fold entirely.[55] World trends, competition from cheaper overseas production, the financial crisis of 1951 and the end of the Korean War (military contracts having kept the industry afloat) all played their part. So, too, did the arrival of the new man-made textiles. I will not be alone in cringing at the fad for Crimplene and Terylene clothing that dominated our sartorial lives in the 1960s. However, both government and economists were rapturous about the employment potential of the new developments. There was considerable debate about attracting new industries and some success in doing so, particularly to identified growth areas around Larne and Carrickfergus and the new industrial estate at Monkstown.[56] Although not the easy walk down the Longlands to the various mills for White City women, there was still more employment available for them than for men.[57]

More serious was the terminal decline of the province's heavy industry. In 1950 the shipyard accounted for one in five of all manufacturing jobs in Belfast, as reflected in the employment profile of the White City. By 1964 it had lost 40 per cent of them and the other heavy industries were experiencing a similar decline.[58] The downturn was reflected in considerable industrial unrest, notably a prolonged strike in the shipyard in 1958 and another the following year after twelve hundred redundancies in the aircraft industry at Shorts.[59] For a while this was offset by the new industries attracted to the Larne/Carrickfergus area. But with the recession of the 1970s and cheaper labour overseas, they disappeared and inward investment became more difficult because of the Troubles.

The Troubles-related political upheaval of the period was accompanied by the disappearance of that sense of post-war well-being that had come from the familiar, in work, home and environment. The new Housing Executive was bigger, more impersonal, the planners and architects – with brave-new-world visions – even more distant.[60] The classic account of this happening is Ron Weiner's *The Rape and Plunder of the Shankill*, which charts the long-drawn-out process of redevelopment from the late 1950s until the 1970s, by which stage almost half the residents had moved out because of the deterioration of the area during the long wait.[61] The considerable publicity given to such developments in the 1960s further contributed to people's disquiet.[62] Something similar happened with the White City. As it disintegrated and residents awaited rebuilding, many moved elsewhere. 'But moving is one of life's traumatic experiences,' Linda Taylor told me. 'Once you'd resettled somewhere else, you didn't want to go through that again to come back.' All over Belfast communities were paying the price of decades of neglect and complacency. The 1981 census showed a city in decline, with some of the worst housing conditions in the UK.[63] 'So it came about,' concluded Charles Brett, 'as a result of fifty years of apathy and neglect ... that by 1970, a first-class housing crisis was one of the principal contributory factors to the Troubles.' In quick succession the 1960s redevelopment chaos and the 1970s bombing would radically alter the physical profile of Belfast, and not for the better.[64]

9

Politics, Normal and Otherwise

*Ordinary people are completely fed up with the whole business
[sectarian politics] ... new ideas have infiltrated ... there is a
restlessness in regard to the whole pace and procedure of politics and
established parties.*

Mass Observation, Ulster Outlooks, 1944[1]

I cannot recall much talk of politics in my home in the 1950s and
early 1960s, or indeed that my parents ever voted. In fact, politics
seemed to figure very little in our lives, and in this we would have
been typical of the rather passive and unquestioning population of
those days. Indeed, even radio and television carried little political
discussion.[2] Nor do I recall mention of any figures in the Nationalist
Party, which should have been our natural political home, possibly
because the Nationalist Party had all but abandoned Belfast, and its
largely working-class Catholic population drifted to labour politics.[3]
Perhaps this is why I remember a real admiration for Paddy Devlin.
This may have been more to do with his trade-union and labour
politics than any Catholic background, for he was heartily disapproved
of by the 'Catholic establishment',[4] as well as his impeccable Belfast
working-class credentials in west and north Belfast, just the areas
where my father had grown up and where my parents had spent their
early days together.

As with others of that generation from the White City, my mother
could not recall that newspapers came into the house – probably
because few actually bought newspapers at the time, as Field-Neill
discovered.[5] 'I suppose we did buy the *Irish News* [an ultra-Catholic,
old-fashioned, nationalist Belfast paper] from time to time,' she told
me, largely for the death notices. I remember her also occasionally

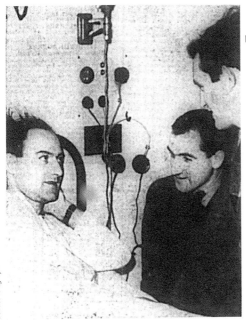

Donal McAteer at the Royal Victoria Hospital, Belfast, in February 1953, following the *Princess Victoria* disaster.

Barbara McGeehan with five-year-old Elizabeth Browne, 1 June 1956.

Ballygolan Primary School, opened 3 January 1955.

The Lido cinema, Shore Road, opened 26 March 1955.

T. Jackson McCormick

The M2 under construction, looking north-west
from the Antrim Road, 1965.

PRONI

Phase one of the M2, opened October 1966.

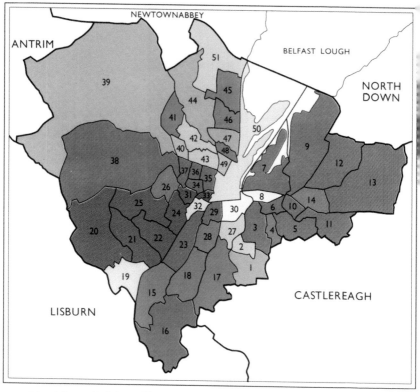

A breakdown of religious affiliation within
the Belfast wards, 1976.
White City is located in number 51.

CATHOLIC/OTHER RELIGIONS
BY LOCAL GOVERNMENT WARDS

PERCENTAGE OF CATHOLICS

UNDER 10%

OVER 10% BUT UNDER 20%

OVER 20% BUT UNDER 30%

OVER 30% BUT UNDER 40%

OVER 40% BUT UNDER 60%

OVER 60% BUT UNDER 70%

OVER 70% BUT UNDER 80%

OVER 80% BUT UNDER 90%

OVER 90%

In December 1984 the Housing Executive approved the demolition of the White City, but it was a long process. This photo was taken *c.* 1990.

The peace wall on the Serpentine Road, at the edge of the White City, 1999.

Flo Kelsey

Gerry Mulholland

Brian Dunn

Shane McAteer

My mother, Sheila Burns

Anna Pearson

buying the southern paper the *Sunday Press* outside Mass on Sundays. The *Belfast Telegraph* – again only bought occasionally and largely for the small ads, in which it had captured the market – seems to have crossed community, though politically it was unionist. Then there was *Ireland's Saturday Night*, the Belfast-produced sports-and-leisure weekly that some of the men on the estate would buy on the way home from work, particularly if they followed the dogs, the Dunmore stadium being just down the Antrim Road, near that other site of pleasure, the Capitol cinema. It was apolitical and gave a good insight into how people spent their leisure time: sport, lots of dancing, cinema, working-men's clubs, shopping, popular music. Set against the newspapers, particularly the weeklies such as the *Irish News's Irish Weekly*, or the *Belfast Telegraph's Belfast Weekly Telegraph*, which tended to concentrate on extremes, *Ireland's Saturday Night* describes another world. But it is a world that working people occupied, and one that is largely absent from the majority of even good scholarly studies of these decades that use only political sources. Belfast and its hinterland, of course, was different. It was the only part of Northern Ireland that produced anything like a modern socialist movement. And people living near the border or in the west of the province – the main market for the weeklies – would have had a different experience.[6]

There was, in fact a very hazy grasp of politics among the population and few sources of information. Nor was there much news or current-affairs coverage on radio. BBC radio, since its arrival in 1924, had been pro-unionist and very nervous about upsetting the Northern Ireland government. There were no Catholic reporters until the 1960s and no Catholic members of the Board of Governors until 1973. Much to the London parent's dismay, the BBC's unionist leanings extended to a reluctance to report on events in the rest of Ireland, let alone cooperate with the Irish national radio station.[7] Of course, you could tune into Irish Radio (Athlone), as my family did. Contrary to external posturing, however, unionism was very nervous about the south and not at all confident that it could always count on London's unquestioning support. The long resistance to Irish or Ulster history programmes, even for schools broadcasting, did not, as the corporation in England – and its Northern Irish controller after 1948 – recognised, accurately reflect audience wishes. The resistance came rather from the director of education in Northern Ireland, Englishman Dr Stuart Hawnt, and the two other Northern Ireland members of the BBC's School Broadcasting Council, who believed that 'it would be a mistake to regard Northern Ireland as in any way different from England'.[8]

Scot Andrew Stewart had come to his new position as controller of BBC Northern Ireland in the late 1940s with the view that even controversial subjects and political discussion needed opening up. The newspapers were not reflecting these accurately, particularly for the NILP, which, unlike unionists and nationalists, did not have a newspaper outlet. And he felt strongly that 'the Catholic Nationalist section of the community has a point of view on local issues which is seldom heard or expressed, for in their own press and speeches they habitually distort it in such a way as to suggest that "Partition" is the cause of every ill'. Stewart was pleased with the introduction of a Catholic voice on a new monthly discussion programme, *Ulster Commentary*, from 1951 – that of noted educationalist and writer, J.J. Campbell. While Campbell's nationalist sympathies were known, he kept to issues of concern to all people in Northern Ireland without confusing them with 'constitutional red herrings'.[9] It was Campbell, now on the BBC's Regional Advisory Committee, who raised the whole issue of history broadcasting. Finally, in 1953, together with T.W. Moody and J.C. Beckett, he launched the series *Ulster Since 1800*, reflecting the revolution in Irish historiography that had occurred and of which Moody and Beckett were pioneers. It proved so popular that a second series was commissioned, though a series on 'Irish' history had to wait until 1965.

The BBC had been looking for a way to get 'a reasonably balanced discussion of current problems'[10] and, in January 1954, they found it in a regional version of the popular London-produced programme *Any Questions?*. Northern Ireland's *Your Questions* tapped into a real public appetite and became even more popular than *Any Questions?* itself – one of the frequent examples of the Northern Ireland populace thinking differently from their political power-brokers. It was chaired by Queen's University academic Desmond Neill (of the Field-Neill Survey), the first panel consisting of *Belfast Telegraph* editor Jack Sayers, J.J. Campbell, Jim Beckett and Charles Brett, and they regularly appeared thereafter.

Commercial channel UTV (from 1959) was even more successful because its support was more broadly based. It declared that it was in the business of 'reconciliation and bridge building' and its arrival 'accelerated' the process of liberalisation in the BBC.[11] By today's standards, however, political reporting was pretty anodyne. UTV did not even have a newsroom until October 1962. As Rex Cathcart shows, Catholics could be forgiven for perceiving the BBC as a largely Protestant/unionist organisation, for there were few Catholics employed before the late 1960s. Although UTV's record was much better, Brum Henderson recalls the novelty of suggesting as much: 'Looking back from this distance in time it may seem incredible that this was not a priority from the outset but it is a measure of how different Northern Ireland was then that it was not.' As happened so often, the prompt to liberalise was coming from England.[12] Arguably, such limited coverage partly underpinned the low-key reaction to the renewed IRA campaign in 1956–62.

Unionism was the dominant force in politics after 1921, when Northern Ireland came into being. Home Rule for the whole island had been on the statute book, but was rejected by southern republicans and northern unionists and the island was partitioned to reflect this new reality. Cheated of victory at the eleventh hour, northern nationalists, who had been overwhelmingly constitutional Home Rulers rather than republicans, remained in a state of sullen shock about partition until the 1960s. They could not be brought to accept the new constitutional position and were very influenced by the Catholic Church, never appreciating that fear and dislike of the Catholic Church was at the heart of northern Protestantism. All of this gave unionist and Orange politicians sufficient excuse to play on Protestant voter fears at times of Orange parades and the surprisingly frequent elections. Whatever the realities of a day-to-day functioning democracy, unionist slogans depicting the Catholic minority as a 'disloyal' Trojan horse, a threat to Protestantism and the union alike, were repeated to keep the Protestant people from straying to other parties or causes. Though nationalists were just as guilty of divisive rhetoric on such occasions, unionism was in power from 1921 to 1972 and many unionist MPs were returned unopposed.[13] In the Stormont debates on the housing issue in 1945, nationalist leader J.P. McSparran had a point when he criticised past unionist governments for 'stirring up internecine strife between people that should have been living in harmony'.[14]

He stressed, however, that he was talking about past unionist governments. There can be no doubt that the twenty years after the end of the war was one of those periods when more moderate voices, even within unionism, were on the increase. Historian of unionism Graham Walker is critical of the unionist leader for all of these years, Sir Basil Brooke, Lord Brookeborough, for not capitalising on that and attempting to conciliate nationalists.[15] Orange parades had been suspended for the duration of the Second World War, but restarted in July 1945. The *Irish News* thought they were not as well attended as before. By the early 1950s, however, parades were back to full strength. There seems to have been little trouble in Belfast, though there was trouble elsewhere. In the mid-1950s the insistence of unionist MP Brian Faulkner on forcing an illegal Orange march through a Catholic area in south Down – the Longstone Road, Annalong – remained for a long time, even in moderate Catholic folk memory, dimming the praise Faulkner should have received for his role in the power-sharing executive of 1974.[16]

The Longstone Road debacle was one of the excessive displays of loyalism that tended to occur around the time of royal visits to the province – 1953, 1954, 1961, 1963, 1966. While the Irish government objected to the inclusion of 'Northern Ireland' in the new queen's title in 1952, its ambassador in London attended the coronation, and flags in Dublin had been flown at half-mast to mark her father's death.[17] Catholics and moderate nationalists were generally respectful of the monarchy. There was particular sympathy for the young queen having to assume her new role in such sad circumstances, which Cahir Healy, anti-partition MP, expressed in the British House of Commons, even though he was protesting at the inclusion of 'Northern Ireland' in her title.[18] Cardinal D'Alton, the head of the Catholic Church in Ireland, sent his congratulations. It would have been difficult for Catholics then to disagree with Pope Pius XII, who, in his message to the British minister to the Vatican, commented:

Scarcely three years have passed since we had the happiness

of receiving Her Majesty in these very halls. But in that brief time what heavy cares have entered into her life. The Lord of all, in his wise providence, has placed the weight of empire on her youthful shoulders, and she has carried the burden with a courageous simplicity and unselfish spirit of devotion.[19]

In the coronation year there was plenty of evidence in the press of tensions, though much less in Belfast than in the west of the province and I do not recall flags being as prominent back then as in recent times. Photos of the coronation street-party in the White City in 1953 show just a few union flags and none on the houses. I asked my mother if she had felt uncomfortable with the flag-waving at this time on the estate. 'No,' she replied, 'it was expected.' Non-elite Belfast was well attuned to living parallel lives and enjoying the prevalent sectarian-themed humour to be found in James Young's hugely popular comedy or Lynn Doyle's popular fiction and Robert Harbinson's autobiography, all favourites in my home. The *Belfast Telegraph* regularly pointed to the ridiculous aspects of our sectarian culture, the horse No Surrender at the 1958 Dublin Horse Show refusing to budge, or the crowds turning up to Bill Haley's film *Rock Around the Clock* not rushing for the exit when 'God Save the Queen' was played.[20]

Gerard McLarnon's play, *The Bonefire*, dramatised that most common of themes in Northern Irish writing, love across the religious divide. When it was staged by the Group Theatre Company at the Opera House in August 1958, there were protests that it was a slur on the Orange Order.[21] These undoubtedly influenced the Group's chairman to reject Sam Thompson's play *Over the Bridge* – dealing with sectarianism in the shipyard – the following year. The rejection led to the resignations of the Group's stars, including James Ellis, who went on to stage it anyway in January 1960. It ran for six weeks at the Empire Theatre, attracting some forty-two thousand theatregoers and very favourable reviews, in which it was hailed as 'saying much that is needed to be said in this part of the world and much that should have been said years ago had anyone the ability or the courage to say it'.[22] Bigger crowds had gathered outside the Opera House on 15

August 1958 (admittedly mostly children) during the visit of the Lone
Ranger (Clayton Moore) as he appeared in all his screen costume to
publicise his film *The Lone Ranger and the Lost City of Gold*.[23] I feel
retrospectively aggrieved that my parents did not take us, since *The
Lone Ranger* was the main programme that our friends came to watch
in our improvised home cinema.

Extreme statements and gestures were criticised by moderate
unionism, which was to the fore during the editorship of Jack Sayers
at the *Belfast Telegraph*.[24] Successive ministers of home affairs, Brian
Maginess and George Hanna, were particularly notable in urging a
more liberal form of unionism. I have not found signs of the nationalist
press giving them any credit for this and all too often such moderates'
careers did not progress because of Orange influences on their party.
In all there was a real gulf of understanding between nationalist and
unionist traditions. Even the *Belfast Telegraph* in the Sayers years was
baffled at the failure of nationalists to recognise the constitutional
position of Northern Ireland and to see that aspiring to a united
Ireland did not prevent them from participating in the system as it
existed. In Northern Ireland people just did not think that things
could be otherwise. As Ken Bloomfield comments on the limitations
of Terence O'Neill's premiership:

> A government that for decades had been based in one
> community was not good about being sensitive to the
> perceptions of others. Monocular vision rather than
> deliberate discrimination was often the problem.[25]

Of course, the swaggering triumphalism of unionist culture
disguised considerable nervousness, which was aggravated by southern
political rhetoric and any resurgence of militant republicanism. By
early 1942 the IRA had all but faded in Belfast. The last of the IRA
internees were released on 21 December 1945.[26] There were some
signs of a more inclusive mood after the war. In 1948, although
commemorations for the 150th anniversary of the 1798 Rebellion were
banned under the Special Powers Act, the lord chief justice granted
an injunction restraining Belfast City Council from prohibiting use of
the Ulster Hall for a 1798 commemoration concert.[27] In November

1950, after the Belfast West bi-election narrowly returned a unionist, conflicting party-political songs, including the Irish national anthem, were sung by the crowd outside the City Hall without any trouble, as the 'relatively strong guard of police stood quietly by'.[28] But there were rumblings in the traditional republican heartlands. There were six incidences of home-made bombs being thrown at Hastings Street police station in 1950–1, as well as an incident of paramilitary tarring and feathering on the Falls Road in February 1951.[29] A ban on flying the Irish tricolour in Northern Ireland came into force that August.[30]

An IRA campaign continued intermittently throughout these years, the most sustained part of which was Operation Harvest in 1956–62. The unionist papers were full of it but, like the megaphone politics, this disguised an underlying normality and Belfast was little affected. Whatever the perception, the operations of the Special Powers Act and the B-Specials, so disliked by – and largely used against – nationalists, Northern Ireland was not a police state. In 1958, even with the ongoing IRA campaign, the RUC changed its uniform from the militaristic kind of the 1920s to a more modern open-neck style.[31] Even Ernest Blythe, Irish minister of finance, cautioned northern nationalist politicians against using emotive and inaccurate language.[32] Nor did the bulk of Catholics support the IRA, despite the republican rhetoric of successive southern politicians. Indeed, militant republicans gave such lack of support as their reason for calling off Operation Harvest in February 1962. The attorney general, Edmund Warnock, responded to local unionists' criticism of the government for its perceived clemency in 1955 that the IRA was not strong in Northern Ireland. About ninety people had been arrested since 1939, he told the Cromac Unionist Association – a great many young men – and, of those convicted or interned and subsequently released, none had come back.[33]

A new mood in the Catholic hierarchy, which denounced the IRA and started to recognise the genuine reasons for Protestant fears, underpinned this. And, like most human situations, and certainly Northern Ireland's, where a terrible pettiness has often had murderous consequences, even small acts of generosity and understanding could melt hostility. The Catholic hierarchy's denunciation of the IRA was welcomed by Northern Ireland premier, Lord Brookeborough, though there was justice in his remark that it had taken them a long time.[34] The post-war thaw in relations owed much to the moderate realism of Cardinal D'Alton during his primacy of the Catholic Church, as reflected in unionist tributes when he died on 1 February 1963. In the worst winter experienced in living memory, the RUC was detailed to assist those travelling over the border to attend the funeral in Armagh on 4 February. As raging blizzards cut off much of the province, they dug Fr Agnellus Andrew out of the snow in Markethill so he could address the TV documentary of the funeral and provided an escort to the Irish president, Éamon de Valera, and members of the Irish government.[35]

In the press and among the political class, there was a lot of mutual watching for the other side to slip up. Unionists watched for any sign of underperformance, economically or otherwise, south of the border. The *Irish News* sought out signs that the reality did not match up to unionist claims that everyone was better off in a union with Britain. And everywhere there was that prickly defensiveness that is such a feature of public life in Northern Ireland. The BBC was taken to task by unionist governments on a number of occasions in the 1950s. Suggestions on flagship programmes such as *Hearts and Minds*, *Tonight* and *What's My Line?* that Northern Ireland might be sectarian produced howls of protest. The legendary Gilbert Harding's comment that Northern Ireland people lacked a sense of humour was deemed particularly offensive. More sensible heads, such as the ever-wise and courageous Methodist leader Eric Gallagher, pointed out that there was enough truth in the remarks to hurt.[36]

The Second World War *had* changed things and might have continued to do so had the IRA campaign not given ammunition to ultra-unionists. In politics, too, there were signs that the old loyalties might be losing some force and, despite a sharp rise in crime in the second half of the 1940s, there was no political crime.[37] By the 1950s public apathy with traditional tribal politics was evidenced by a slump in the unionist vote and the development of something like normal class politics. There was a leftward swing among the Belfast working class after the war, which had shown the failure of the unionist government to address working-class issues and their disastrous unpreparedness for the Blitz. Various labour parties took 40 per cent of the vote in the

1945 election in Belfast, against unionism's 50 per cent.[38] Support grew for the NILP. It lost a lot of nationalist support when, under pressure from its core working-class, trade-unionised Protestant base, it declared for the current constitutional position, continued union with Britain.[39] The labour vote, then, was split among several different parties. But the party campaigned hard to restore its non-sectarian ethos and gradually won back a Catholic vote, particularly among the young. In the 1958 election old nationalism as well as unionism did badly and there was a major shift to the NILP, which won four of the eight seats contested in Belfast, coming second in another three.[40] That year it assumed the role of official opposition at Stormont, after the Nationalist Party's continued refusal to be so recognised.[41]

In a post-mortem, the *Belfast Telegraph* depicted the election as a vote against unionist monopoly, as well as traditional nationalism: 'In Belfast at least, it reflects the view that today Anti-partition has little to offer anyone, and that were it not for the eternal abrasion of Protestantism and Roman Catholicism, Northern Ireland would be close to being at peace with itself.' The Unionist Party needed to take its stand less on self-preservation and loyalty and appeal more widely: 'A body of moderates – Catholics among them – is being mobilized and their votes will go to the party that offers reasonable discussion and impartial dealings.'[42] It was the kind of moderate, inclusive unionism which the paper's editor, Jack Sayers, spent his career promoting. Even so, such an analysis shows a distinct lack of understanding of even moderate nationalism, or recognition that there might be something wrong with continuous one-party domination. But it did show that the unionist government was looking increasingly out of touch. Brookeborough went off on an extended winter holiday to Gambia, his messages home and pictures in the press creating the image of an old-style colonial governor.[43]

Northern nationalism was also experiencing internal debate on whether it should accept the status quo, without abandoning the aspiration of reuniting the country.[44] The independent unionist candidate in north Belfast – seen as more extreme than mainstream unionism – attributed his defeat to Catholics actually voting unionist to keep him out. But if there was ever any realistic chance of 1950s unionism accepting Catholics, it died in the Orange denunciation of such a suggestion in November 1959.[45] And even if some Catholics had voted for moderate unionists in the recent election, there is little sign of many seeking to join the Unionist Party. Indeed, the *Irish News* dismissed such a suggestion as 'a strange ambition' of 'stray Catholics'.[46] Leading unionists agreed. Sir Clarence Graham, chair of the UUC's standing committee, caused outrage in the party for telling a Young Unionist conference that there was nothing to stop Catholics joining the Unionist Party. 'Much rage ... Graham's speeches on the line of allowing R.C.s to enter the Unionist Party,' Brookeborough recorded in his diary for 4 November 1959, and he sought to calm those who wanted the two to resign. 'The point is, there is no indication from either the nationalists or the Church that they agree with us in the policy of the maintenance of the constitution, but they may come later − speeches will only delay matters.'[47] Efforts at bridge-building continued through Orange–Green talks in 1962–3, developing from good relations between nationalist and Orange leaders in the Stormont Senate and welcomed in the press, though here again coming up against the absolutes of the constitution − Orange insistence that nationalists accept the union with Britain prior to talks − and nationalist insistence on talking about discrimination.[48]

At the local-council elections in 1958, the NILP had also polled well. By 1962, it was the second-largest party in Belfast. Newtownabbey, with its large working-class population in the new housing estates, was one of the NILP's strongholds. The party was respected in the area for having helped the strikers in the shipbuilding and engineering industries with interest-free loans.[49] The *Belfast Telegraph* thought it could become the first urban council in the province with a strong labour opposition.[50] As the NILP's historian, Aaron Edwards, comments, its success in this period rested on Catholics and Protestants having lived together in harmony for a generation.[51] But it was vulnerable to underlying sectarianism − there were plenty of flashes of this even in this more hopeful period − and the influx of Catholics caused tensions among its grass-roots loyalist members.[52] The decline of Protestants in the south, and a number of anti-Protestant scandals there in the 1950s, fuelled fundamentalist Protestantism in the north.[53] These were the years of the rise of Ian Paisley, his and others' protests leading to restrictive legislation over nationalist flags, when the RUC would have preferred a less-confrontational approach.

Arguably the IRA's Operation Harvest had deterred demands for equal rights for nationalists and strengthened the hardliners in unionism. It was an embarrassment to Catholics. Awareness of underlying sectarianism made moderates – a majority of both Protestants and Catholics – excessively cautious and ill equipped to deal with serious issues. However, from 1963–4 onwards a number of groups, including the NILP and the Belfast and District Trades Union Council, started to demand equal civil rights for Catholics as part of living in the UK.[54] But in starting to address Catholic working-class issues (when the base of the NILP was Protestant working class) the 'Protestant-Catholic thing' began to 'rear its head',[55] leading to the defeat of David Bleakley as MP for Woodvale. In north Belfast and south Antrim the party continued to poll well into the 1960s and early 1970s, its Newtownabbey branch continuing to pursue cross-community and civil-rights issues. But it was all very low key and Edwards is critical of the party for failing to push a number of issues and thereby playing a part in progressive polarisation along old lines.[56] Newtownabbey remained a stronghold of the NILP into the 1970s, when the party was collapsing elsewhere. However, the Troubles made things increasingly difficult for the party and, in the loyalist Ulster Workers' Council strike of 1974, it sided with its main constituency, the Protestant workers. Essentially the NILP had ceased to exist by 1982–3 and was formally disbanded in 1987, its history appearing to support the idea that underlying sectarianism deterred class politics.

I was too young to benefit from the explosion of youth culture and its music revolution in the first half of the 1960s. Belfast, often so backward, seemed mainstream then, with its own screaming Beatlemania and world-famous names such as Roy Orbison and the Rolling Stones ('polite boys', as one dance-hall owner recollected) playing in the local dance-halls. Things were also just changing for me. I had my first proper job as a Saturday girl in British Home Stores and the new independence and social life that came with it. Amidst that new world of the sixties also came some clues to the undercurrents that would explode in 1968–9. It was 1966, the year of the anniversaries of the 1916 Easter Rising and the Battle of the Somme – republican and loyalist milestones respectively. Amid fears that the IRA would use the centenary as an excuse to restart its campaign and that Paisley's growing movement would ensure sectarian clashes, trains and buses from the south were banned and all police leave was cancelled. My family had gone to Toomebridge to attend a 1916 rally. It was surrounded by police and Black Marias – my first ever experience of hostile policing. Even more intimidating was a call on the crowd from one of the speakers to attack the police. But we were moderate nationalists and quickly realised that we should not really have been there. The 1916 commemorations passed off peacefully and, contrary to the large police presence at Toomebridge, the RUC on the whole did not intervene in the commemorative events. But the language used by republicans, the displays of flags and the playing of the Irish national anthem unsettled Protestant people.[57] Paisley and his new Ulster Protestant Volunteers were gathering more support and many Protestants felt that the commemorations should have been banned.[58]

Two months later, a series of sectarian attacks and murders in Belfast intruded into what had seemed until now to have been such a newly liberalising atmosphere. The first signs of the revival of militant loyalism came on 11 June. A twenty-eight-year-old Catholic storeman, John Patrick Scullion, had been drinking and was walking across the Falls Road shouting 'Up the Republic', when he was picked out by loyalist assassins and murdered. The largely Protestant nearby Shankill Road was not considered out of bounds for Catholics in those days, and on 26 June three Catholic barmen had gone there for a late-night drink after finishing their shift at the International Hotel on Royal Avenue. As they left they were shot by the Ulster Volunteer Force (UVF). One, eighteen-year-old Peter Ward, was killed and the Malvern Street attack entered the prehistory of the Troubles. The following day, seventy-year-old Protestant widow Matilda Gould was killed in a botched attack on a neighbouring Catholic business.[59] In a veiled criticism of Paisley and his supporters, as well as unionists, the *Belfast Telegraph's* editorial talked of 'crazy people leading the province on a path to self-destruction … it is in danger of being thrown back into a dark past by sectarian forces which have too long been winked at by many who should know better'.[60] For the first time the Special Powers Act was invoked against Protestants. My mother knew many people in the hospitality and catering industry and this attack on young barmen from a well-known city hotel made the public personal. UVF leader Gusty Spence, who was convicted of the murder, was added to the small gallery of figures causing a frisson in my family lore. It all came back as I saw him enter the lecture hall at the 1993 Blackpool Labour Party Conference, where I was on a Northern Ireland panel at a fringe meeting, talking about the recent Opsahl Commission. It was difficult to recognise the bogeyman of the 1960s in the genial pipe-smoking intellectual whom I joined in the bar afterwards, along with David Ervine. And, as always, I reflected on how much should have united rather than divided Belfast's working classes.

By 1993 former loyalist prisoners were blaming Ian Paisley's pronouncements for driving them to such acts. In the later 1960s at Queen's University we used to laugh at one of our friends who could imitate perfectly the guldering roar of Paisley. Such apparent Old Testament rhetoric and denunciations of 'rampant popery' seemed so out of place in the optimistic 1960s. We know now that they were not. For Paisley was just the extreme end of that undercurrent in Protestant thinking, so honed by unionist electioneering and Orange culture, which saw Éire's constitutional claim over the north, the clear power of the Catholic Church and the rumblings of republicanism as collective popery closing in. The loyalist news-sheets of the early Troubles make this very clear. Such fears were latent when unionism was in firm control and Catholics kept in their place, as the intermittent protests over Catholics getting social housing or jobs reveal. Indeed, in the hopeful 1950s they were dismissed as a throwback. However, the 1960s also saw those old certainties weakening – not just economically, but politically too.

An opinion poll in 1967 showed that most people sought moderation, including better north–south relations, although there was still a significant unionist minority against them.[61] In nationalism the old refusal to participate in Northern Ireland's civic and political life was being challenged by a younger generation. Prominent among these people were future leaders of constitutional nationalism such as John Hume and Austin Currie, as well as Conn and Patricia McCluskey and other professional Catholics who were demanding equal rights within the existing system.[62] The world seemed to be full of people abandoning old deference and seeking change by peaceful protest.

Even Belfast in recent years had witnessed Campaign for Nuclear Disarmament (CND) marches, though they were very 'respectable', as the *Belfast Telegraph* observed. The CND badge started to appear in my school – hardly an act of major rebellion, though considered so by the nuns.[63] By 1967 the McCluskeys' Campaign for Social Justice had produced the Northern Ireland Civil Rights Association and Britain, under Wilson's Labour government, was taking note. This was important to the then-prime minister of Northern Ireland, Terence O'Neill, as he courted the British Treasury in support of his modernising programme.

Unionism, too, seemed to be liberalising, with O'Neill keen to build bridges to the Catholic community. The growth of ecumenism and the reforming papacy of John XXIII were also challenging the old beliefs. But once again the populist fundamentalism of Paisley spoke for an older certainty. O'Neill's very public gestures of welcoming successive taoisigh to Stormont and visiting a Catholic school did not play well with loyalists or with traditional unionists. He was also under pressure from his own cabinet, many of whom had remained unhappy at his appointment as Brookeborough's successor. At the time it seemed that this well-meaning liberal unionist was being held back from his declared cross-community programme by obdurate unionism. And there was considerable cross-community support for him. But his natural shyness and English accent translated into snobbishness in working-class Protestant minds, while his modernising programmes seemed to be at the expense of the old industries and traditional neighbourhoods, which they believed were being destroyed to accommodate the new vision.[64] In retrospect, however, some historians have argued that O'Neill never really intended more than 'gesture politics', believing instead that long-term regional development would bring Catholics to recognise how much better off they were in the north. Even his good friend and closest ally in the years of his premiership, Ken Bloomfield, believed that he was too timid in his reform agenda.[65] In moderate, mixed communities in Belfast we might have seen O'Neill as the great hope for the future. I recall my entire family gathered around the television in December 1968 to watch his 'Ulster at the crossroads' broadcast and signing up to the *Belfast Telegraph*'s 'Back O'Neill' declaration. But all this Catholic support did him little good in working-class loyalist communities.

Now, as the expected reforms failed to materialise, civil rights marches of largely Catholic campaigners and then of students – all of whom were on state grants ('*our* state', thought less advantaged Protestants who traditionally did not progress to third-level education) – were on the march. And everywhere they went they were stopped by increasing numbers of Paisleyites, claiming that these were the 'papish rebels' of Protestant demonology. Even if they believed that Catholics were changing and accepting the legitimacy of Northern Ireland, it was discomfiting at a time when guaranteed Protestant employment in the shipyards and engineering industries was no longer a certainty. Even the NILP and the trade unions, both strongholds of Protestant skilled workers, were taking up civil-rights issues. 'Nobody seemed to be talking about the hardships of poor Protestants,' Sarah Nelson found in her talks with loyalists in the 1980s:

> Thus one role of Paisley's campaigns was to articulate the social grievances of people left out of the new affluence, squeezed on one side by the middle class, on the other by Catholics … Social and community awareness was vulnerable to being harnessed for sectarian political ends by those who sought to convince the poor that the rewards they had earned through loyalty to the regime were being snatched away by avaricious Malone Road snobs and pampered rebels.[66]

Was that sectarian-themed humour that we had so indulged in a form of liberal condescension? Were we in denial that our society did not live up to western democratic norms and actually perpetuated the stereotypes we thought we had risen above? Such evasion may well explain why so many of us had not detected signs of the forthcoming Troubles.

10

Troubled Community

He'd never loved his native town;
But now with buildings torn apart,
His generation's bridges blown
And future generations hurt,
He could not quench his smouldering heart
With cold disdain.

Roy McFadden, 'Fire Bomb'[1]

I had gone up to Queen's University in the autumn of 1967 and found it abuzz with political and debating clubs. It seemed perfectly in tune with the times to march for civil rights and what seemed like half the university turned out to do just that on 9 October 1968, only to find our routes barred by angry Paisleyites. After our three-hour sit-down protest within sight of the City Hall, our intended destination, I do not recall the meeting afterwards in Queen's at which People's Democracy was formed. In all honesty, being a fair-weather protester, I think I just caught the bus home. No one then expected the Troubles. I had just finished my second year at Queen's when they erupted in 1969. I had left Belfast on a beautiful June morning to work for the summer in the United States. I returned in September to a war zone. The Belfast in which we had moved without inhibition, ranging freely with no sense of restricted zones, had gone. It has never returned.

Familiar landmarks disappeared. The 1893-built Grand Central Hotel, which I passed on every journey to university, where celebrities had stayed in the 1950s and 1960s and where, as a teenager, I had dreamed of some day joining the glamorous and important people who seemed to frequent it, was first turned into an army barracks, repeatedly bombed by the IRA and finally replaced by a shopping mall.[2] Smithfield, one of the oldest shared spaces in the city, an Aladdin's cave of curiosity shops and old book-stalls and such an integral part of my growing up that I painted it as part of my portfolio for art-college entrance, disappeared in an orchestrated arson attack in May 1974. Patricia Craig, in her evocative memoir *Bookworm*, recalls people crying in the street as they viewed 'the smouldering wreckage' the following morning. 'Even now, I cannot bear to approach the spot where Smithfield stood. Its absence encapsulates for me the badness of Belfast, its drive towards self-immolation.'[3] In the worst decade of the Troubles, 'it was the last haven of antique ease', wrote the *Belfast Telegraph* in a poignant editorial, and 'its rumbled, careless jumble of stalls' run by people whose families had traded there for generations gave it 'an intimacy and impulsive warmth':

> We offer our sympathies to those who have so suddenly lost their stalls and their medley of merchandise. The elements who conspired to create a fire of such proportions will probably never be known, but they cannot take much satisfaction in having destroyed one more Belfast landmark. It is just another senseless act of destruction.[4]

The article is a requiem for pre-Troubles Belfast.

Initially the White City seemed little affected. In contrast to west and north-west Belfast, the situation in Newtownabbey was sufficiently peaceful in October 1970 for the Housing Trust to take the governor of Northern Ireland on tour to a number of its estates, including the White City.[5] One Catholic resident, whose family remained into the 2000s, told me that she was more worried about going into Belfast, where she then worked: 'You would hear the music for BBC Radio Ulster in the morning and just know that news of some atrocity there would immediately follow.' And that was the point. Although the full horror of the Troubles impacted most on a few areas, the constant flood of atrocity headlines, and the flight of families from affected areas, spread fear, intimidation and ultimately paramilitary power. As IRA atrocities intensified and the unionist government fragmented before the threat of direct rule from Westminster (which was imposed in March 1972) Larne and Carrickfergus, where so many locals worked and went to school, became the centre of extreme unionism. Under Larne's MP, Bill Craig, that extreme unionism was expressed in his new grouping, Ulster Vanguard (February 1972). By September it included Ian Paisley's Democratic Unionist Party and the emerging loyalist paramilitary organisation the Ulster Defence Association (UDA). Huge rallies involving all three were held in Carrickfergus.[6]

The sectarian reordering of space in Belfast had started with the flight of 3,570 families from mixed areas in the west and north-west of the city in 1969. The next period of significant movement was the three weeks following the introduction of internment on 9 August 1971, as families abandoned mixed areas for safety 'among their co-religionists'.[7] By 1973 the CRC estimated that between eight and fifteen thousand families (6.6–11.8 per cent of the Belfast urban area) had been intimidated out of their homes.[8] It was in late 1971 and early 1972 that the Newtownabbey area was first affected – largely, it seems, by movements into Greencastle (almost certainly of Catholics, as this was a Catholic enclave) and movements of Catholics out of Rathcoole and the Shore Road and Protestants into the latter, as well as Monkstown and Glengormley.[9] There is no mention of the White City being affected at this time. Rathcoole figures prominently in the CRC report as experiencing major intimidation against Catholics and those in mixed marriages. But those intimidated needed police recognition of such intimidation to get onto the emergency housing lists, and the CRC criticised Whiteabbey RUC for its unwillingness to recognise intimidation. There was a belief that the security forces found mixed areas difficult to manage and criticism that they dealt inadequately with intimidation as a result. One woman told me that her family endured extended intimidation in Rathcoole because the RUC would not facilitate their desire to be rehoused in another mixed area, when the tendency of the authorities was simply to remove Catholic families to increasingly ghettoised west Belfast.[10] The East Antrim [Larne] Times at this period is still dominated by the typical stories of a local newspaper. But its young people's picture competition in February 1972 presents a different story – of riots, armed soldiers and destruction.[11]

By then we have the first real detail of what was happening in Whitewell because of the creation of the CRC and the courage of its officers on the ground. The impressive one-time television engineer Joe Camplisson – who would go on to forge a career in international conflict resolution but remain firmly rooted in working-class Belfast – was its officer in Greencastle. In contrast to 'the abnormal political situation' elsewhere in Belfast, community relations in the Whitewell/ Greencastle area still seemed good and there were contributions he felt he could make. 'The village of Greencastle straddling the Belfast/ Newtownabbey boundary is one of the oldest communities in Belfast,' he reported in June 1971. It was the 'natural hub' for surrounding areas, including the White City. But the same old problem – that the area fell between local councils – meant that it was neglected and the 'development of social and recreational facilities … did not keep pace with the housing programme … Relationships in Greencastle across the religious divide have always been good and this influence was strongly felt in the new estates.' The area became the centre of his community-development programme. He was approached by a cross-community group of men and asked to help provide facilities for 'the increasing number of youths in the area'. Among these was 'a loosely-organised football club' in 'the densely-populated' White City, with three hundred and fifty houses and flats but 'no sport and recreational facilities'. Two neighbouring estates, the 'mainly Catholic' Belfast Corporation estate of Bawnmore, with two hundred and fifty houses and high unemployment, and the mainly Protestant Belfast Corporation Longlands estate, also lacked any facilities and the construction of the urban motorway was eating away even more open space.[12]

Despite rising tensions, Camplisson speaks highly of the quality of leadership in the area. A Greencastle Savings Group, drawing members from many of the estates, had gained an offer of premises from Belfast Corporation. A Concern Group composed of a number of students anxious to take part in community projects, as well as the Whitewell Social Group, were providing youth leadership to a large number of teenagers and organising camping expeditions: 'They have successfully undermined a gang of youths calling themselves "The Dartan"' (Tartan gang). That was the name adopted by groups of youths in 'militant Protestant areas … in many parts of the city after the Scottish troops fell into disfavour in the Catholic areas'.[13] In Greencastle, the

St Mary's Hall Committee suggested a programme of events such as a bowls tournament 'to provide opportunities for both Protestants and Catholics in the area to meet and mix'. This might help defuse growing tensions, particularly in the difficult months of the traditional summer marching season. But by July 1971 Camplisson thought that community relations in the White City were 'deteriorating rapidly'.

And he was right. That summer was when things seriously unravelled. Trouble broke out for the first time in Greencastle in July 1971. He set up the Greencastle Protestant and Catholic Relief Committee because of the intimidation of families. This committee was instrumental in helping to 'prevent intimidated families from over-reacting by leaving their homes prematurely'. It was formed after the first Catholic family had to leave Mount Vernon on the Shore Road and took refuge in a Greencastle school. 'Unfortunately the Security Forces and the Police have been unable to contain intimidation activity[,] it being so widespread. I can do nothing to resolve the problem.'

Internment of those suspected of paramilitary violence was introduced on 9 August and 'complete chaos' ensued. There is a sense of firefighting by the local groups in an effort to contain intimidation, which was now widespread. The areas in north Belfast where White City people had traditionally come from were badly affected. Some four and a half thousand people were displaced from Ardoyne, the New Lodge, Duncairn, Oldpark Road, Ballysillan and Glencairn in the weeks following internment, and the new residents coming in from Belfast were adding to the tensions and social problems in the area.[14] Most of the flow into the wider area was Protestant, for Newtownabbey, as a largely Protestant area, was deemed safe. By December community relations had broken down. Tartan gangs – now seen as the junior wing of the UDA – from Mount Vernon, Parkmount, Rathcoole, White City and the Shankill Road had come together and a gang of about two hundred attacked Catholic businesses in Greencastle on 8 December.

A group of Catholic youths from Bawnmore was seen as part of the problem. Attempted recruitment there by the Ardoyne Provisonal IRA was spurned by Bawnmore residents, who took no part in the civil-disobedience campaign that affected many other Catholic areas in the wake of internment. However, Bloody Sunday – 30 January 1972, when paratroopers opened fire on unarmed civil-rights marchers in Derry, killing thirteen – like internment, saw IRA recruitment escalate. Among the new recruits were three teenagers from Bawnmore. Two of the families had traditions of serving in the British armed forces and most recently in the Ulster Defence Regiment (UDR). 'This was a non-political family,' the father of one told a reporter many years later. 'We never talked politics, Irish history never meant anything to us.' But three days after Bloody Sunday his seventeen-year-old son and his two close friends travelled into a republican area and joined the IRA. Two months later they were blown to pieces by their own bomb in a lock-up garage on the estate.[15]

Thereafter, the estate was targeted by loyalist paramilitaries from Rathcoole and, despite the continuing efforts of the Bawnmore and District Tenants' Association, both the Official and Provisional IRA gained members in Bawnmore. For a while the surrounding Protestant areas were reluctant to work with the tenants' association. But this did not last. On 3 January 1973 there was a joint meeting of representatives from Bawnmore, Graymount, White City, Shore Crescent and Greencastle to tackle the growing youth problems, and indeed until that point the trouble seems largely to have been youth driven. Camplisson reported the White City attitude to Bawnmore as 'guarded', though Graymount, by now a UDA stronghold, was 'cold'. The army command in the area – Major Peter Clarke, Queen's First Regiment – was also involved and helped bring about an amalgamation of all the tenants and community organisations in the area to try to prevent such confrontations. Graymount declared itself 'not ready to join', but did consent to be involved in a pilot project of a joint children's party.[16]

These years saw a real struggle by community leaders to retain the traditionally good communal relations in the area. On Sunday, 16 January 1972 Camplisson took an urgent call from the Shore Crescent Tenants' Association about intimidation of Catholic families and a sustained campaign to destroy the interdenominational tenants' association. The year 1972 was the worst of the Troubles. This, too, was the first year of sectarian killings in the area. By early 1973 attempts at cross-community action in the Whiteabbey, Rathcoole and

Greenisland areas were disintegrating in the face of a UDA takeover of the Newtownabbey Friendship Group, which had brought together the various factions. The moderate Alliance Party and its one Catholic member had withdrawn, as had NILP councillor Bob Kidd, 'a dedicated strong-willed socialist politician who has devoted his life to the community ... a Protestant loyalist', as Camplisson described him. He also reported that some unionist members of the group refused to acknowledge that intimidation was taking place, so the NILP was reluctant to make case files available to them.

No further detailed reports of community relations in the area are available because of the abolition of the CRC in 1975.[17] Thereafter it becomes difficult to track developments in the White City. In time the estate came to be known as a UDA stronghold, though this appears not to have been the case in the period during which Camplisson was reporting.[18] The UDA had emerged from the post-internment chaos in September 1971 and would become the largest paramilitary force in Northern Ireland. Recruits were largely working-class males aged between seventeen and twenty-two. Partly legitimised by Craig's Vanguard movement, it reflected the belief that Protestants were being 'sold out' by both Britain and traditional unionism, as well as the disintegration of normal politics in these years. However, as so often in the past, the long-established Protestant stereotype of Catholics as disloyal rebels now caused them to be conflated with the IRA in the Protestant paramilitary mind. 'The campaign revealed a perennial truth of Northern Irish life,' wrote Sarah Nelson, 'when political alienation and frustration were high among Protestants ... whoever was responsible for their grievances, the first and major victims would be Catholics.'[19] As the press filled with news of IRA bombings and atrocities, 'Protestant killer squads' responded by killing innocent Catholics. Indeed, as Nelson points out, they were responsible for most of the civilian killings in 1972–3, though she points to the killing spree declining as the political situation settled down after the reintroduction of direct rule in 1975.[20]

Since the estate in recent years has experienced considerable interface tensions and violence, residents are understandably guarded in what they say. I found myself constantly interrogating silences to explain the absence of information about the White City during the

Troubles. Nor does communal memory conform to the historian's instinct of pinpointing events and trends in a chronological framework. Also, most of those who talked with me tended more often than not to stress the basic communal decency of the neighbourhood, rather than any nastiness. It seems that the White City did not fall apart quite to the same extent as other areas in the city, though of course this was partly the result of Catholics having left. Even so, I heard of a murderous White City group, which one informant called the 'Window Cleaning Gang', targeting Catholics in the 1970s and shock was expressed at some they had known as children ending up as paramilitaries. 'It was hell, hell, hell and you were scared,' recalled one, 'and then having to go to work after a night of it.' The same person recalled an incident when a young male in a balaclava addressed a friend by name, adding, 'You thought you knew people until the Troubles.' Another recognised a neighbour as one of the masked men halting traffic on the Serpentine Road. There are accounts of residents trying to prevent the youths from getting involved and women in particular standing up to the paramilitaries. I was told of one mother who went out to pull her own son back from possible involvement. She saw the older paramilitaries all lined up on the wall of Gunnell Hill and the younger lads gathered in apparent admiration. 'You fuckin' bastards!' she shouted at them. 'Hard men putting the youngsters out to go to prison!' She succeeded. None of her family became involved in paramilitarism.

'I have experienced good and bad from them,' one White City resident commented to me of the UDA, a sentiment endorsed by a 2002 report into the area:

> Paramilitaries exert influence (and in parts, control) over some areas in North Belfast. They are regarded by some people as protectors of their communities. There are those associated with them who try to exercise constructive leadership and have worked to improve their communities and in some cases to build relationships across the divides. However, there are others who exercise a malign influence and are barriers to progress.[21]

I was told of two Liverpool Orangemen who came to the estate in the mid-2000s on a 'mission', as they called it, to 'fight the cause'. They were the only paramilitaries mentioned to me as having a really malign effect on the estate and as criticising peacemaking initiatives. The Scouse accent was also considered very aggressive – they were 'the Scousers who did all the slabbering'. They were eventually expelled by the UDA.

Brian Dunn recalled two Troubles-related fatalities affecting the White City. Brian's neighbours were Catholics, the Kellys. Mary Kelly was a friend of his mother's and they would socialise together. Her brother was an early victim of the Troubles. The Shore Road became one of the murder arteries of these years, with the bars in Greencastle regular targets. On Friday, 29 March 1974 Mrs Kelly's twenty-four-year-old brother, Joe Donnelly, had been trying to save people by carrying a UVF bomb out of Conway's Bar in Greencastle, when it blew up, scattering pieces of his body everywhere.[22] He was finally identified by his shoes – Brian's old trainers, given him by Brian's mother. The other was forty-two-year-old Jimmy Frazer, who was killed as he walked home from playing pool nearby in July 1989. He had no paramilitary connections and the court that found three young men from Bawnmore guilty of his killing pronounced it sectarian, their drink-fuelled attack following a question about his religion.[23] Brian also recalled Constable Lindsay McCormack, the community policeman who would help the children cross the road from Ballygolan school, killed by the IRA outside the school in March 1983, again by youths whom a witness thought were secondary-school boys because of their height.[24]

All of this raises the question: did the White City retain its mixed character through the Troubles? The answer is yes, but to a very limited extent. 'There are still Catholics on the estate,' I was told in 2013, though only four was the estimate. 'Oh, really!' retorted a former Catholic resident, when I told him this. 'Probably because they were in the UDR or some such.'

There was an element of truth in this. Some were also in mixed marriages. The UDR was a part-time force, established in 1970 following the recommendations of the Hunt Report (1969) that the Ulster Special Constabulary (B-Specials), who were 100 per cent

Protestant, should be disbanded and replaced by a new, locally recruited and non-denominational body. South-east Antrim had the highest level of UDR recruitment in Northern Ireland. Initially Catholics did join, making up some 18 per cent of the force. But by the time of a 1973 British Military Intelligence report, Catholic numbers had dropped to 4 per cent, although the main Catholic newspaper, the *Irish News*, continued to publish recruitment notices.[25] The report found evidence of UDR collusion with the UDA in particular and of UDR weaponry having been used in a number of murders and thwarted murders by loyalists in the north Belfast and Newtownabbey areas.[26]

In the 1950s some 27 per cent of the estate was Catholic, while 23 per cent was recorded in the 1971 census, although the numbers are likely to have been higher because some Catholics refused to state their religion in the 1971 census and many more boycotted that of 1981.[27] By the time of the 1991 census, however, they were down to only 5 per cent, and the figure was 4 per cent by 2001.[28]

'There was a mass exodus of Catholics from the White City' at that time, I was told by a former Catholic resident. That the area was resorting to sectarian polarities in these years is undeniable, although there is evidence that the White City was not immediately affected. By 1974 numbers of Catholics in the parishes of Whitehouse and Whiteabbey were down by 55 per cent – reflecting the move out of Rathcoole and Monkstown. But Greencastle was only marginally down, while the number of parishioners at St Gerard's had risen by 15 per cent and in Glengormley by 70 per cent.[29] Some current residents I spoke with denied that Catholics were intimidated.

'Nobody was attacked,' I was told. 'I saw Catholics leaving and no one had touched them.'

'The government gave them money to get out, intimidation money,' said another.

'I don't think they were intimidated. They chose to go,' said a third.

Tony Kennedy, who had been the Housing Executive's north-Belfast area manager at this time, had not heard of the term 'intimidation money' when I asked him. He thought it might have been referring to the assistance with removal expenses for such families. But 'it wouldn't have been enough to make you want to give up your home', he added, and 'rehousing due to intimidation had to be supported by a statement from the RUC'.

I had clear information that intimidation had indeed occurred in a number of cases. Bonfires became bigger and bigger in the mid-1970s. In 1975 the police advised one Catholic woman to go away for the Twelfth. When she returned, she found her house wrecked and subsequently moved out. Nine other Catholic families on the estate were named to me as also having been intimidated and some went to England. Others, particularly if they had boys in the family, 'saw the way things were going' and moved, one person told me. 'Protestants did too.' A street-by-street analysis of the *Belfast Street Directory* shows a small spike in Catholic departures in 1974–5, but most longstanding residents remained, tenancies being transferred to the wives (as husbands died) or occasionally to sons when their mothers also grew old. The Catholics who remained seem to have been accepted and, to some extent, protected. However, they were always vulnerable. I learnt of one elderly man, who had lived in the estate since it was first built, finally being intimidated out during the sectarian tensions of the early 2000s. The Housing Executive would not have been allocating new tenancies to Catholics in this now loyalist estate and most remaining Catholics appear to have gone with the demolition of the old estate in the late 1980s and early 1990s. John Darby found that those in mixed marriages who stayed after the Troubles 'identified closely – sometimes extravagantly' – with whichever of the two communities now prevailed, thereby assisting the transformation of the estates into single-religion ones. 'The tensions raised by intimidation forced everyone to opt for one side or the other. An ambiguous position was untenable.'[30] And this is what happened in the White City. 'They [the remaining Catholics] joined with us to defend the estate' – against republican attacks – I was told.

The Housing Trust (as well as Belfast Corporation) was in the process of being subsumed into the Housing Executive in the early 1970s. It was a traumatic birth. Normal housing policies had to be torn up, as 'emergency' lists of the new homeless – those intimidated out of their homes – were prioritised. 'Our efforts to provide better housing,' it reported in April 1974, 'have continued to be frustrated by bomb damage, sectarian murders, intimidation, homelessness, vandalism and squatting associated with the political upheavals.'[31] Prefabs made a comeback, this time brought in from the Greater London Council, with the assistance of the homeless charity Shelter.[32] There is a sense of a real struggle to cope by the housing authorities. Squatting, even in half-built new houses, held back the redevelopment programme. By 1976 squatting in new schemes was being organised by the paramilitaries and the Housing Executive thought it might have to stop building entirely. The collection of rent was becoming dangerous and a number of robberies lay behind the introduction to the area of payment by Giro in February 1973.[33] Perversely, though predictably, squatting and intimidation was less of a problem by 1977 as religious polarisation had become the norm.[34]

Even those families intimidated out of mixed areas still expressed a desire to live in such areas and I have been struck that so many compelled to move during the Troubles have remained in the general area, so identified with their families' histories. By now, however, the trend was being orchestrated by the paramilitaries – the IRA in west Belfast, the UDA in Newtownabbey. In public housing at least the vision of integration was fading. Charles Brett recalled 'the distress and mortification' of the Housing Trust in its fading days at 'the final collapse of their well-intentioned attempts to create wholly integrated estates'. The new Housing Executive at first followed the same policy, until it had to admit that it was 'hopeless' in Belfast and 'with much distaste and dismay' felt it necessary to ask applicants whether they preferred to live on mixed, Protestant or Catholic estates.[35]

The notion of spatial freedom and movement – such a large part of my memories of the White City and of Greater Belfast – was one of the victims of the Troubles. There was a sense of horizons narrowing, particularly among the young. Only those who remember a time before the Troubles are comfortable moving wider afield. In the worst years of the 1970s walking was no longer safe, particularly in the evenings. Random sectarian attacks were common. As the Troubles segregated working-class areas, it was all too easy to presume the religious identity of those attacked. Visiting friends in the old areas could be a death sentence. The Catholic Rolston family had lived in Rathcoole for over twenty years, but moved to the Catholic enclave of Fairyknowe, near the White City, in 1974. John, at sixteen the youngest of five children, still spent every Saturday night with a friend in Rathcoole. On Saturday, 28 June 1975 he was celebrating having finished his schooldays at the local Catholic secondary school, Stella Maris. As he walked back he was followed by two Rathcoole teenagers, members of the UVF youth wing, who knew him. He was murdered just as he reached the Throne hospital on the edge of the White City. Padraig O'Malley, in his moving book about the IRA hunger strikers, visited Stella Maris school in the late 1980s. He recalled the sadness of the vice-principal as he listed the twenty pupils who had died in the Troubles, some as IRA members, one as a member of the RUC murdered by the IRA, as many more, like John Rolston, victims of sectarian murder by loyalist paramilitaries. Stella Maris had been one of those schools set up to accommodate the new estates, notably Rathcoole. The site on Church Road had been offered by the Housing Trust in the late 1950s and opened in 1964. It had to close in 1993, a victim of the Troubles reconfiguring mixed areas into the new polarised ones, as well as competition from new schools set up to accommodate this new reality. By then twenty-seven of its pupils had been Troubles-related casualties.[36]

A new statistic started to blight the area in 1973 – the use of the old scenic Cave Hill/Bellevue 'playground' to dump the bodies of those murdered by the paramilitaries, both republican and loyalist. A favourite spot was the Hightown Road just behind the Cave Hill, the most notorious the grisly killing by the Ulster Freedom Fighters (UFF) of Social Democratic and Labour Party Senator Paddy Wilson and his Protestant secretary Irene Andrews in June 1973 following blatant sectarian incitement by the *Loyalist News*.[37] The low point was 1974, with four bodies found in the area – one murdered by the IRA, three by loyalists.[38] It was also a year marked by IRA 'spectaculars' – the Birmingham, M62 and Guildford bombings – and loyalist 'spectaculars' – the Ulster Workers' Council strike (centred on south-east Antrim) and the Dublin and Monaghan bombings. Little wonder the plea for more recreation and sports areas in the locality took on a new vigour. A lower level of killings continued into the early 1980s, peaking in 1981 following the deaths of the IRA hunger strikers. Again there was youth rioting. One of those killed by an RUC plastic bullet in Bawnmore was a respected Catholic community leader trying to stop youths from stoning the police. By now the area had settled into a new, segregated pattern, though it was a patchwork-quilt one that reflected the recent mixed-living history. In Charles Brett's maps of 1985 the White City is a small 'wholly or predominantly Protestant' patch surrounded by small 'wholly or predominantly Catholic' enclaves, in turn surrounded by some mixed and largely Protestant areas, including Rathcoole and the Shore Road.[39]

'Traditionally the Whitewell Road was perceived as an area with a good level of community integration,' reported a Housing Executive survey of 2014, 'until 1997 when the crisis at Drumcree – the prohibition of Orange parades along the now largely nationalist Garvaghy Road in Armagh – polarised the two communities in the area and brought increased tension and segregation.'[40] Along with other loyalist areas, Whitewell had erupted in the summer of 1997 in response to Drumcree. Republicans being brought into the peace process thereafter, and then into government in 2007, was unsettling for many Protestants. In particular it fed a popular Protestant perception that Catholics wanted them out. Loyalists played upon this, although that is not to say that it was not a genuine belief. Certainly the decline in Greater Belfast's Protestant population assisted this perception, while Catholic areas were bursting at the seams. Yet there was huge resistance to using the boarded-up houses in Protestant areas to relieve Catholic overcrowding. Indeed, in one newspaper a nationalist resident of the Whitewell area claimed that when the White City was rebuilt residents demanded that no Catholics be housed there, even though she accepted that there was fear on the estate and that 'decent people' also lived there.[41]

The truncation of the estate in the 1990s rebuilding had taken away most of the Antrim Road end and funnelled communications towards the lower Whitewell and Serpentine Roads, an interface which Joe Camplisson had called 'Agro corner' in the 1970s. It now saw regular clashes between loyalists and nationalists. In several nights of rioting in July 1997, police were called repeatedly to deal with sectarian clashes between Whitewell/Serpentine Road nationalists and White City loyalists. As with so many other housing developments in Belfast during the Troubles, the rebuilding of the White City incorporated security planning into the new layout and there were fewer entry points than before. Now those few entry points, at Gunnell Hill, Navarra Place and Mulderg Drive, were repeatedly attacked.[42] While loyalists from the White City retaliated in kind on neighbouring Catholic homes, and provocative marches were organised by both sides, there can be no doubt about the sense of vulnerability in the White City in these years. The estate was 'like the bullseye in a dart board', one community worker told me, the implied sense of vulnerability the result of sectarian disturbances that broke out in 1997–8 and continued far into the 2000s.

One man told Suzanne Breen of the *Sunday Tribune* that his daughter's house 'on the frontline' in the White City had been attacked fifty-six times in one year. Eventually she gave up and moved out. A grandmother on the much-attacked Gunnell Hill pointed to the huge bag of missiles that had been thrown at her house and told of threats that they would be burnt out. Another resident told of how they were taunted and attacked when walking to shops or the doctor's surgery in the adjacent nationalist part of the Whitewell Road.[43] It was a war zone, White City resident Linda Taylor told me. 'We seriously could have been wiped out.' Brian Dunn recalled having to glue himself to the back wall of one house to avoid the rain of petrol bombs. A siren would warn residents of impending attack and the women would walk about with first-aid boxes. Linda advised her daughter not to go out in fashionable wedge shoes in case she had to flee any trouble. They could not put their lights on – if they did, their windows would be broken. Partially-sighted grandmother Anne Ash would make them all tea. She was the only one who could do so in the dark. 'We couldn't go back to that,' Linda concluded.

In 1999 I returned with my mother to the White City to find the Serpentine Road side ringed by one of those euphemistically named peace walls (which are, in actuality, forbidding-looking forty-foot-high metal fences) and the immediate vicinity showing signs of the neglect that blights the surrounds of such security structures. Another ran from Gunnell Hill to the Serpentine Road and, to complete the embattled ring-fenced feel of the estate, another was added at the other side between the primary school and Old Throne Park, this time to protect residents on the Catholic/mixed Throne estate from White City missiles.[44] As elsewhere in Belfast, over succeeding years the peace walls got higher.

Community worker Brian Dunn recognised that attacks were also being made on Catholics in the area, which he and others condemned. But, in a claim to Suzanne Breen that I had heard before from such vulnerable Protestant enclaves, White City residents thought their plight often went unrecognised, with Catholics always being seen as the victims.[45]

'That each community in Whitewell has experienced historical traumas at the hands of the other community is irrefutable,' commented the 2008 Whitewell Youth Mediation Project, 'but many within the Whitewell area continue to see only themselves as victims and only their enemies as aggressors and perpetrators.'[46]

In 2002 the Northern Ireland government commissioned a report into the Troubles as they affected north Belfast, including the White City. One of its public sessions was held in the White City Community Centre for the Protestant enclaves of Graymount and Shore Crescent, as well as the White City itself. The main themes emerging were of a community under considerable stress. The team found the 'level of harassment, conflict and hatred at [an] all-time high'.[47] People felt hemmed in and misunderstood and had difficulty accessing facilities outside their immediate area. There were few facilities within their area – no shop, no children's playground, no mobile library. Apathy and lack of youth leadership, lack of parental discipline, alcohol and drug abuse continued to pose problems. Young people were underperforming at school and were being harassed by police. The White City had become a dumping ground for the Housing Executive, as 'good' families moved out and 'problem' ones moved in, particularly when frequent loyalist internal feuds involved 'all those mad families moving from the Shankill', as one resident said. The area was going downhill, with dog-fouling and very poor street-cleaning, a waste ground where demolished Orlit houses had not been rebuilt, attracting antisocial activities and littering, and fewer buses on the Whitewell Road than before. The old village atmosphere had gone. A narrower definition of territory had developed over the past six to eight years, and the longstanding complaint about the estate falling between the Belfast and Newtownabbey local authorities, and the lack of coordination between the two, acquired new relevance. The meeting confirmed the sense of low morale in the declining Protestant communities. There were fewer issues raised by representatives of the nearby Catholic areas of Fairyknowe, the lower Whitewell, Greencastle, Bawnmore and, by now, the Longlands.[48]

Ten years of sporadic intercommunal violence have created no shortage of historical trauma for both sections of the Whitewell community. In addition to three deaths in 2001–2 and several stabbings in 2007–8, another report in 2008 recounts arson attacks, bricks being thrown at schoolgirls, sustained and often riotous attacks on communities, constant intimidation and a litany of assaults. The idea of neutral space was entirely missing from this battle over access to the Whitewell Road. Gangs of young vigilantes lay in wait, the direction you came from or turned to a crude communal identifier. The disappearance of the shops from the White City in its redevelopment was a particular loss, since the nearest shops were now in adjacent, largely Catholic, areas. A real sense of White City residents feeling trapped emerges from the report:

> You are walking up to the shop, and out of house windows, or out of car windows, people are shouting 'orange bastards' or 'get back into your estate', or threats like, 'you have two seconds to get out of here'. This was everyday in life. Its [sic] not their shops, we have no other shops to go to. We have been brought up all our lives to get used to not being able to get on the Whitewell (Road). (Protestant female).[49]

Young Catholics were unsympathetic, for they too were being blocked from access to the loyalist Shore Road and also experiencing sectarian attacks. A twelve-year-old Catholic girl, walking back from the large Abbey Centre shopping complex in March 2005, was jumped by 'about five wee boys and three wee girls' as she turned towards the Catholic top end of the Whitewell Road. 'Don't you dare walk down this road you Fenian B,' they shouted, as they pulled her to the ground and kicked and jumped on her, before running back into the White City. UDA spokesman John Montgomery, while condemning the attack, explained it as part of 'the anger the Protestant community feel' because of recent decisions by the Parades Commission and 'an ongoing campaign of intimidation and attacks on Protestant White City residents by nationalists'.[50]

A group of volunteers from the White City, described in the report as 'Interface Workers', dated the increase in sectarian violence in the Whitewell Road area to the sectarian killings of three youngsters in 2001–2: 'The deaths of Thomas McDonald and the two Catholic boys, Daniel McColgan and Gerard Lawlor, were senseless killings which fucked up everything on the Whitewell Road for years.'[51] The killings occurred against the background of heightened sectarian tension arising from the loyalist dispute over Catholic schoolchildren accessing the Holy Cross school through another interface in north Belfast. On 29 July 2001 the loyalist Red Hand Defenders, a cover name for the UDA, killed Gavin Brett, an eighteen-year-old Protestant student of Glengormley high school outside the GAA club in Glengormley, mistaking him for a Catholic.

Five weeks later a sixteen-year-old student who attended the same school, Thomas McDonald, from the White City, rode his BMX bike to the neighbouring nationalist Longlands estate and hurled a brick at a car, knowing the driver likely to be Catholic. The female driver, a thirty-six-year-old Catholic mother of six, pursued him back towards the White City, mounting the pavement, destroying the bike and killing the teenager. She was later imprisoned for manslaughter.

The following January twenty-year-old Daniel McColgan from the Longlands was the target of the Red Hand Defenders/UDA as he arrived for work as a postman at Rathcoole sorting office. They struck again at the top of the Whitewell Road in July 2002, killing nineteen-year-old Gerard Lawlor as he walked home. The memorial for Thomas McDonald on the Whitewell Road was vandalised so often in the ongoing clashes in the area that it was removed into the estate. It had become a 'shrine' and as such 'seen as a magnet for confrontation', young Whitewell Road Catholics told the Belfast Interface Project in 2008. Daniel McColgan's grave in Carnmoney cemetery was also repeatedly desecrated by loyalists.

'The deaths of the three local young men have profoundly affected both communities,' reported the Youth Mediation Project:

Their deaths and the manner of their deaths were tragedies

for their families and disastrous for local intercommunity relations. Constant sectarian taunting and the regular desecration of memorials have ensured that community wounds were never given the chance to heal ... [and] instilled within each 'wronged' community a profound sense of victimhood.[52]

The young people admitted that much of the violence was recreational rioting, though they were encouraged by older members of their community to attack anyone coming out of the White City:

If someone came out of White City onto the Whitewell Road, sometimes, most times, we would get into them, 'cause if you did not hit them, our ones, especially older ones would say 'what are you doing letting them snouts onto the road for'. But if there was just you and your mate and no one else saw nothing, you might just let the guy go.[53]

However, the 2007 stabbings of two youths in these nightly riots caused everyone to draw back. The clashes at the Serpentine Road interface were 'spiralling out of control'. Stop going there, community workers as well as the UDA told the teenagers from the White City.

By 2007, as things calmed down politically in Northern Ireland with the formation of the new governing institutions, as well as the UDA declaration that it would decommission weapons, the recognition grew that more would be achieved by cross-community work to address shared issues. The Belfast Interface Project (a north-Belfast-based charity) funded the Whitewell Youth Mediation Project, quoted above. It tells of efforts through 2005–8 to address the problems of the area and to develop 'trustful relationships ... between community activists from both communities'. Also notable was a certain mutual respect that was developing between former paramilitaries now involved in community work. 'Whether you like it or not,' a long-term resident told me, 'paramilitaries live in our community and you have to include them.' The detente was, of course, fragile and flag protests and controversial parades threatened it.

The community leaders' efforts were bearing fruit, not least on cross-community issues. By 2012 they were sharing the facilities of the Greater Whitewell Community Surgery in Greencastle. And, although the White City/Whitewell Road interface at Gunnell Hill was again a flashpoint during the flag protests of January 2013,[54] the recognition that they could win more for their area together than apart culminated in the Greater Whitewell Community Survey of May 2014. In responses to a widely distributed questionnaire, there was significant support for a shared community facility on the Serpentine Road, in the now-closed Ballygolan school, and even a return to mixed housing at some stage in the future. Though it is impossible to extract White City opinion – and a greater percentage of Catholics than Protestants responded – Brian Dunn remarked that he was struck in the responses at 'how safe people feel in the area', how much mixing was already going on and how committed they were to sharing. 'I think that bodes well for the future,' he concluded. In the summer of 2015 some fifty local young people were organised to clear graffiti by a voluntary neighbourhood group which included Sinn Féin and Ulster Unionist councillors as well as the Presbyterian minister. It was facilitated by St Ninian's, where its meetings were held.

I have returned regularly to the estate since embarking on my research for this book in 2010. The smallness of the rebuilt estate is very noticeable. The loss of the large green space on Thorburn Road and lack of the old open access to the Snaky Path and onward to the fields and forest has accentuated the 'hemmed-in' feeling. At the lower Serpentine end of the estate the large metal railing and gate is still there, though it is now usually open. At the Snaky Path side of the original White City, however, there is now a derelict area as bad as one would expect to see in the notorious 'sink' estates of Britain, although until now I would never have thought of the White City in such a category. In 2015–16 I found mounds of rubbish and the space clearly being used as a dumping ground for old fridges, old furniture and other such debris. There were also signs of drug-taking, a big problem for both communities in the Greater Whitewell area. There are still tensions and worries that the waste ground might be used for antisocial activities. However, I was told of much support for cross-community activities and that attendance at events in the community centre is mixed. The community workers are proving very effective.

Two of the peace walls in the area have been removed and there are plans to take down the one separating the White City from the Serpentine Road in 2018–19. In May 2017 I found the waste ground partially decluttered and there is a hope that the territorial integrity of the old White City might be recaptured with plans submitted for new housing to be built there. A return to mixed housing, however, is very unlikely in the foreseeable future.

Afterword

*Castle electoral area … is a socio-economically varied electoral area
with both some of the richest and some of the poorest areas of the
City. The solidly loyalist areas of the Shore Road and York Road
suffer high levels of economic deprivation. There are other isolated
Working Class Protestant areas … White City, Kilcoole, Westland
and Henderson. There are also a few isolated Working Class Catholic
areas – Fairyknowe, Lower Whitewell, Lower Cavehill, Kansas and
Glandore. The rest of the constituency is middle class or even better off.*

'Castle', *Belfast City Council elections 1997*[1]

I recently walked the Antrim Road/Whitewell area to see how things
had changed since I lived there. Although the grounds of Belfast
Castle have lost some sense of wildness, their openness to public use
remains, as does the very obvious public respect for them.[2] But whilst
Hazelwood/Bellevue retains its green and wooded aspect, the old
spirit has gone. Now it is just called 'the zoo', and the zoo occupies
the entire area, serviced – with echoes of Joni Mitchell – by a huge
car park, covering the entire area of the old open dance platform, the
playground and Barry's amusement park. The old Hazelwood entrance
is totally blocked off. There is no easy pedestrian access, except by a
long trawl from the Glengormley end, through the car park. The old
cottages have long gone in the road-building which has so changed
the lived landscape. The majestic Bellevue staircase is overgrown
and decaying. To see the old pleasure park today, you have to pay an
entrance fee, for it has been entirely encompassed by the zoo. The
pond and crannog are still there and there are still people picnicking.
But the Floral Hall is in a state of decay and collapse, even though it
was granted listed status in December 1994, its doors having closed
for the last time in January 1974. Nostalgic regret aside, I had to admit
that such developments were probably inevitable. The Corporation

Transport Committee had struggled to make it pay and the zoo has at least maintained the basic outline of the original pleasure gardens. With this sobering bow to modernity, I headed towards the rest of the White City's remembered landscape.

The forest is now a woodland park, sensitively done – although, with new money and plans to further develop it announced in October 2016, I fear this may not last. On the lower field, where we played summer games, and children and pets roamed freely, a very colourful integrated primary school has been built. The old steps down to the Throne, already semi-ruined in the 1950s, are still there. The Snaky Path is more manicured, largely with side walls, but its steepness and semi-wildness are just as evident, the rivulet running down the side still prone to flooding.

I proceeded back to the Antrim Road at the top of the path and this is where the image of leafy suburbs is most apparent. As my walk continued past the houses there, I began to understand something of the resentment that their owners must have felt at the working-class invasion represented by the White City. The housing sprawl that so concerned commentators in the 1950s has gone on unabated. New developments now totally cover the green fields that once separated the White City from the older villas on the Antrim Road.

As I walked on towards the Serpentine Road, St Gerard's Catholic Church, overlooking Fortwilliam golf course, looked very big – brash, almost. Opposite St Gerard's I turned into the Serpentine Road. In my childhood the Serpentine Road was considered 'posh'. Today it looks shabby and decaying, having become, until recently, one of the new interfaces in north Belfast's intercommunal conflict. As I continued my walking survey, I descended past the semi-derelict site where Dunlop Memorial Presbyterian Church had been built to service the new estate. Dropping attendances caused it to close in 1999. St Ninian's Church of Ireland on the Whitewell Road acquired separate parish status in 1949 because of the new estate population in area. This too closed in 2015 because of declining congregations.

I walked past the closed building and noted activity in the church hall. I entered and found it had been turned into a large charity shop until the whole site and buildings could be sold. I joined the small group of volunteers and, as so often in Belfast, we entered into conversation about past times. One of the volunteers, Warren, travelled over regularly from east Belfast, but had come from the area and been involved with scouts and other such activities in the church for many years. He corrected me, though not in a hostile fashion, when I made the fundamental mistake of using the term 'Catholic' in Protestant company rather than 'Roman Catholic', the former firmly identifying the user as definitely non-Protestant. It is a mistake that I rarely make in Northern Ireland, since this is one of those social niceties that have papered over divisions for generations. He thought the area was now 99.9 per cent 'Roman Catholic' – a figure not quite sustained by the last census, but reflective nevertheless of Whitewell Protestants' perceptions of being surrounded.

At this point Belle entered, whose family were Greencastle people going back generations. Like others, they all remembered good communal relations. The Rainbow Guides organised at St Ninian's they thought largely Catholic. Even in 1995, when a sectarian arson attack on the church destroyed the choir area, they said the Catholic priest from Greencastle had offered crucial assistance. It is characteristic of sectarian cultures everywhere in the world that we often do not realise that sectarianism lurks somewhere in our subconscious and, when it involuntarily outs itself, we quickly backpedal to make amends. Greencastle Methodist Church (founded in 1939, its present building dating from 1966) was now the only Protestant church left on the Whitewell Road and the group thought it, too, was in trouble. They believed the main reason for falling attendances was the decline in the older population. While attendances at St Gerard's are holding up – a feature of the growing Catholic middle class in the Antrim Road area – those at Greencastle's Star of the Sea are low, reflecting the decline of the lower Whitewell/Greencastle area.

As I walked along the Whitewell Road I thought how shabby it too now looked, particularly nearing Greencastle, which has entirely disappeared as a historic village under Northern Ireland's equivalent of Spaghetti Junction. Recent sectarian tensions and clashes are reflected in the neglected appearance of some houses and boarded-up buildings, including the old Orange hall, though the one small grocery store was clearly doing well. I ascended the road towards the old bus terminus and Throne hospital, now a business centre, though the original exterior is preserved. I was particularly struck by the quietness of the Snaky Path, once such a thronged thoroughfare of young people travelling to and from school. The houses at the edge of the White City were less neglected than those on the lower Whitewell, despite some racist attacks on them in 2013 and intermittent sectarian clashes where the White City faces the exit from the largely Catholic Arthur Road/Longlands area – recognisable as such by the occasional tricolour. Today the success of the community workers in the entire area is reflected in the relative absence of flags in comparison with some neighbouring areas.

Children's space experience is personal and very localised, which is why our remembered worlds, so big at the time, seem to have shrunk when we return as adults. Though only a short walk from my home at the Antrim Road end of the estate, the Whitewell Road had been a strange country to me. Today I could recognise few landmarks apart from the Throne hospital. And, while some of the best views of the Cave Hill can be had from here, there is and was a sense of a less-leafy lower part of the estate than the Antrim Road end, a difference that was accentuated when the North Approach Road (1955), then the M2 motorway (1966), tore through the remaining green fields on that side of the estate. I felt quite disorientated by the constant noise so soon after refinding continuing traces of the semi-rural living on the Antrim Road side. That disorientation increased as I turned into the bridge crossing the motorway. I recognised my former piano teacher's house at the other side, but where was the Longlands Road that had taken me there from the White City and along which was sited one of those tiny 'parlour' shops where I had frequently been sent on errands? After a short detour I found it. Its upper part had been moved to accommodate the motorway, and the Mill Dam and former flax-mill site lie somewhere underneath the huge Abbey Centre shopping complex.[3] Today no one from the White City would have the freedom to pass through what is now the republican Longlands area, and crudely written sectarian threats regularly appear to ensure that Protestants recognise this.[4]

I set out to tell the story of the housing estate I grew up in with a sense of urgency, given the passage of time and the progressive loss of its original tenants. I was just in time to catch a handful. Memory, of course, is not an exact science. However, the recollections of those who shared their memories with me were in broad agreement: this mixed-religion estate was a good place to live in, even if the quality of the housing itself left much to be desired. I was struck at how residents from the 1940s and 1950s, both those remaining and those who had left – even Catholics who had left during the Troubles – became excited when I mentioned the names of former neighbours and streets of the old estate. Place and neighbourhood memory was still shared despite the divisiveness of recent history. Unexpectedly, there was virtually unanimous praise for the housing authority, the Housing Trust, despite a paternalism which today we would consider intolerable. My study accordingly encompassed its story also, for I was surprised to find how little research had been done on it.

Eliciting clear answers about signs of sectarianism was difficult. Was this just that polite, or some would say evasive, 'whatever you say …' culture so characteristic of Northern Ireland? Up to a point, yes. However, researchers need to be aware of how stereotypes can underpin our questions and cause us to adopt a polarising mentality, which may not be there in reality. 'We didn't think like that,' was what I was being told by female interviewees, and I came to respect that. I quickly abandoned the formal interview in favour of informal conversations and I returned frequently to visit.

Sectarianism in Northern Ireland is, of course, a huge issue and it is unrealistic to assume that it was not present in the original White City estate. I certainly recall children's comments about inappropriate flowers in gardens. Sweet William, London pride and orange lilies were deemed strange in Catholic gardens, though in reality they existed in every garden. There were families, too, whose adults were known to be sectarian, even though it did not stop interaction and friendship between the children. I have often mentioned White City-raised Marjory Alyn's semi-autobiographical novel in this book. It captures nicely how those in mixed-religion areas negotiated neighbourliness and identity issues. The talk within the family walls might have included stereotypical stories of the 'other side' and handed-down memories. But outside the home a mixture of a 'don't mention the war' pattern of behaviour and genuine neighbourliness prevailed. With considerable comic effect, Alyn recounts how the young Catholic heroine and her

Protestant best friend negotiate the tricky question of what religion Smokey the cat should be in a mock christening. This was dangerous ground. 'You watch what you say to them,' her grandmother warns her. It involved 'little things' like not referring to Mass or Father Sheridan: 'I knew what the consequences were if I didn't "Watch the road," but I had no idea what would happen if I didn't "Watch what I said."' All the stereotypes heard at home then come out, though they are so garbled that they sound nonsensical, and the children move on very quickly to more important things, like playing.[5] Sectarianism then, was low key, though real enough for some families, and the balance started to be disrupted by incomers in the early 1960s. As I have shown, family ties to north Belfast, which accounted for the majority of the original estate's inhabitants, were with traditionally mixed areas. This started to change as those from redeveloped single-culture areas began arriving and today the north-Belfast identity that I recall has given way to a patchwork of small, very localised and highly sectarian identities.[6] But for over a generation people lived as good neighbours in the White City.

This raises the question: does mixed-religion housing work? Certainly, along with the concept of integrated education, it has majority support in opinion polls.[7] However, a recent study of Hazelwood College is salutary. Hazelwood is the integrated secondary school which, with the integrated primary school on the old Throne school site, flanks today's White City and is attended by many young people from the area. The integrated-education movement has fought hard to promote shared education against vested interests and reluctant governments. But it can only do so much when the underlying culture is inherently sectarian. The study of Hazelwood found that, while there were generally good cross-community relationships and friendships within the school, this did not translate into similar attitudes outside. Indeed, many of the pupils involved in the study (2001–2) were participants in the sectarian rioting outside, where group identities prevailed.[8]

It is unrealistic to expect integrated education, even if it were more than the current 7 per cent of schools, or shared housing to fundamentally alter the canker of sectarianism. However, today mixed-religion or shared housing is back on the agenda, though with much higher obstacles to overcome, given the 94 per cent polarisation in Belfast's housing estates. It was part of the Good Friday Agreement agenda and is currently being inched forward by the Housing Executive, working with various housing associations. However, it may be some time before it returns to north Belfast. Here housing waiting lists are 76 per cent Catholic and only 22 per cent Protestant. The Protestant decline has given rise to the fear that Protestants are being squeezed out, a fear I also heard in today's White City. The excessive displays of flags and other forms of territory- or boundary-marking witnessed in recent years are part of this. And, just as in the White City in the 1960s, the display of flags, emblems and graffiti can seriously jeopardise such mixing.[9] Social geographers Ian Shuttleworth and James Anderson legitimately ask how we can accept the idea of such territorial claims in today's society.[10] They have, however, been around for a very long time. We must be patient.

The ups and downs of politics can also be a 'chill factor' and that will continue until (and if) Northern Ireland ever achieves anything like a normal political system. Worryingly, the Northern Ireland Assembly's most recent community-relations strategy document, *Together: Building a United Community Strategy*, seems to think that 'a united community' can be built by embracing and celebrating 'cultural expression'.[11] Sadly, the terms 'culture' and 'community' have been transformed and narrowed by the Troubles. We have moved a long way from the old Housing Trust's avoidance of all such 'cultural' symbols. A 2006 examination of shared housing, commissioned by north Belfast's Institute for Conflict Research and funded by the Community Relations Council, found similar traits to those presented in this book: that mixed housing delivered positive experiences, that residents tended to be more moderate than those in single-culture estates, that length of residency and a strong sense of belonging and attachment to place overrode communal background.[12]

It is important not to exaggerate the transforming potential of mixed-religion housing. Any such policies now fall under Stormont's Good Relations Strategy's watered-down, though perhaps realistic, aims.[13] Even good relationships are no defence against sectarian structures and mindsets, or paramilitary intimidation. Yet this history of the White City estate shows that neighbourliness and neighbourhood identity can prevail over sectional awareness and be remembered and valued even after they appear to have disintegrated. In 1956, in the last of a series of newspaper articles on planning in Belfast, Emrys Jones mused on what then was a new concept of 'neighbourhood'. Before the war no one had ever thought of building such communities. Since the war 'we no longer build estates, but neighbourhoods', with schools, shops and recreation facilities. He wondered whether 'neighbourhood' was a reality or 'merely the fancy of American sociologists' and he lamented the absence of follow-up studies.[14] Belatedly, this history of the White City goes some way towards providing an answer. The current aspiration to building such new communities was very much that of the Housing Trust and in 1969 its chairman, Herbert Bryson, thought that it had generally been successful in its aims. Asked by the Cameron Commission about levels of integration on its estates and whether better personal relationships between Catholics and Protestants had resulted, he thought 'definitely yes … particularly in the estates in Belfast' and, from his time with the Housing Trust, he had learnt 'that when you get Catholics and Protestants in the same estate it breaks down barriers'.[15]

Notes

1. A Desirable Suburb

1 Michael Longley, 'Colin Middleton – an Interview', *IT* (7 April 1967).

2 Map showing position of water board 'easement' (PRONI, VAL/8/415, 21 Sept. 1950).

3 Lynsey, Hanley, *Estates: An Intimate History* (London, 2007), 124; Guy Debord, 'Introduction to a Critique of Urban Geography', in Harald Bauder and Salvatore Engel-Di Mauro (eds), *Critical Geographies: A Collection of Readings* (Kelowna, B.C., 2008), 23–7.

4 See: the articles by Gerry Kearns and Nuala C. Johnson in James S. Duncan, Nuala C. Johnson and Richard H. Schein (eds), *A Companion to Cultural Geography* (Oxford, 2004), 194–206 and 316–30; Karen M. Morin, 'Landscape: Representing and Interpreting the World', in Sarah Holloway, Stephen P. Rice and Gill Valentine (eds), *Key Concepts in Geography* (2nd ed., London, 2009), 286–99; D.W. Meinig, (ed.), *The Interpretation of Ordinary Landscapes: Geographical Essays* (Oxford, 1979), particularly contributions by Pierce F. Lewis and D.W. Meinig; Tim Cole, '(Re)visiting Auschwitz: (Re) encountering the Holocaust in its Landscapes', *Cultural History*, vol. 2, no. 2 (2013), 232–46; Jaromir Benes and Marek Zvelebil, 'Historical Interactive Landscape in the Heart of Europe: The Case of Bohemia', in Peter J. Ucko and Robert Layton (eds), *The Archaeology and Anthropology of Landscape: Shaping your Landscape* (London, 1999), 73–93; Barbara Bender (ed.), *Landscape: Politics and Perspectives* (Oxford, 1993), particularly essays by Bender and Cosgrove; T. Hägerstrand, 'Presence and Absence: A Look at Conceptual Choices and Bodily Necessities', *Regional Studies*, vol 18, no. 5 (1984), 373–9. Hägerstrand gave birth to 'Contextual Theory', which argues that the contexts in which human activity takes place – the time, the space, and the place in the sequence of events – are crucial to the nature of that activity. My thanks also to Dr Hilary Bishop and Dr Karen Morrissey for further advice on this.

5 Donald Graham and North Belfast Community Resource Centre, *WhiteCity: Crumbling Orlits* (Belfast, 1986), unpaginated introduction, also 12.

6 See essays by Ruairí Ó Baoill and Philip Macdonald in S.J. Connolly (ed.), *Belfast 400: People, Place and History* (Liverpool, 2012), 63–122.

7 Emrys Jones, *A Social Geography of Belfast* (London, 1960), 247.

8 A map of Belfast Lough with a plan of the town of Belfast … by … James Lawson (PRONI, D2156/1, 1789); E.K. Proctor, *Belfast Scenery in Thirty Views* (Belfast, 1832).

9 Jones, *Social Geography*, 168, 173, 205, 244–50, 264, 276–8; idem, 'Belfast: A Survey of the City', in British Association for the Advancement of Science, *Belfast*

in Its Regional Setting: A Scientific Survey (Belfast, 1952), 208: 'In the north there was an established squirearchy with large villas commanding the higher land overlooking the lough.'

10 *NW*, 4 Aug. 1953.

11 Dorita E. Field and Desmond G. Neill, *A Survey of New Housing Estates in Belfast: A Social and Economic Study of the Estates Built by the Northern Ireland Housing Trust in the Belfast Area 1945–1954* (Belfast, 1957) (hereafter Field-Neill Survey), 1.

12 Angélique Day and Patrick McWilliams (eds), *Ordnance Survey Memoirs of Ireland, vol. 2: Parishes of County Antrim I, 1838–9* (Belfast, 1990), 34; John Dubourdieu in his *Statistical Survey of the County of Antrim* (Dublin, 1812), had also noted problems with the soil, 'a strong loam upon clay. The substratum of clay … is however not unattended with disadvantage; it makes it tenacious of moisture' (Part I, 21).

13 Day and McWilliams (eds), *Ordnance Survey Memoirs*, 38.

14 Ibid., 35.

15 Ben Simon, *Voices from Cave Hill* (Belfast, 2010), 28.

16 Ibid., 46–7.

17 W.A. Maguire, *Belfast: A History* (Lancaster, 2009), 7–9; Cathal O'Byrne, *As I Roved Out* (Belfast, 1946), 238–9.

18 George Benn, *A History of the Town of Belfast from the Earliest Times to the Close of the Eighteenth Century* (London, 1877), 272–5.

19 T.R.O. Beringer, 'The Throne Hospital: A Short History', *Ulster Medical Journal*, vol. 67, no. 2 (Nov. 1998), 115–16.

20 F.J. Bigger, 'The Cave Hill and Its Story: Sports on Easter Monday', in F.C. Bigger and J.S. Crone (eds), *In Remembrance: Articles and Sketches, Biographical, Historical, Topographical by Francis Joseph Bigger* (Dublin, 1927), 141–2. John Gray thinks their route would rather have been via Gray's Lane, nearer today's White City, which could accommodate wheeled vehicles.

21 Day and McWilliams (eds), *Ordnance Survey Memoirs*, 53.

22 Benn, *History of the Town of Belfast*, 615; Day and McWilliams (eds), *Ordnance Survey Memoirs*, 53.

23 William Grimshaw, *Incidents Recalled: Or, Sketches from Memory* (Philadelphia, PA, 1848), 32.

24 Ibid., 28.

25 J. O'Laverty, *An Historical Account of the Diocese of Down and Connor, Ancient and Modern* (5 vols, Dublin, 1878–95), vol. 3, 20.

26 Mary McNeill, *The Life and Times of Mary Ann McCracken, 1770–1866: A Belfast Panorama* (Dublin, 1960), 174–8, 194–5; Robert M. Young (ed.), *Historical Notices of Old Belfast and Its Vicinity* (Belfast, 1896), 183–4.

27 Derek Mahon, 'Spring in Belfast', *New Collected Poems* (Oldcastle, 2011), 15.

28 Frederick W. Boal and Stephen A. Royle (eds), *Enduring City: Belfast in the Twentieth Century* (Belfast, 2006) – see 311 for the best view of the promontory as a sleeping man.

29 Hilary Maginnis, 'Some Belfast Business Families and Their Houses', *North Irish Roots*, vol. 13,

no. 2 (2002), 31; *Culture Northern Ireland: Belfast Galleries*, www.belfastgalleries.com.

30 *BNL*, 30 Oct. 1956. I have John Gray to thank for this, though even he – the recognised expert on all things to do with the Cave Hill – has been unable to trace the exact origins.

31 Patricia Craig, 'Village Voices', in Boal and Royle (eds), *Enduring City*, 309–25, shows how Belfast is a collective of 'little village communities'; Marjory Alyn, *The Sound of Anthems* (London, 1983), 22.

32 John Gray, *The Great Cave Hill Right of Way Case* (Belfast, 2010), 20–1, 45. In those days the area was much more densely inhabited than later.

33 Bigger, 'The Cave Hill and Its Story', 141–5. Bigger claims the Easter Monday celebrations went back to the eighteenth century. Maginnis, 'Some Belfast Families and Their Houses', 32; C.J. Robb, 'Easter Monday on Cavehill', *BT*, 30 Mar. 1956.

34 Gray, *Cave Hill Right of Way Case*, 35; Proctor, *Belfast Scenery* – the Georgian mansions, in romantic settings, of Belfast's industrialists.

35 Complaints about children from the Whitewell Nissen huts trespassing and interfering with cattle on grounds of the Whitewell laundry (PRONI, LA/59/2F/23, 16 May 1946); also carcases of sheep that perished on the hills in recent snowstorms polluting the streams (ibid., 17 Apr. 1947); vesting orders for the new estate also refer to much of it 'in use as grazing land' (PRONI, VAL/8/415, 1946).

36 'Carndhu', 'Belfast Fifty Years Ago', *IN*, 7 Mar. 1951.

37 See, for example, 'Belfast Castle: 200 Acres of Beautiful Grounds Open Free to the Public', *Ireland's Saturday Night*, 20 Apr. 1957, an advertisement for Easter amusements. There was a bus, too, operating from Strathmore Park.

38 *NW*, 20 Jun. 1951.

39 *The City of Belfast Official Handbook* (London, 1950), 30.

40 Memorandum of agreement between the earl of Shaftesbury and Belfast Corporation (PRONI, HLG/4/48, 21 Mar. 1935); see also Archdale's report to the ministry (ibid., 22 Mar. 1937) and newspaper coverage of the inquiry, *BNL*, 20 Mar. 1937; 'Belfast Castle Presented to the City,' *BT*, 27 Jan. 1934, 5; 'Shaftesbury Estate', *BT*, 13 Nov. 1933.

41 Bigger, 'The Cave Hill and its Story', in Bigger and Crone (eds), *In Remembrance*, 144.

42 Alyn, *Sound of Anthems*, 29.

43 Stewart McFetridge, *Bellevue: Belfast's Mountain Playground – Things You Didn't Know or Had Forgotten* (Belfast, 1995), 40.

44 Ibid., 14.

45 Day and McWilliams (eds), *Ordnance Survey Memoirs*, 101.

46 Frank Mitchell and Michael Ryan, *Reading the Irish Landscape* (3rd ed., Dublin, 1997), 262.

47 McFetridge, *Bellevue*, 24, 47–51.

48 'Opening of Hazelwood Floral Hall: Completion of City's Playground – Triumph Over Difficulties', *NW*, 5 May 1936.

49 John Gray, 'New Future for

the Floral Hall', *The Cave Hill Campaigner* (Summer 2011), 1.

50 *BT*, 23 Jun. 2010; the story of how the animals were shot during the Blitz and the distress of the keepers was reported in *BT*, 19 Apr. 1941.

51 *BWT*, 3 Apr. 1959.

52 *BNL*, 8 Jun. 1953; *City of Belfast Official Handbook*, 152.

53 'Bellevue Gardens' aerial photo, *City of Belfast Official Handbook*, 19, 29; *Belfast Official Industrial Handbook* (Belfast, 1952), 100; Sean Girvan, *Cavehill: A Short Illustrated History* (Belfast, 1994), unpaginated; *Ireland's Saturday Night*, 20 Apr. 1957, lists the attractions, also of Belfast Castle.

54 *City of Belfast Official Handbook*, 152.

55 Simon, *Voices from Cave Hill*, 12.

56 McFetridge, *Bellevue*, 69; 'Floodlit Floral Hall', front-page picture, *NW*, 5 May 1936; also Archdale on the castle grounds (PRONI, HLG/4/48, 22 Mar. 1937).

57 Americans in Ireland (Sussex University, MO1306, Jun. 1942); Moya Woodside, Diary (Sussex University, MO5462, Dec. 1940, 26 Jan. 1941, 30 Apr. 1941).

58 *BNL*, 3 Oct. 1956; *BT*, 19 Sept. 1956; 'Zoo to Stay Open on Sundays', *BWT*, 5 Oct. 1956. See also Joe Moran, *Armchair Nation: An Intimate History of Britain in Front of the TV* (London, 2014), 106–7. The strength of Sunday observance movements in Britain (against the more silent majority) defeated a 1953 bill in parliament to permit more Sunday amusements. The postmaster general now permitted Sunday TV, though even then schedules not permitted to start until 2 p.m. to allow for churchgoing and children's programmes did not begin until 4.30 p.m. to allow for Sunday school.

59 *BT*, 19 Sept. 1956.

60 *BT*, 31 Dec. 1966.

61 Ian Budge and Cornelius O'Leary, *Belfast: Approach to Crisis – a Study of Belfast Politics 1613–1970* (London, 1973), 161–2; BDTUC, *Annual Report* (1964), 4, had made representations to the press about this.

62 Day and McWilliams (eds), *Ordnance Survey Memoirs*, 36–7; Jones, *Social Geography*, 18–20.

63 Conrad Gill, *The Rise of the Irish Linen Industry* (Oxford, 1925 (reprinted 1964)), 232, also 50, 144; Jones, 'Belfast: A Survey of the City', 125.

64 Alyn, *Sound of Anthems*, 3.

65 Day and McWilliams (eds), *Ordnance Survey Memoirs*, 43 and 40–1; Abstract of title of the executors of the will of the late Robert Grimshaw (PRONI, D3521/5, 1871).

66 Ordnance Survey: County Series 6" (1:10560) maps: Antrim sheet (PRONI, OS/6/1/57/1A-2, 1832–3); Valuation records: parish of Carnmoney, first valuation, Ballgolan(d) (PRONI, VAL/1B/115A, 1836); Grimshaw leases (Registry of Deeds, 369/538/249691, 432/66/280034, 619/467/425914, 646/69/443054, 1786–1812).

67 Belfast RDC minutes (PRONI, LA/59/2F/23, 28 Aug. 1947).

68 Newtownabbey Urban District

Council minutes (PRONI, LA/59/2CA/3, 18 Jul. 1960), on one of the dangerous dams, inadequately fenced.

69 Ordnance Survey maps (PRONI, OS/6/1/57/3–6, 1832–3, 1901–2, 1920–2).

70 Jones, *Social Geography*, 264; 'Challenge': Housing Trust promotional film (PRONI, FILM18/8, *c.* 1965).

2. 'A Benevolent Public Body'

1 Eric L. Bird, 'The Work of the Northern Ireland Housing Trust', *Journal of the Royal Institute of British Architects* (Nov. 1949), 7–8.

2 Transcript of Cameron's meeting with Housing Trust representatives (PRONI, GOV/2/1/197, 2 Jul. 1969); Howard-Drake (Home Office), 'Discrimination in N. Ireland' (Nat. Arch., CJ3/60, Apr. 1969) 2–3.

3 C.B.E. Brett, *Housing a Divided Community* (Dublin, 1986), 22.

4 *IN*, 4 Jan. 1945. The inter-war neglect is reflected in the indexes to *Northern Ireland Parliamentary Debates: 50 Years of Northern Ireland Parliamentary Debates Online* (Belfast, 2006), http:// stormont-papers.ahds.ac.uk. There is hardly anything – single figures – for the period 1921–39, followed by an explosion of references to housing in 1944–50.

5 *UYB* (1950), 230; *Northern Ireland Parliamentary Debates*, vol. 27 (1944, 1945), 2,648, 2,699–700. A further 3,581 labourers' cottages were built in rural areas. 'The Northern Ireland Housing Trust: Summary of a Talk at the Housing Centre, London, on 27th February, 1951 by Sir Lucius O'Brien' in NIHT, *Annual Report* (1950–1).

6 *Housing in Northern Ireland: Interim Report of the Planning Advisory Board* (Belfast, 1944), 35.

7 Field-Neill Survey, 4, 9.

8 *Housing in Northern Ireland*, 8; NIHT, *Annual Report* (1945–6), 7.

9 Debate in Stormont on Housing Bills, *IN*, 13 Jan. 1945; Brett, *Housing a Divided Community*, 25. The report is hard hitting and very compassionate towards working people.

10 *UYB* (1950), 231.

11 Medical officer's 1944 report, *IN*, 5 Sept. 1945; *Report on the Health of the County Borough of Belfast for the Year 1947, by the Medical Officer for Belfast* (Belfast, 1948), 3; *Report on the Health of the County Borough of Belfast for the Year 1949* (Belfast, 1950), 9.

12 *Housing in Northern Ireland*, 15, 43.

13 First annual meeting of the Belfast Child Welfare Voluntary Workers' Association, *IN*, 27 Jan. 1945.

14 *IN*, 29 Mar. 1945.

15 Notes for lord mayor, allocation of houses, Belfast Corporation (PRONI, LA/7/3/B/16, 11 Jun. 1947); Brian Barton, *The Belfast Blitz: The City in the War Years* (Belfast, 2015), 494–8, discusses the conflicting evidence of where most damage was sustained.

16 *IN*, 1 Sept. 1945.

17 A. Robinson to H.E. Jones, Ministry of Commerce (PRONI, HLG/6/1/12, 26 Aug. 1943), giving him 'the sort of dope' the Ministry of Supply likes. The press also reflects such frustration. See,

for example, letters to the editor, *IN*, 20 Sept. 1945.

18 James McSparran, Nationalist Party leader, in the Stormont Housing debate, *IN*, 19 Oct. 1945.

19 John A. Oliver, *Working at Stormont: Memoirs* (Dublin, 1978), 70 and 19–20.

20 John Andrews to William Grant (PRONI, HLG/3/19, 29 Jul. 1944); see also Ronald Green's reports on Housing Associations in Scotland (PRONI, HLG/3/21, e.g. 14 Jul. 1944), again showing central frustration with the local authorities, and George Ross to Ronald Green (PRONI, HLG/3 /21, 19 Dec. 1945). See also Sir Roland Nugent, leader of the Senate, moving the second reading of the bill on 2 January 1945, criticising the way subsidies to local authorities operated, producing 'shoddy workmanship', in *IN*, 3 Jan. 1945.

21 Talk by Sir Lucius in London, 27 Feb. 1951, in NIHT, *Annual Report* (1950–1).

22 Ronald Green, 'Housing Association' (PRONI, HLG/3/21, 13 Jul. 1944).

23 Ronald Green to Capt. C.H. Petherick at the Ministry of Finance (ibid., 14 Jul. 1944).

24 Correspondence between Green and Campbell (ibid., 13–20 Oct. 1944); J.I. Cook, Stormont Finance Ministry to D.F.C. Blunt, Treasury (Nat. Arch., T233/442, 27 Feb. 1945), anticipating criticism from such bodies; also various correspondence on the establishment of the Housing Trust.

25 Brett, *Housing a Divided Community*, 27.

26 *Northern Ireland Parliamentary Debates*, vol. 27 (1944–5), 2,077–8.

27 Ibid., 2,085.

28 Ibid., 2,085–6.

29 Ibid., 2,093.

30 Ibid., 2,196. The criticism was from Dr William Lyle, unionist MP for QUB and former member of Tyrone County Council.

31 *IN*, 17 Jan. 1945; also the less-extreme editorial in the same paper, which acknowledged the good treatment of Irish war workers by Britain; *BNL*, 5 and 17 Jan. 1945.

32 *BNL*, 5 Jan. 1945, responding to comments made by Senator J.G. Leslie.

33 Green to George Ross [Scottish Housing Department] (PRONI, HLG/6/1/13, 6 Dec. 1944).

34 Editorials, *IN* and *BNL*, 15 Feb. 1945; Heads of legislation, establishment of the Housing Trust (PRONI, HLG/6/1/13, 1945); amendment to replace term 'working class' with 'workers' (ibid., 6 Dec. 1944). See also *Northern Ireland Parliamentary Debates*, vol. 27, 2,176, 2,218, where the unionist MP for North Down sought to include those on higher wages than understood by the term 'working-class' in previous acts.

35 In fact the Irish republic had a good post-war record in building working-class housing, even though that had slipped by the 1960s. See: David Dickson, *Dublin: The Making of a Capital City* (London, 2014), 512–13; Diarmaid Ferriter, *The Transformation of Ireland 1900–2000* (London, 2004), 466; Erika Hanna, *Modern*

Dublin: Urban Change and the Irish Past, 1957–1973 (Oxford, 2013), ch. 5; '1969: The Housing Crisis', supplement to *Build* (April 1969); also Derek Birrell, Alan Murie and J.G. Calvert, 'Housing Policy in Northern Ireland: Facts and Findings', *Community Forum*, no. 2 (1972), 19.

36 Brett, *Housing a Divided Community*, 26.

37 *UYB* (1950), 232.

38 [Green] to 'Secretary' [Ministry of Finance] (PRONI, HLG/6/1/13, 7 Nov. 1944).

39 Grant's address to the Newtownards Chamber of Commerce, *BNL*, 13 Feb. 1945.

40 Press conference of 15 February 1945, *BNL*, 16 Feb. 1945.

41 Oliver, *Working at Stormont*, 71. Oliver was recognised within the department as having a particular interest and knowledge of the housing issue (see PRONI, HLG/3/21). He and some others from the department had taken a part-time course in social studies at QUB in 1941–2, 'kept together as a study group in the years 1943 and 1944 and taken a special interest in social problems as we actually found them in Ulster, not just as they were told in textbooks' (Oliver, *Working at Stormont*, 73–4).

42 Profile of Sir Lucius, *BNL*, 6 Dec. 1961.

43 *NW*, 9 Jun. 1949.

44 Moya Woodside, Diary (Sussex University, MO5462, 20–1 Apr., 5 May 1941).

45 *BNL*, 16 Feb. 1945.

46 Larmor resigned in 1957; until

then the original team was intact (NIHT, *Annual Report*, 1957–8). Sir Lucius resigned as chair in February 1960 (though he remained on the board). Bryson remained with the Housing Trust for twenty-five years, and was chair in 1960–70.

47 Brett, *Housing a Divided Community*, 27.

48 *IN*, 15 Feb. 1945; *BNL*, 15 Feb. 1945.

49 HLG: list of staff employed by the NIHT (PRONI, SO/1A/229, 31 Mar. 1945); NIHT, *Annual Report* (1945–6), 24.

50 Grant to O'Brien (PRONI, HLG/6/1/24, 7 Feb. 1945).

51 *BNL* and *IN*, 16 Feb. 1945.

52 *IN*, 4 Jan. 1945; *BNL*, 5 Jan. 1945.

53 NIHT, *Annual Report* (1945–6), 9; Jones, *Social Geography*, 99: densities in the old industrial core of Belfast were between fifty and a hundred, and twenty-eight to thirty per acre in Ardoyne, built in the 1930s. Even the interim report of 1945 recommended twenty to the acre. A. Murie, W.D. Birell, P.A.R. Hillard and D. Roche, 'Housing Policy Between the Wars: Northern Ireland, England and Wales', *Social Policy and Administration*, vol. 5, no. 4 (Oct. 1971), 263–79.

54 Northern Ireland Planning Commission, *Planning Proposals for the Belfast Area: Interim (Second) Report of the Planning Commission* (Belfast, 1945), 5. The Ulster Garden Villages project was only set up in 1946, and Merville Garden Village was built in 1947–9.

55 Talk by Sir Lucius in London, 27 Feb. 1951, in NIHT, *Annual Report*

(1950–1); PRONI, HLG/3/21, 1944. In the background research HLG had investigated such developments in Britain. See, for example, a pamphlet by Reginald Browne and National Federation of Housing Societies, *The Housing Society Movement in Britain* (London, 1943).

56 NIHT, *Annual Report* (1945–6), 18–20; NIHT: minutes (PRONI, HLG/6/5/3A, 28 Apr. and 5 May 1948).

57 Don Anderson, *Oaklee: The First 30 Years* (Belfast, 2010), 18–22; Mark K. Smith, 'Octavia Hill: Housing, Space and Social Reform', *The Encyclopaedia of Informal Education* (2008), www.infed.org/thinkers/octavia_hill.htm. In England at the time there was resistance to giving people gardens in redevelopment schemes. See David Kynaston, *Austerity Britain 1945–48: A World to Build* (London, 2007), 43–4.

58 NIHT, *Annual Report* (1945–6), 22. By the time of the *Annual Report* of 1959–60, 12, disappointment was being expressed that 'greater numbers of suitably qualified women are not presenting themselves for training'. Housing managers' salary was £350 per annum and £475 for senior housing managers (considerably higher than the £172 earned by Housing Trust shorthand typists) see HLG: list of staff employed by the NIHT on 31st March 1947 (PRONI, SO/1A/255, 1947).

59 Bird, 'Northern Ireland Housing Trust', 7–8; NIHT, *Annual Report* (1950–1), 10.

60 NIHT, *Annual Report* (1947–8), 6.

61 NIHT, *Annual Report* (1957–8), 14.

62 Housing Act (Northern Ireland) 1945 (PRONI, HLG/6/1/13, 1945).

63 NIHT, *Annual Report* (1945–6), 22–3.

64 NIHT, *Annual Report* (1949–50), 10; NIHT, *Annual Report* (1951–2), 7–8; also reports for 1946–7, 3, 1947–8, 3, and 1948–9, 1; Bird, 'Northern Ireland Housing Trust', 2, also details the financial arrangements. Brett, in *Housing a Divided Community*, 25, 34–6, is also damning on the way the subsidy operated with the private building industry.

65 NIHT, *Annual Report* (1949–50), 9.

66 NIHT, *Annual Report* (1950–1), 9–10; See Kynaston, *Austerity Britain 1945–48*, 155, 900 for the ideal for public housing.

67 W.R. O'Brien to J. Kennedy, Esq, in the Ministry of Finance (PRONI, VAL/8/409, 13 Apr. 1948). This file contains extensive information about the rating values of Whitewell, 1947–48, as do VAL/8/408 and VAL/8/410.

68 Valuation records: Housing Trust, Poor Law valuation (PRONI, VAL/8/409, 1948).

69 Correspondence with Ministry of Finance (PRONI, HLG/6/1/24, 1947–50). This is undoubtedly Freer, HLG permanent secretary; he sounds frustrated. See *BNL*, 13 Jan. 1948, Grant and Freer in London trying to speed up house-building, falling behind Britain. See also *UYB* (1950), 234.

70 Brett, *Housing a Divided Community*, 8–9.

71 John Whyte, *Interpreting Northern Ireland* (Oxford, 1990), 54–64;

Marianne Elliott, *The Catholics of Ulster: A History* (London, 2000), 386–7; John Cameron and Northern Ireland Government, *Disturbances in Northern Ireland: Report of the Commission Appointed by the Governor of Northern Ireland* (Belfast, 1969), 58–61.

72 *BNL*, 16 Feb. 1945.

73 R.D. Megaw and Northern Ireland Ministry of Home Affairs, *Report of Enquiry into the Housing Schemes of Belfast Corporation* (Belfast, 1926); Budge and O'Leary, *Belfast: Approach to Crisis*, 145–9.

74 Belfast Corporation/County Borough Council: file marked: 'Miscellaneous', mainly concerning housing issues, in particular a series of letters between RUC Headquarters and the City Hall Estates Department (PRONI, LA/7/3/B/16, Mar.–Apr. 1949); Brett, *Housing a Divided Community*, 33. Brett also absolves Belfast Corporation of sectarianism in the allocation of houses.

75 The case of Annie Copeland (PRONI, HSS/27/39, 1953–4); also Belfast Corporation Housing Allocations Inquiry (PRONI, HSS/27/2 and HSS/27/7, 1953–4).

76 Northern Ireland HLG, *Inspector's Report on Belfast Corporation Housing Allocations Inquiry* (Belfast, 1954), paragraphs 44–7; *BNL*, 10 Mar. 1954.

77 Oliver, *Working at Stormont*, 74.

78 UUC: file containing documents relating to the Housing Sub-Committee (PRONI, D1327/15/14, 1950–1).

79 E.T. Herdman to W. Douglas, UUC secretary (ibid., 5 Jun. 1950).

80 Report of the meeting (ibid).

81 Cabinet Secretariat: Dame Dehra to Sir Robert Grandsen (secretary to the cabinet), 22 June, and briefing paper, 'The Political Aspects of Housing', also exchange between Sir Lucius and Basil Brooke, 7–8 May 1949, who is very supportive (PRONI, CAB/9/N/4/17, 1949–50). Indeed, Sir Lucius comes out rather well from these trials and he is not overruled by government.

82 *Housing in Northern Ireland*, 10.

83 Graham Walker, *A History of the Ulster Unionist Party: Protest, Pragmatism and Pessimism* (Manchester, 2004), 116–17. Walker considers the Housing Trust as 'one of the most progressive innovations on the Unionist record', but is critical of Brooke for not taking things a stage further to appease the Catholic minority in these positive years after the war.

84 Oliver, *Working at Stormont*, 72. The merger into the Housing Executive was part of overall local-government reform consequent on the Cameron Report.

3. The New Estate

1 Oliver, *Working at Stormont*, 71–2.

2 John W. Blake, *Northern Ireland in the Second World War* (Belfast, 1956), 218–21; Robert Fisk, *In Time of War: Ireland, Ulster and the Price of Neutrality, 1939–45* (Dublin, 1983), 478–9; Moya Woodside, Diary (Sussex University, MO2505, 7 Oct. 1940 and MO5462, e.g. 26 Aug. 1940, 16 and 26 Oct. 1940, 2 and 8 Apr. 1941). Moya Woodside's diary confirms both a lack of shelters and how blasé Belfast people were about the war.

3 *BWT*, 7 Apr. 1961. Then aged 80, Hawthorne gives his recollections on the twentieth anniversary.

4 *BWT*, 14 Apr. 1961; *BT*, 25 Apr. 1941 had run the story.

5 *BWT*, 14 Apr. 1961 – recollections of the seventy-three-year-old air-raid warden, Alfred Ambrose.

6 Belfast Civil Defence Authority: Demolition and Clearance Section. Lists of Premises Demolished and Sites Cleared (PRONI, HLG/6/1/11, 1944); Letters of the city surveyor (PRONI, HLG/3/10, Oct.–Dec. 1943).

7 Barton, *Belfast Blitz*, 281.

8 Moya Woodside, Diary (Sussex University, MO5462, 20 and 27 Apr. 1941, 14 May 1941).

9 *BWT*, 7 Apr. 1961; *BT*, 19 Apr. 1941 has the account of the shooting of the animals. The head keeper, Dick Foster, 'with tears streaming down his face as the executioners proceeded from cage to cage' shooting 'the animals he loved so much' (thirty-three of them, plus a vulture). This also describes very moving scenes of mass public funerals of the victims through the Belfast streets.

10 Account of German air-raid on Veryan Gardens, Belfast (PRONI, T3756, 1941); also Rev. Finlay Maguire's account (PRONI, D2742, 1941–8); 130 homes were destroyed in Veryan and Vandyck Gardens (Barton, *Belfast Blitz*, 190).

11 David Brett, 'Geologies of Site and Settlement', in Nicholas Allen and Aaron Kelly (eds), *The Cities of Belfast* (Dublin, 2003), 22; *BT*, 18 Oct. 1941 and *BNL*, 23 Oct. 1941, reporting on the 15 October ceremony at City cemetery, a memorial to 154 unidentified victims of the Blitz (other unidentified victims were buried in Milltown cemetery).

12 William Ward notebooks (PRONI, D2742, 1941–8); *BWT*, 8 Nov. 1957, on the redevelopment of the blitzed area in Bridge Street.

13 *IN*, 2 Mar. 1945; *BWT*, 18 Mar. 1949; *UYB* (1950), 365.

14 Belfast RDC minutes (PRONI, LA/59/2F/23, 18 Jul. 1946).

15 *BWT*, 2 Feb. 1951; *UYB* (1953), 318–19. However, food rationing does not appear as a category in the *UYB* for 1956). *BT*, 30 Dec. 1950 reports that petrol rationing ended on 25 May 1950, coal not until 1958; *BT*, 15 Jul. 1958 has a picture of a man taking down the sign at Ministry of Commerce office following the decontrol of coal.

16 *BT*, 15 Jul. 1958.

17 *NW*, 22 May and 27 Oct. 1951; *BNL*, 7 Jan. and 23 Jun. 1955; *BT*, 4 Jun. 1958 asks 'How long will it be before all the bombed sites in the centre of Belfast are re-developed?'

18 'Blitz Market Story', *Ireland's Saturday Night*, 7 Dec. 1957.

19 *IN*, 22 May 1948; Belfast County Borough War Damage Act 1941, City surveyor to the Ministry of [Home Affairs] (PRONI, HLG/3/10, 19 Oct. 1943). This file is full of letters from people about war damage to their homes. *BWT*, 17 Aug. 1956, on a thirteen-year-old, Victor Devlin, killed in Corporation Street when a blitzed building collapsed.

20 John Campbell, *Memories of York Street* (Belfast, 1991), 5.

21 One of the earliest requests to rebuild came from Malcolm McKibbin Esq, of Balmoral Ave. in south Belfast for his thirty houses destroyed on Serpentine Road: McKibbin to Grant (PRONI, HLG/6/1/16, 23 Sept. 1944); 'Bombed Houses: Rebuilding Proposals in Belfast', *BNL*, 17 Jan. 1945.

22 War damage: compensation on dwellings affected by planning schemes (PRONI, HLG/6/1/11, 1944). There is much here about the inferior standard of housing built between the wars.

23 Oliver, *Working at Stormont*, 66.

24 'Huts as Homes', *BNL*, 19 Jan. 1945.

25 This was 1951. See council minutes (PRONI, LA/59/2F/26, 16 May 1951); see PRONI, LA/59/2F/23–4, 1946–52 for numerous references to the Whitewell Nissen-hut camp and Newtownabbey Urban District Council minutes (PRONI, LA/59/2CA/2, 1959) for prefabs in the area. Whitewell, conversion of hutments, 24 temporary dwellings by Belfast Rural DC (PRONI, ED/13/1/2283, Dec. 1947); also J. Donaldson, HLG to A. Wilson, Education Ministry, '2000 prefabs needed for Belfast, 390 on Shore Road – the largest site in Belfast', enclosing spreadsheet, 'Hutments – conversion: position at 30th June, 1947', twenty-four conversions completed for Whitewell (PRONI, ED/13/1/2283, 2 Jul. 1947); *UYB* (1947), 208; *BNL*, 3 Jan. 1948. By 1947 1,609 'prefabricated temporary houses' had been built and there were another 391 in progress; 1,022 hutments had been converted, with 40 per cent more in preparation.

26 *BNL*, 19 Jan. 1945, on the occasion of the inaugural luncheon of the Federation of Building Trade Employers, addressed by Prime Minister Brooke, where discussion of the Housing Trust was the major item, Brooke using soothing language towards private enterprise.

27 *BWT*, 6 Apr. 1962.

28 'The Belfast of the Future' and editorial, 'Post-War Belfast', *BNL*, 17 Jan. 1945; 'Big Plan for Improving Belfast', *IN*, 17 Jan. 1945.

29 'Around and About', *BNL*, 20 Jan. 1945.

30 It straddled Belfast County Borough, Belfast Rural District and Antrim County Councils, though PRONI, HLG/6/1/24, 1950, shows 24 Whitewell houses in Belfast City Urban Council and 290 in Belfast RDC.

31 NIHT, *Annual Report* (1945–6), 8.

32 Green to Calvert (PRONI, VAL/8/415, 29 Aug. 1945).

33 Northern Ireland Housing Trust: Whitewell Road site (ibid.,1945).

34 Housing Trust: Whitewell estate, the 1946 survey in file: investigation of interests in Housing Trust estate at Whitewell (PRONI, VAL/8/415, 1946).

35 Megaw and Ministry of Home Affairs, *Enquiry into Belfast Corporation*, 58–61; Whitewell arbitration proceedings, with notice of application for vesting order and vesting map, showing Barron land largely near the Serpentine and Whitewell Roads (PRONI, VAL/8/415, 1945–65).

36 Belfast RDC minutes (PRONI, LA/59/2F/23, 22 Dec. 1947).

37 [Green] to W.D. Scott, Ministry of Finance (PRONI, HLG/6/1/13, 27 Dec. 1944).

38 Housing: land purchase – Housing Trust application for vesting order, Carnmoney, Belfast (Whitewell), date of vesting order (21 December 1945), and various correspondence about vesting the Whitewell estate (PRONI, FIN/18/26/122, 1945–9); Sites for houses to be built by the Housing Trust (PRONI, HLG/6/1/24, 24 Feb. 1945); Bird, 'Northern Ireland Housing Trust', 1–2; NIHT, typed document, detailing processes (NIHE Library, HT.2.NORT, 1968).

39 Alyn, *Sound of Anthems*, 2.

40 McKibbin's valuations (PRONI, VAL/8/415, 1 Apr. 1946).

41 J. McMullan to J.G. Calvert (PRONI, VAL/8/344, 13 Oct. 1945).

42 McKibbin's valuations (PRONI, VAL/8/415, Apr. 1946).

43 Valuation records: Housing Trust – Whitewell site, document dated 15 Apr. 1946, attached to McKibbin's foregoing letter, also folder: investigation of interests (PRONI, VAL/8/415, 15 Apr. 1946), 5.

44 NIHT, Whitewell site: award of arbitrator (PRONI, FIN/18/26/122, 24 May 1950).

45 NIHT, *Annual Report* (1946–7), 8–9.

46 Grant to Sir Basil Brooke (PRONI, HLG/6/1/12, 3 Sept. 1945).

47 Draft cabinet memorandum (PRONI, HLG/6/1/24, 16 May 1946).

48 NIHT, *Annual Report* (1946–7), 4–5, 16 and plate XI, showing these houses on the Whitewell estate; see Belfast RDC minutes (PRONI, LA/59/2F/23, 17 Apr. 1947) for the weather conditions, particularly a late snowstorm in April.

49 *BNL*, 24 May 1946, headlined 'Cement Shortage: Supplies Being Sent from Éire' – misrepresenting the 23 May session at Stormont as being critical of the minister for seeking supplies from Éire. See also *Northern Ireland Parliamentary Debates*, vol. 30 (1946–7), 819–20.

50 Adrian Robinson to H.E. Jones at the Ministry of Commerce (PRONI, HLG/6/1/12, 18 Aug. 1943); Graham, *WhiteCity: Crumbling Orlits*, introduction.

51 For the defects of Orlit housing see Graham, *WhiteCity: Crumbling Orlits*, intro, 1–7 and Appendices I–III. NIHT Orlit estates were built all over Northern Ireland at this period, but the White City was the biggest.

52 Letter (PRONI, HLG/6/1/12, 23 Apr. 1947). This file also has the building schedule for June 1947.

53 Progress can be traced through the NIHT *Annual Reports* (1947–50); see also PRONI, LA/59/2F/23 (1946–52); LA/1/2/GA/48, 22 Jul. 1947; ED/13/1/2263 and 2283 (1947–9); see also Grant to Sir Basil Brooke (PRONI, HLG/6/1/12, 3 Sept. 1945) on the expected shortage of materials.

54 NIHT, *Annual Report* (1946–7), 5.

55 *BWT*, 28 Jan. 1949.

56 Bird, 'Northern Ireland Housing Trust', 7.

57 Brett, *Housing a Divided Community*, 19.

58 Bird, 'Northern Ireland Housing Trust', 6–7; NIHT: minutes (PRONI, HLG/6/5/3A, 23 Jun. 1948): Bird and Osborn were taken to view the Cregagh and Whitewell estates; NIHT, *Annual Report* (1949–50), 9.

59 Calvert to education minister, W.H. Smyth (PRONI, ED/13/1/2283, 5 Jul. 1946).

60 NIHT, *Annual Report* (1945–6), 8–9.

61 NIHT, *Annual Report* (1952–3), 13; Jones, *Social Geography*, 99; idem, 'How Can We House These New Thousands?', *BT*, 10 Jul. 1956.

62 NIHT, *Annual Report* (1945–6), 12.

63 Jones, 'These New Thousands', *BT*, 10 Jul. 1956; Mass Observation studies showed that people in England also disliked flats – see Hanley, *Estates*, 59, 60, 78, 93. The final map of the estate is in PRONI (VAL/8/415, 1945–65), as is the detail of the Throne lands.

64 NIHT, *Annual Report* (1951–2), 19; Spreadsheet showing NIHT completions (PRONI, LA/7/3/E/13/9, 1961–2).

65 Oliver, *Working at Stormont*, 72.

66 *BT*, 10 Jul. 1956.

4. The First Residents

1 Hugh Shearman, *Ulster* (London, 1949). Born in 1915, he lived in north Belfast. This is quoted in Patricia Craig, 'Village Voices', in Boal and Royle (eds), *Enduring City*, 309–10, a wonderful essay in which she shows how so many Belfast writers are actually writing about the small patch in which they grew up (John Hewitt, Cal McCrystal, Bernard McLaverty, Brian Moore, Gerald Dawe, all from north Belfast).

2 There was friendliness and neighbourly behaviour, but not 'visiting' – a trend noted also of 'aspirational neighbourhoods' in 1950s Britain. See, for example, Peter Scott, 'Visible and Invisible Walls: Suburbanisation and the Social Filtering of Working-Class Communities in Interwar Britain' (discussion paper, Reading, 2004), 22–4.

3 UUC inquiry (PRONI, D1327/15/14, 1950–1); NIHT, *Annual Report* (1967–8), 58; NIHT, Manual of Housing Management (NIHE Library, 009827, 1965), 1–30.

4 Field-Neill Survey, 18, 70–2 and map of estate locations at back. *BT*, 16 Jan. 1953: in the choice of where to live, a 'potent factor seems to be the young wife's desire to live in a familiar district, preferably close to her mother'.

5 Field-Neill Survey, 72: table showing some 88 per cent of trust tenants on incomes 'above standard'.

6 UUC deputation to Sir Lucius O'Brien (PRONI, D1327/15/14, 23 May 1950); NIHT: minutes (PRONI, HLG/6/5/3A, 29 Sept. 1948).

7 Belfast RDC minutes (PRONI, LA/59/2FA/24, 25 Nov. 1948, 24 Feb. 1949, 21 Jul. 1949).

8 Belfast RDC minutes (PRONI, LA59/2FA/23, 16 Oct. 1947).

9 'Era of the Lamplighter Nears Its Close', *BT*, 11 Apr. 1957; 'Electric Lighting to Extend to Shore and

Whitewell Roads in 1958', *BT*, 13 Dec. 1957.

10 *BT*, 18 Apr. 1957. Lamp-post swinging was declared a 'very dangerous sport' by the Belfast coroner at the inquest into the death of a Larne schoolboy killed when the rope broke.

11 NIHT, Manual of Housing Management (NIHE Library, 009827, 1965), 56.

12 Ibid., paragraphs 92–4, 123–9. NIHT, *Annual Report* (1956–7), 14.

13 NIHT, tenancy agreement (PRONI, VAL/8/408, 1946–58), which is rather defective in punctuation.

14 NIHT, Manual of Housing Management (NIHE Library, 009827, 1965), 127, 262: aerials should be 'as inconspicuous as possible'; there are worries about those for ITV, 'which may have to be at a great height', and about potential damage to houses.

15 Bird, 'Northern Ireland Housing Trust', 6–7.

16 *BT*, 10 Jul. 1956; Jones, *Social Geography*, 216–19, about the 'sea of smoke' over Belfast and the pervasive smell of coal. Clean-air legislation came in England in 1956, to Northern Ireland in 1964. See also: NIHT, *Annual Report* (1968–9), 11, and (1961–2), 11, on the painting and maintenance schedule; NIHT, Manual of Housing Management (NIHE Library, 009827, 1965), 336, March 1968 insertion – new guidelines for replacement of open fires with electric ones, immersion heaters replacing back boilers; BDTUC, *Annual Report* (1956), 9, campaign on air pollution in Belfast (though

at the same time complaining of rising coal prices); 'Smog Inquiry', *BT*, 30 Dec. 1959, welcoming the fact that the Ministry of Health has set up an inquiry, but concluding that the government should act with more urgency.

17 NIHT, *Annual Report* (1945–6), plate 6: plan of the Orlit house, four bedroom, one in every block of four.

18 NIHT, *Annual Report* (1960–1), 11.

19 Calvert to A.H. Blair, Esq, superintending valuer (PRONI, VAL/8/409, 7 Nov. 1947); First appeals, Whitewell estate (PRONI, VAL/8/410, May–Jun. 1949).

20 Field-Neill Survey, 42.

21 Joint Council of Furniture Industry (Northern Ireland) to Grant (PRONI, HLG/6/1/13, 22 Nov. 1944).

22 *BNL*, 20 Feb. 1945, listing prices of utility furniture; also *IN*, 4 Jan. 1945 and 2 Apr. 1948.

23 Field-Neill Survey, 34; NIHT, *Annual Report* (1963–4), 12. K.S. Isles and N. Cuthbert, *An Economic Survey of Northern Ireland* (Belfast, 1957), 222–3, cites 148–66s. per week for skilled workers, 113–33s. for unskilled.

24 NIHT, Manual of Housing Management (NIHE Library, 009827, 1965), 300–1; Field-Neill Survey, 76.

25 Graham, *WhiteCity: Crumbling Orlits*, G/18; also complaints about shoddy and unchecked workmanship.

26 Octavia Hill, *Octavia Hill's Letters to Fellow Workers 1872–1911: Together with an Account of the Walmer Street Industrial Experiment* (Robert

Whelan, ed.) (London, 2005), 54–5; *BT*, 27 Aug. 1956, containing Cyril Lord talking to the Belfast Rotary club about the need for 'brightness in textiles' and brightness in life; *BT*, 10 Jul. 1956, containing Emrys Jones's complimentary article on the new housing: 'architects … have not been afraid of using bright colours'.

27 *IN*, 1 Apr. 1948: article on the colours of utility 'units'.

28 Brett, *Housing a Divided Community*, 30.

29 The total of 100.1 per cent appears as 100 per cent in Field-Neill; female heads of households, unfortunately, have been excluded.

30 Field-Neill Survey, table 3; *BSD* (1949–50); *BT*, 16 Jan. 1953: because of the variety of NIHT designs, estates have a more 'heterogeneous' mix rather than just 'workers'. Brett, *Housing a Divided Community*, 50, explains the religious complexion of certain trades – slaters and tilers were traditionally Catholic, bricklayers Protestant.

31 *BT*, 7 Oct. and 22 Nov. 1957; *BNL*, 29 Aug. 1957; Henry Patterson, *Ireland Since 1939: The Persistence of Conflict* (Dublin, 2006), 141–3; Jones, *Social Geography*, 162–3, on high female employment; 'Whitehouse Training Centre for Unemployed Also Offers Needlework Classes for Women', *BT*, 16 Jun. 1958; NIHT, *Annual Report* (1962–3), 7, on the shortage of skilled labour and the restrictive practices of the trade unions. The trust has to resort to non-traditional building again because of a shortage of bricklayers. See also *BT*, 20 Apr. 1955, on the new factories being sited nearby, and *BNL*, 25 Oct. 1957.

32 See also *BT*, 3 Jul. 1956, in which Emrys Jones confirms this – one in five women were working in textiles, one in six in clothing. The 1954 report, *Juvenile Delinquency: Interim Report of the Northern Ireland Child Welfare Council* (Belfast, 1954), 8, 15, fretted about the impact of so many mothers of school-age children working in the textile industry.

33 Newtownabbey Urban District Council minutes (PRONI, LA/59/2CA/3, 8 Feb. and 7 Mar. 1960). By now mobile shops were considered a problem.

34 *Northern Ireland: Planning for Prosperity* (supplement to *Advertisers Weekly*, no. 4) (1956), back cover.

35 Plans for shops and flats on the estate (PRONI, VAL/8/415, Oct. 1951); also NIHT, *Annual Report* (1951–2), 17 and (1952–3), 15.

36 Jones, *Social Geography*, 86.

37 *BNL*, 29 Sept. 1951; Field-Neill Survey, 82–3.

38 *BSD* (1953), 480, (1954), 485–6 and 496, on the 'chippy'.

39 Sale of council houses discussion document (PRONI, HLG/6/5/2, 30 Nov. 1951); NIHT, Manual of Housing Management (NIHE Library, 009827, 1965), insertion 335, 4 Mar. 1968: 'Public Relations. Housing Managers and staff dealing with the public should bear in mind that the Trust is judged on such contacts', and they needed always to explain things carefully.

40 NIHT, *Annual Report* (1947–8), 3–5 and (1949–50), 8. Rents in 1948 (PRONI, VAL/8/408, 1948).

41 NIHT, *Annual Report* (1949–50), 8; Protests at rents going up (PRONI, DEV/9/57, 1962–8).

42 Cameron Commission: evidence submitted by NIHT per F.W. Hornibrook (general manager), Belfast (PRONI, GOV/2/1/197, 2 Jul. 1969), 18–19.

43 NIHT, Manual of Housing Management (NIHE Library, 009827, 1965), 327, 276.

44 Ibid., 137.

45 NIHT, typed document (NIHE Library, HT.2.NORT, 1968).

46 NIHT, Manual of Housing Management (NIHE Library, 009827, 1965), 112–19, 191–7.

47 NIHT, *Annual Report* (1969–70), 12.

48 Belfast RDC minutes (PRONI, LA/59/2FA/24, 15 Jan., 5 Apr. 1948).

49 Octavia Hill, *Letter to Fellow Workers*, 5.

50 NIHT, *Annual Report* (1957–8), 16.

51 Ken Bloomfield, *Stormont in Crisis: A Memoir* (Belfast, 1994), 226.

52 Andersonstown (PRONI, DEV/9/576, Jun. 1965).

53 NIHT, *Annual Report* (1951–2), 11; the trust also reported only £40 having to be written off as irrecoverable since 1945: *Annual Report* (1957–8).

54 NIHT, *Annual Report* (1957–8), 11.

55 Gillian Darley, *Octavia Hill* (London, 1990), 332.

56 Brett, *Housing a Divided Community*, 30.

57 NIHT, *Annual Report* (1963–4), 9–10, (1964–5), 18–19, (1966–7), 11–13, (1969–70), 13.

58 NIHT, *Annual Report* (1947–8), 1.

59 Jones, *Social Geography*, 263–5.

5. The Dramas of Not-So-Everyday Lives

1 NIHT, *Annual Report* (1957–8), 12.

2 *IN*, 6–7 Apr. 1948; *BWT*, 16 Jan. 1953, on the 'alarming increase of crime in Belfast'.

3 'Talk on Capital Punishment by Dr J.L.J. Edwards of QUB', *BNL*, 22 Mar. 1955. See also *BWT*, 4 Aug. 1961, 22 Dec. 1961 and 9 Feb. 1962, expressing shock at the two hangings in 1961. The death penalty was provisionally abolished in Britain in 1965 and permanently in 1969, but not in Northern Ireland until 1973.

4 'Trial of 21-Year-Old Painter, Ponsonby Avenue Murder', *BWT*, 29 Jul. 1949; *Belfast Forum*, www.belfastforum.co.uk. The McGowans were a middle-class family, the father a publican.

5 John Linklater, 'The Boy Who Fitted the Bill', *The Herald*, 11 Mar. 1995.

6 *BNL*, 14 Nov. 1952 and 17 Jan. 1953; *BWT*, 30 Jan. 1953, 6 and 13 Feb. 1953, 6 and 13 Mar. 1953. Judge Curran's obituary, *BT*, 22 Oct. 1984.

7 Duncan Webb, 'This Boy Did Not Kill Pat Curran', *The People*, 9 Feb. 1958, front-page spread; *The People*, 16 Feb., 2 Mar. and 9 Mar. 1958.

8 Jeff Dudgeon, article in *BT*, 14 Oct. 2000; 'Ulster Version of *White Mischief*', *BT*, 27 Oct. 2009, reviewing the TV documentary *Scapegoat*; *Sunday Life*, 4 Oct. 1998; *Empire News and Sunday Chronicle*, 2 Feb. 1958; *The People*, 16 Feb.,

23 Feb., 9 Mar., 16 Mar. 1958; *IN*, 25 Feb. 1958; 'Petition for Release Rejected', *BT*, 10 Jun. 1958.

9 *BNL*, 6 Jan. 1953; *BWT*, 9 Jan. 1953, on Irish taoiseach's message of sympathy, and the gracious response from the Northern Ireland premier, Lord Brookeborough.

10 Bloomfield, *Stormont in Crisis*, 24.

11 Stephen Cameron, *Death in the North Channel: The Loss of the* Princess Victoria, *January 1953* (Newtownards, 2002), 21. Cameron concludes that the ship should never have sailed. The BBC shipping forecast had warned of gales.

12 *Irish Independent*, 2 and 26 Feb. 1953.

13 *Timewatch* (BBC, 7 Mar. 2003); Cameron, *Death in the North Channel*, 19; *IW*, 7 Feb. 1953; Jack Hunter, *The Loss of the* Princess Victoria (2nd ed., Stranraer, 2010), 19.

14 *IN*, 2 Feb. 1953; Photo of the McAteer brothers, *BT*, 2 Feb. 1953.

15 *BT*, 26–7 Feb. 1953; Cameron, *Death in the North Channel*, 37.

16 *IN* and *BT*, 2 Feb. 1953.

17 *Ulster Herald*, 7 Feb. 1953.

18 Cameron, *Death in the North Channel*, 66–9, which provides an entire list, with biographies and photographs; *BT*, 2 Feb. 1953.

19 *IW*, 4 Apr. 1953.

20 *IW*, 7 Feb. 1953; Report on the inquiry, *IW*, 4 Apr. 1953.

21 *BT*, 31 Jan. and 1 Feb. 1953, and on the fiftieth anniversary, 31 Jan. 2013; *Belfast Forum*, www.belfastforum.co.uk.

22 *IN*, 2 Feb. 1953; Report on the firing party for Sgt James Sumner, from Clonmel, of the Royal Inniskilling Fusiliers, at the Sacred Heart Catholic Church, Omagh, *Ulster Herald*, 7 Feb. 1953.

23 *IN*, 1 Aug. 1955; Barbara McGeehan's statement to the RUC, *IN*, 22 Dec. 1954.

24 *BSD* (1950): listings for Lonsdale Street show a lot of rooming houses; Jones, *Social Geography*, 222, 226, 247; BDTUC, *Annual Report* (1952), 5, (1953), 6; *IW*, 10 Jan. 1953, reporting on the Trades Union Council joining with the Young Christian Workers' organisation to raise the issue with MPs and the health officer, for example, of a family of eight living in one room, with four of the children suffering from TB.

25 Court report, *IN*, 20 Jan. 1955. Mr Justice Curran thought her history no excuse for her conduct.

26 *IN*, 18 Jan. 1955; *IW*, 15 Jan. 1955; Picture of Mrs Teresa McCreedy, of 29 Lonsdale Street, who rented the room to the McGeehan family in 1947, *IN*, 8 Jan. 1955.

27 *IW*, 15 Jan. 1955.

28 Ibid.

29 *IN*, 22 Jan. 1955.

30 *IN*, 21 Jan. 1955.

31 *BWT*, 11 Feb. 1955 and *IW*, 12 Feb. 1955; also *IN*, 5 Feb. 1955.

32 *IN*, 20 Jan. and 7 Jan. 1955. Judge Curran seems very fair here and shows some compassion, including towards the parents of the stolen child.

33 *BWT*, 8 Apr. 1955.

34 Picture of Barbara McGeehan

with Elizabeth and her brother in Garton Way, *BT*, 1 Jun. 1956, prominently on front page.

35 P.T. D'Orbán, 'Baby Stealing', *British Medical Journal*, vol. 2, no. 5,814 (1972), 635–9. I am grateful to Dr Lindsey Earner-Byrne for making me aware of this article. This crime is very rare and there has been little research on it done in Ireland.

36 *IT*, 16 Apr. and 21 May 1957.

37 June Considine (Laura Elliott), 'Memories of a Stolen Child', *Irish Independent*, 5 Jun. 2010, www.independent.ie/entertainment/books/memories-of-a-stolen-child-2665965. The author also had been disturbed by this story as a child and it inspired her fictional work, *Stolen Child* (Avon, 2015); Interview, *BT*, 10 Jun. 2010.

38 *IW*, 1 Jan. 1955.

6. Having It So Good, Belfast Style

1   The voice of Marjory Alyn's ten-year-old heroine, *Sound of Anthems*, 2.

2   'Irishman's Diary', *IT*, 24 Jan. 1955.

3   Norman McNeilly, *Exactly 50 Years: The Belfast Education Authority and Its Work (1923–73)* (Belfast, 1974), 116–17; *NW*, 3 Apr. 1957, on the Field-Neill Survey.

4   NIHT, *Annual Report* (1959–60), 11.

5   Graham, *White City: Crumbling Orlits*, 13.

6   Field-Neill Survey, 15–16, 27–35, 66; W.D. Flackes, *BT*, 16 Jun. 1958, article on the operation of the welfare state ten years on, finding that those on new estates have more difficulty living on unemployment benefit because rents, heating and hire-purchase payments are higher than in the old, crowded streets.

7   *BT*, 16 Feb. 1956.

8   Field-Neill Survey, 66, 23, 38; in the Belfast workforce, the figure was 36 per cent in 1951: A.C. Hepburn, *A Past Apart: Studies in the History of Catholic Belfast, 1850–1950* (Belfast, 1996), 109.

9   NIHT, *Annual Report* (1955–6), 7–8.

10 *BT*, 18 May, 5 Jun. and 30 Jun. 1965; Communication from NIHT tenants' federation, as well as considerable documentation on this issue, May–July 1965 (PRONI, DEV/9/57, 7 Jul. 1965); NIHT, *Annual Report* (1963–4), 12: a table of average incomes of applicants in 1954–63 shows a big increase (though rents have remained low). In fact, incomes in Northern Ireland doubled between 1937 and 1951 (*BNL*, 29 Aug. 1957).

11 Field-Neill Survey, 41–2.

12 David Kynaston, *Austerity Britain 1948–51: Smoke in the Valley* (London, 2008), 317–20.

13 *NW*, 17 Jul. 1958, containing Sir Lucius talking about pride in gardens on Housing Trust estates as witnessed by their success in garden competitions; NIHT, *Annual Report* (1956–7), 15, reporting that tenants' interest in gardens was very high.

14 Field-Neill Survey, 44–7, 76, although they single out Cregagh (which at this stage had entirely open front gardens) and Andersonstown as the main estates making this suggestion.

15 Ibid., 54–60; *BT*, 16 Jan. 1953.

16 Field-Neill Survey, 61.

17 *BNL*, 28 Mar. 1955.

18 *BWT*, 20 Feb. 1953.

19 *BWT*, 9 Jan. 1953.

20 *IT*, 24 Jan. 1950; Barton, *Blitz*, 519–33; Jonathan Bardon, *A History of Ulster* (Belfast, 1992), 575.

21 Romie Lambkin, *My Time in the War: An Irishwoman's Diary* (Dublin, 1992), 42, 96; Americans in Ireland (Sussex University, MO1306, 8 Jun. 1942), which confirms Flo's account and is very complimentary.

22 *BWT*, 28 Mar. 1958; *NW*, 26 Mar. 1954, on the royal dressmaker; *BWT*, 8 Jan. 1954, on Frankie Laine.

23 *Ireland's Saturday Night*, 14 Dec. 1957.

24 *BWT*, 25 Mar. 1955; see, for example, *Ireland's Saturday Night*, 14 Jan. 1956, for the various entertainments offered by the cinema, amateur musicals and dance venues.

25 *UYB* (1950), 358 and (1957–9), 324–5; *IN*, 8 Jan. 1955; *BT*, 31 Dec. 1951 – this also has the most popular books borrowed. As for library newspaper readership, 142,117 and 88,000 were reported as using the magazine and newspaper rooms respectively in Belfast Central Library in 1947 (*IN*, 4 Apr. 1948).

26 War damage to property files for Belfast County Borough and Belfast Rural District: Duncairn Ward – Whitewell Road (PRONI, VAL/20/5/74, 1941–9).

27 Advertisement for Ferguson TV and radio sets, *IN*, 15 May 1953; *BT*, 29 Dec. 1953; Moran, *Armchair Nation*, 74–5, 81; Gillian McIntosh, *The Force of Culture: Unionist Identities in Contemporary Ireland* (Cork, 1999), 122–4. The number of licences in Northern Ireland increased from 558 in 1953 to 10,353 in 1954, largely in the Antrim/Down (i.e. Belfast) area (information courtesy of Sam Manning of QUB).

28 *BT*, 3 Jun. 1953; Moran, *Armchair Nation*, 129; Maurice Walsh, 'Media and Culture in Ireland, 1960–2008', in Richard Bourke and Ian McBride (eds), *The Princeton History of Modern Ireland* (Princeton, 2016), 254.

29 *BNL*, 3 Jun. 1953.

30 *IN*, 8 May 1945; *BNL*, 8 May 1945, reporting Catholic bishops in Northern Ireland and other church leaders instructing their priests to schedule thanksgiving masses.

31 'Ike Given Freedom of the City', *BNL*, 15 and 24 Aug. 1945; *IN*, 15 Sept. 1945, on Montgomery.

32 There were regiments returning, march-pasts etc. (e.g. 'Inniskillings Back after 17 Years Overseas Service', *BT*, 11 Apr. 1951); 'Freedom of City for RUR', *BNL*, 8 Feb. 1954. This comprised a big event at City Hall, with streets lined with people for the march-past; there were also marches for the centenary of the Boys' Brigade; 'War Rumblings with Russia', *BT*, 30 Dec. 1950.

33 George Fleming, *Magennis VC: The Story of Northern Ireland's Only Winner of the Victoria Cross* (Dublin, 1998), 172, 181–2, 196–9, 211–12. Magennis's homecoming is played down in the *IN*, with no pictures

(15–27 Dec. 1945). Even the visit to his school is just a paragraph hidden away on p. 3 of the 18 Dec. 1945 issue. His mother was upset at how nationalist MPs were using him for political purposes.

34 *IN*, 15 Dec. 1945. In fact, Magennis had arrived by a different route, unknown to those gathered to welcome him, on news of which the official car was sent to his home so that he could be officially welcomed home at the City Hall.

35 *NW*, 10 Jan. 1946, announcing plans for the 19 January ceremony; *BT*, 13 Nov. 1945, on the letter awarding the VC; *NW*, 13 Dec. 1945, containing pictures of him and his mother at the palace, also of bunting and union flags in Ebor Street to welcome him home; Report of his homecoming, *BNL*, 15 Dec. 1945.

36 *IN* and *BNL*, 24 Mar. 1948.

37 *NW*, 2 Jun. 1958.

38 Preachers' book of Whitehouse Church of Ireland parish, Co. Antrim (PRONI, CR/1/76/E/6 and 8, 1940–76). Significant amounts of money – often ten times the normal collections – were raised for Orange charities at these services – for example, on 3 May 1959, for Greencastle and District Orange Lodges, when four hundred people attended. There would be similar increases in numbers for big British patriotic events – the Festival of Britain (August 1951), the Baden-Powell centenary (February 1957) and Remembrance Sunday – as well as for the British Legion and junior Orange Lodge. See also *BT*, 11 Jul. 1959, reporting a decline in the number of Orange arches.

39 Sale advertisement for Arnott's, *BT*, 29 Dec. 1953, for comparison with average wage rates as discussed in ch. 4; other references to the different stores: *NW*, 26 Mar. 1954, *BT*, 5 Apr. 1955, *BNL*, 6 Apr. 1955, *BT*, 4 Jun. 1958 and *BT*, 5 Nov. 1958.

40 *BT*, 17 Sept. 1954.

41 BDTUC, *Annual Report* (1965), 1, (1964), 1, 4, 9, (1963), 3, (1960), 3.

42 *IN*, 28 Jan. 1955: Co-op's profile as an all-round supplier, particularly of coal.

43 BDTUC, *Annual Report* (1959), 8–9.

44 Ibid., 45, also 42, 75; Sean O'Connell, 'An Age of Conservative Modernity, 1914–1968' in Connolly (ed.), *Belfast 400*, 301–2; David Kynaston, *Family Britain 1951–57* (London, 2009), 400; BDTUC, *Annual Report* (1954), on government trying to restrict the growth of hire-purchase and trade unions taking this up.

45 *BT*, 21 Oct. 2015.

46 As more appeared, the housing manager expressed her concern about the large number of 'unsightly' aerials, needed because of poor reception: Newtownabbey Urban District Council minutes – Housing Committee (PRONI, LA/59/2CA/9, 3 Oct. 1966).

47 Moran, *Armchair Nation*, 106, 128; Brum Henderson, *Brum: A Life in Television* (Belfast, 2003), 77.

48 Newtownabbey Urban District Council: papers to the Local Government Conference at Portrush (PRONI, LA/59/2CA/2, Sept. 1959); *BNL*, 22 Sept. 1956 and 1 Jan. 1957; *BT*, 29 Sept. 1956,

containing a front-page photo of a big queue in Ormeau Avenue to obtain driving licences before the test was brought in on 1 October. There were 1,500 before noon (when the office closed) and 5,000 in the week; also a letter from a Whitewell resident complaining that the speed limit had not been extended to there: 'This part of the Antrim Road is a built-up area,' and six people had been killed in it.

49 BDTUC, *Annual Report* (1960), 2, (1962), 4, (1964), 7, on the introduction of the five-day week.

7. The Impact of the Welfare State on Everyday Lives

1 Eric Gallagher, *At Points of Need: The Story of the Belfast Central Mission, Grosvenor Hall, 1889–1989* (Belfast, 1989), 85.

2 Memorandum of a conference held at the Housing Trust offices with the minister of education (PRONI, ED/13/1/2283, 20 Jun. 1946).

3 NIHT, *Annual Report* (1949–50), 15; Ministry of Education: school provision – NIHT's general manager, John Calvert, to W.H. Smyth (PRONI, ED/13/1/2283, 5 Jul. 1946); Valuation records: Housing Trust – Whitewell site (PRONI, VAL/8/415, 1949): a map has written on it, 'Plot 120'x 120' [corner of the green space on Thorburn Road] to be acquired by U.D.C. for Play Centre'; Eric Waugh, *BT*, 5 Dec. 1955, article on Rathcoole and how the estate was built before any proper amenities. A cinema was in the planning stage, called the Alpha, and 'many Rathcoole residents no doubt would wish that the time of its

appearance had better harmonised with its name'.

4 McNeilly, *Exactly 50 Years*, 86, 112.

5 The BDTUC was against the eleven-plus as 'iniquitous' and called for its abolition. See BDTUC, *Annual Report* (1962), 4 and 12; (1964), 1.

6 County Borough of Belfast Education Committee Report (PRONI, HLG/6/5/4, Mar. 1950). The Irish National Teachers' Organisation was still calling for such a facility at new schools in 1960: see *IN*, 1 Jan. 1960.

7 County Borough of Belfast Education Committee: development scheme for primary and secondary schools (PRONI, HLG/6/5/4, Mar. 1950).

8 Belfast RDC minutes (PRONI, LA/59/2FA/24, 12 Sept. 1949).

9 *BWT*, 28 Jan. 1949.

10 *Larne Times*, 2 Feb. 1961.

11 The *UYB* charts the casualties: 147 killed and 2,396 injured in 1949 (*UYB* [1950], 126), 167 and 2,975 in 1951 (*UYB* [1953], 134), 160 and 4,561 in 1955 (*UYB* [1956], 141); *IN*, 28 Jan. 1955: there were 3,315 road accidents in 1954 with 159 killed, 163 in 1953.

12 *BWT*, 18 May 1951.

13 *BNL*, 29 Sept. 1951.

14 Newtownabbey Urban District Council minutes (PRONI, LA/59/2CA/2, 19 Jan. 1959); Antrim County Council: minute book, quarterly and annual meetings (PRONI, LA/1/2/ GA/48, 9 Sept. 1947); *BWT*, 30 Mar. 1955: Belfast RDC were told that the numbers of accidents on

the Antrim Road between the city boundary (roughly Serpentine Road) and Ballyhenry, just beyond Glengormley, was due to bad lighting (numbers rising from 1953 and four killed in 1955); *NW*, 13 Apr. 1954, gives figures over the years as an argument for the development of motorways; *UYB* has annual figures: *UYB* (1956), 139–40, shows the increase.

15 Trust selling site for school (PRONI, VAL/8/415, 1951–2); *BNL*, 4 Jan. 1955 and 13 Oct. 1955, reporting the opening of the Throne school at Ballygolan.

16 *BT*, 24 Apr. 1958 and 23 Apr. 1949, on the opening of Graymount.

17 *BSD* (1957), 35a.

18 *BT*, 14 Jan. 1959; *IN*, 14. Jan. 1959; and *BWT*, 6 Mar. 1959, on the school flags, including a picture of Dunlambert.

19 QUB/J/1/7, 5 Feb. 1953, 28 Feb. 1955, 22 Oct. 1956, 4 Feb. 1958, box 14.

20 Richard Hayward, in *Ulster and the City of Belfast* (Ballycastle, 1950), 46, rails against the terrible town planning in Belfast and the habit of planners of eradicating what went before, though he depicts a city quite at ease with itself. Not until 1972 did Northern Ireland have listed-buildings legislation.

21 *BNL*, 4 Jan. 1955.

22 Patrick Shea (then a civil servant at the Ministry of Education), covers this from the inside: *Voices and the Sound of Drums* (Belfast, 1983), 160–4; D.H. Akenson, *Education and Enmity: The Control of Schooling in Northern Ireland, 1920–50* (Newton Abbot, 1973); Elliott, *Catholics of Ulster*, 461–2;

Fionnuala O'Connor, *In Search of a State: Catholics in Northern Ireland* (Belfast, 1993), 312–13; *Northern Ireland Parliamentary Debates*, vol. 30, 2,268–87, the second reading of the Education Bill, 23 Oct. 1946.

23 Ironically, this was the same complaint as facing Brooke from his own party and the UUC. See John Privilege, 'The Northern Ireland Government and the Welfare State, 1942–8: The Case of Health Provision', *Irish Historical Studies*, vol. 39, no. 155 (May 2015), 447.

24 Editorial, *IN*, 16 Jan. 1948: while accepting its merits, the bulk of this editorial denounces the legislation as 'unjust to the Catholic community', an example of English secularism and agnosticism that 'will strengthen further the control of the State'; 'The Aggression of the State: We Will Resist', *IN*, 9 Feb. 1948; McNeilly, *Exactly 50 Years*, 68–9; Bardon, *History of Ulster*, 593–5.

25 Michael McGrath, *The Catholic Church and Catholic Schools in Northern Ireland* (Dublin, 2000), 112–26, 144–5; Elliott, *Catholics of Ulster*, 462.

26 I have analysed the literature and various arguments about this in my *Catholics of Ulster*, 258–65; Akenson, *Education and Enmity*, remains the most powerful account.

27 McNeilly, *Exactly 50 Years*, 80–90, 134–5.

28 Progress was charted in *UYB* (1950), 174–6, (1953), 171–2, (1956), 179–80, (1957–9), 183–4, (1960–2), 186–8; PRONI, Education Archive, historical introduction, 83.

29 For example, the Star of the Sea club on the Shore Road, the subject of the BBC 1982 documentary *Old Scores*.

30 Oliver, *Working at Stormont*, 69; Romie Lambkin, in *My Time in the War*, 55, described being 'spellbound' by a lecture she attended in Belfast in 1943 on Beveridge: 'a kind of Utopian way of things … when everyone, no matter how poor, will be properly cared for'.

31 Thomas Carnwath, *Report to the Special Committee of Belfast Corporation on the Municipal Health Services of the City* (Belfast, 1941); *see* Boal and Royle (eds), *Enduring City*, 242, 247; *UYB* (1957–9), xix.

32 'Tuberculosis in Retreat', *BT*, 21 May 1956 and 30 Dec. 1957, describing plenty of food supplies now in the shops; *UYB* (1957–9), xxii–xxiii, (1950), 46, (1953), 44; significant number of chest hospitals in 1950 (PRONI, VAL/8/435, 1950); Caoimhghín S. Breathnach and John B. Moynihan, 'Brice Clarke (1895–1975) and the Control of Tuberculosis in Northern Ireland', *Ulster Medical Journal*, vol. 78, no. 3 (2009), 179–84; Greta Jones, *'Captain of All These Men of Death': The History of Tuberculosis in Nineteenth and Twentieth Century Ireland* (Amsterdam, 2001), 192, 217–19, 229–30, shows a wartime peak in Northern Ireland of 104 deaths per 100,000, then rapid decline after the war (the biggest decline in the British Isles). The figure dropped to twenty-three by 1953 and eight by 1963.

33 *BT*, 29 Jan. and 1 Feb. 1963. *Annual Report. 3rd, 1950 on the Health of County Antrim* (Belfast, 1951),

12, reports a steady decline in the previous three years; Antrim County Health Committee, *Medical Officer's Report for the Year 1957* (Ballycastle, 1957); *Formation of the Northern Ireland Tuberculosis Authority*, supplement to *Ulster Medical Journal*, vol. 58 (1989), 30–41, www.ncbi.nlm.nih.gov/pmc/articles/PMC2448157/pdf/ulstermedj00082-0030.

34 *UYB* (1950), 47.

35 Belfast RDC minutes (PRONI, LA/59/2F/23, 28 Aug. 1947, 5 Apr. 1948).

36 *BWT*, 14 Jan. 1949; medical services and supplies were only nominally free, of course, because the public paid for it in taxation.

37 'Surveying the Working of Ulster's New Health Service: Public Rush Effect', *BWT*, 14 Jan. 1949. This gave as one of the reasons for the rush to acquire spectacles the 'old custom' of existing users simply inheriting them from parents or grandparents; *BWT*, 11 Mar. 1949.

38 *BT*, 27 Aug. 1958.

39 *BWT*, 6 May 1949, 25 May 1951; see also Peter Hennessy, *Having It So Good: Britain in the Fifties* (London, 2006), 8. The sweet ration was reimposed later that year because of the rush and lasted until 1953; 'Forgotten Men', *BNL*, 9 Mar. 1954, on dentists earning less because fewer people needed dentures; also, the sudden rush for treatment after the 1948 act. See also *BWT*, 5 Jan. 1951; 'More Bad Teeth Since Sweets De-rationed', *IN*, 26 Jan. 1955.

40 Antrim County Health Committee, *Medical Officers' Report for the Year 1957*, 66.

41 *BWT*, 25 May 1951.

42 Antrim County Health
Committee, *Medical Officers' Report
for the Year 1957*, 47; *BNL*, 6 Jan.
1947, on measles epidemic; *Report
on the Health of the County Borough
of Belfast for the Year 1949*, 50, shows
quite an outbreak of measles,
scarlet fever and whooping cough
in the area; also, a list of inspections
of schoolchildren shows head
infestation the main 'ailment' (ibid.,
46).

43 Dr F.F. Main, chief medical
officer, talk entitled 'Our
Health Services', to the Local
Government Conference (PRONI,
LA/59/2CA/2, 26 Sept. 1959);
Kynaston, *Smoke in the Valley*, 66–7,
on the terrible fear of polio, which
was rife, with outbreaks every
summer (late 1940s); *UYB* (1950),
240–2, on the 1947 outbreak.

44 John Ditch, *Social Policy in
Northern Ireland between 1939 and
1950* (Aldershot, 1988), 95–9;
Cabinet Secretariat: the position
of the Mater Hospital (PRONI,
CAB/9/C/65/5, 1966–70;
CAB/9/C/65/7, 1951–75).

45 Peter Martin, 'Social Policy and
Social Change Since 1914', in Liam
Kennedy and Philip Ollerenshaw
(eds), *Ulster Since 1600: Politics,
Economy, and Society* (Oxford, 2013),
308–24.

46 *UYB* (1950), 234, (1957–9), 217.

47 Editorial, *BT*, 8 Jun. 1956,
criticising the measure as out of
touch with public opinion and the
Unionist Party's own backbenchers;
*Northern Ireland Parliamentary
Debates*, vol. 40 (1956–7), 1,340,
1,785–99, 1,872–7.

48 UUC, *Southern Ireland: State or

Church?* (pamphlet, Belfast, 1951);
Marianne Elliott, *When God Took
Sides: Religion and Identity in Ireland
– Unfinished History* (Oxford, 2009),
208–9; Ferriter, *Transformation of
Ireland*, 501–4, on the importance
of class as well as religious outlooks.

49 Field-Neill Survey, 81. Statistically,
they find family allowances a
significant portion of income of
the poorer families (accounting
for as much as 17–18 per cent of
family income), 31–2.

50 *BT*, 31 Dec. 1948.

51 *BT*, 31 Dec. 1959, says that wages
are up 50 per cent, which is
confirmed in NIHT, *Annual Report*
(1963–4), 12.

52 *BT*, 31 Dec. 1959.

53 F.S.L. Lyons, 'The Twentieth
Century', in T.W. Moody and
J.C. Beckett (eds), *Ulster Since
1800: Second Series – a Social
Survey* (London, 1957), 60 – one
of 22 talks broadcast by the BBC
Northern Ireland Home Service
between October 1956 and March
1957.

8. Arcadia Undone

1 Campbell, *Memories of York Street*, 11.

2 Newtownabbey Urban District
Council minutes (PRONI,
LA/59/2CA/2, 12, 16 Feb., 14 Apr.
and 20 Apr. 1959).

3 Newtownabbey Urban District
Council minutes (PRONI,
LA/59/2CA/2, Dec. 1959), report
of the conference held on 23–6
September; NIHT, *Annual Report*
(1964–5), 8–9, recounting the
NIHT's utter frustration with
the 'depressingly slow' planning
system in Northern Ireland, one
of reasons why Northern Ireland

was so far behind Great Britain in slum clearance. See also *BT*, 16 Apr. 1957, on differences between rural/urban councils and how protective they are of their boundaries.

4   Belfast Corporation/County Borough Council: City Surveyor's Office – commentary on the Matthew Report (PRONI, LA/7/3/E/13/7, 3 May 1963).

5   'The North's Housing: New Towns or Dormitories', *IT*, 16 Feb. 1959; *IN*, 7 Mar. 1951, reflecting on Belfast fifty years previously: 'the city has overlapped its boundary posts to such an extent that its former green belt, which was fairly extensive in 1900–1, has now completely disappeared'; 'Can Belfast's Sprawl Be Halted?', *NW*, 4 Aug. 1953; John Cole, 'Space Is the Key to a New Belfast', *BT*, 16 Jan. 1956, describing overdue slum clearance creating space for similarly overdue developments in Belfast centre, including the blitzed sites and the neglected planning reports of 1945 and 1951.

6   Jones, 'These New Thousands', *BT*, 10 Jul. 1956; Jones continued his attack in his influential book *A Social Geography of Belfast*, 67–70, showing how the expansion had engulfed former villages like Greencastle and Whiteabbey and continued to creep through the Carnmoney gap to give Glengormley 'all the undesirable features of a suburb'.

7   '"Nasty" Letter on Housing from Ministry Irks Councillors', *BT*, 26 Jan. 1960; 'Stormont Hates City Council Says Sir Cecil McKee', *BT*, 1 Jan. 1964; (very stiff) Letter from HLG's John Oliver to the town clerk (PRONI,

LA/7/3/E/13/7, 27 Jan. 1964); 'Belfast Corporation Meeting Says Decisions by the Council Overruled by Stormont', *IN*, 4 Jan. 1955.

8   'Can Belfast's Sprawl Be Halted?', *NW*, 4 Aug. 1953; Parliamentary notice establishing Newtownabbey Urban District Council, *Belfast Gazette*, 23 Nov. 1956.

9   *BNL*, 2–3 Jan. 1957; *IN*, 28 Sept. 1956, though they claimed that the name was chosen from one of the 130 letters they did receive, some from outside the area.

10 *Larne Times*, 3 Apr. 1958; *BWT*, 4 Apr. 1958.

11 *BT*, 4 Feb. 1958.

12 *Larne Times*, 14 Aug. 1958.

13 *BT*, 1 Apr. 1958.

14 *BT*, 20 Apr. 1961, on a meeting representing Cave Hill, Bellevue and Hazelwood, and 27 Apr. on a meeting with the local-government minister.

15 *NW*, 18 Dec. 1958.

16 Bill Morrison, 'Planning the City; Planning the Region', in Boal and Royle (eds), *Enduring City*, 145; Brett, *Housing a Divided Community*, 32: Newtownabbey was 'a missed opportunity to develop a proper New Town'.

17 Robert H. Matthew and Northern Ireland HLG, *Belfast Regional Survey and Plan, 1962: A Report Prepared for the Government of Northern Ireland by Sir Robert H. Matthew* (Belfast, 1964) (hereafter Matthew Report); Mark Hart, 'From Smokestacks to Service Economy: Foundations for a Competitive City?', in Boal and Royle (eds), *Enduring City*, 103.

18 Matthew Report, 9–15, 148–50.

19 Oliver, *Working at Stormont*, 79–80; 'Belfast House-Building … Renewed Demand for Extension of Boundary', *IW*, 8 Jan. 1955; *BT*, 18 Apr. 1957.

20 Oliver, *Working at Stormont*, 81–2; Belfast Corporation/County Borough Council: City Surveyor's Office (PRONI, LA/7/3/E/13/7, 3 May 1963), Matthew Report.

21 Morrison, 'Planning the City', 146–7.

22 NIPC, Linen Hall Library, 614, Housing; *Sunday News*, 28 Jul. 1974. Even when building finally began, there were further delays and chaos caused by those refusing to move out.

23 Oliver, *Working at Stormont*, 86.

24 *BT*, 7 Apr. 1955; *BWT*, 15 Apr. 1955; *BT*, 30 Jan. 1956, article on the approach road, with an artist's sketch. The road had been one of the 1945 report's recommendations: Planning Commission, *Planning Proposals for the Belfast Area*, 7. However, it was still being constructed in 1963–4: Newtownabbey Urban District Council Housing Committee: re-housing of families in Whitewell houses due for demolition yet to take place (PRONI, LA/59/2CA/6, 26 Nov. 1963).

25 *NW*, 13 Apr. 1954.

26 Morrison, 'Planning the City', 148–9; *Sunday News*, 14 Jan. 1973 (NIPC, Linen Hall Library, press cuttings), on working-class people badly affected by the M2 going through their area and never given a chance to voice their opposition.

27 *BNL*, 29 Sept. 1951; Building Design Partnership, *Belfast Urban Area Interim Planning Policy* (Belfast, 1967) shows many of the recommendations of the 1944 report still not achieved.

28 NIHT, *Annual Report* (1952–3), 20, a sentiment reiterated in the report for 1953–4, 11.

29 PRONI, LA/7/3/E/13/7, 3 May 1963. The need to rehouse families from urban motorway and redevelopment schemes is a major theme in trust reports by the end of the 1960s. See NIHT, *Annual Report* (1966–7) and (1968–9).

30 Meeting held at Stormont 15 March 1965 between the Ministry of Development and representatives of the Housing Clearance and Redevelopment Committee (PRONI, LA/7/3E/13/7, 1965); NIHT, *Annual Report* (1957–8), 11–15.

31 Ibid., 13–14; *BT*, 4 Jul. 1958 and *NW*, 17 Jul. 1958, on the NIHT report.

32 NIHT, *Annual Report* (1958–9), 16–17, 23. Rathcoole was the largest NIHT estate in Northern Ireland (*Annual Report* [1964–5], 18).

33 *BT*, 18 Apr. 1957, on Belfast Corporation's slum-clearance report.

34 NIHT, *Annual Report* (1962–3), 33, 40–3; Copies of reports on meetings between Belfast Corporation and NIHT officers (PRONI, LA/7/3E/13/2, Nov. 1964), and Calvert to Dunlop (ibid., 16 Sept. 1964), reporting that seventeen of the White City re-lets went to Belfast families; see also the city surveyor on the Matthew Report (PRONI, LA/7/3E/13/7, 3 May 1963), the

'undeveloped portions' of existing NIHT and Belfast Corporation sites; Graham, *WhiteCity: Crumbling Orlits*, introduction. Thirty-eight dwellings were added in the early 1960s, thirteen of these one-bedroom units for the elderly.

35 Newtownabbey Urban District Council minutes (PRONI, LA/59/2CA/4, 30 Nov. 1959, 10 Apr. 1961; LA/59/2CA/6, 21 Jun. 1963; LA/59/2CA/7, 20 Jan. 1964; LA/59/2CA/4, Mar. 1961), the last on worries about Matthew and rehousing from cleared slums into the wider area.

36 Brett, *Housing a Divided Community*, 33–4, 49; the quote is from city surveyor on the Matthew Report (PRONI, LA/7/3/E/13/7, 3 May 1963).

37 'Slum Clearance', NIHT, *Annual Report* (1954–5), 14–15.

38 Three residents – one Catholic, two Protestant – told me this. John Darby, in *Intimidation and the Control of Conflict in Northern Ireland* (Syracuse, 1986), 32, found the same happening on other mixed estates.

39 CRC: North Belfast Group – second quarterly report, June 1971 (PRONI, CREL/5/2/1, Jun. 1971), 9; Minutes of first to seventy-seventh meetings of Chairman's Committee of Northern Ireland Housing Executive (PRONI, HE/2/1/3/1, 15 Oct. 1975), 164, on problems associated with those coming in from the emergency housing list.

40 Brett, *Housing a Divided Community*, 29.

41 NIHT, *Annual Report* (1961–2), 11; NIHT, *Annual Report* (1965–6),

10–11. Altogether the NIHT built 917 Orlit houses, but almost 7,000 other forms of system-built houses in 1945–66, and Orlit was the only form not still in use by 1966.

42 'No Place Like Home', *Burton Latimer Heritage Society*, 1987, www.burtonlatimer.info/history/proposed-demolition-orlits.html; Jayne McCoy, 'Homes Scandal?', *Diary of a Sutton Councillor*, 2012, jaynemccoysblog.wordpress.com/tag/orlit-homes/; 'Report of the HCT Seminar on 7 December 1983', *Housing Review*, vol. 33, no. 2 (March–April 1984), 69.

43 Graham, *WhiteCity: Crumbling Orlits*, foreword by Vivienne Anderson.

44 *BT*, 6 Sept. 1994.

45 *For Your Benefit* (Ulster Folk and Transport Museum, BBC Northern Ireland Community Archive, 1691, Feb. 1986).

46 Graham, *WhiteCity: Crumbling Orlits*, introduction by Brian Dunn.

47 Ibid., 10–13.

48 Minutes of meetings of board of Northern Ireland Housing Executive (PRONI, HE/2/1/1/18, 25 Feb. 1987), on shops and dwellings at Navarra Place, Whitewell to be demolished: Ordnance Survey 1:2,500 Series, sheet 114-13 (QUB School of Geography, Archaeology and Paleoecology Map Library, 1997).

49 Graham, *WhiteCity: Crumbling Orlits*, 10–11.

50 Editorial: 'Unionist and Labour', *BT*, 7 Apr. 1953.

51 Editorial, *BT*, 30 Jan. 1956, commenting on the economic report by Isles and Cuthbert

(reporting in 1955 but publishing in 1957). Their *Economic Survey of Northern Ireland*, 8–16, stressed that although income in Northern Ireland more than doubled in 1938–51, in 1951 it was only 67 per cent of the average income in the UK as a whole and unemployment was higher. It pointed to the slump in the linen industry and concluded that Northern Ireland needed to attract new industries.

52 *BT*, 2 and 9 Jan. 1956. The weekly articles from 2 January to 20 February 1956 carry upbeat sketches of proposed buildings, roads, amenities etc.

53 See, for example, *BWT*, 2 Feb. 1951, when nineteen-year-old Rose Campbell, a warper, was chosen.

54 NIHT: survey of housing needs in rural areas (PRONI, COM/63/1/389, 1948–50); *BWT*, 2 Feb. 1971.

55 *BT*, 28 Sept. 1956, 21 Jan. 1957 and 22 Nov. 1957; *BNL*, 4 Mar. 1959, on Whiteabbey Bleaching Company going into liquidation, the fifth textile factory to close. Whiteabbey had also been finishers for cotton. There was lots of discussion at the time of the decline of the linen industry – for example, *BT*, 21 Jan. 1957, and the series of articles in January–February 1956 in *BT*; also *BT*, 15 Feb. 1959.

56 *NW*, 17 Jul. 1958; *BT*, 1 Apr. 1958, on new concerns of ICI, Courtaulds, Chemstrand and DuPont; *BT*, 1 Apr. 1955, waxing lyrical about the new fibres and diversification at Doagh Flax Spinning Company; *BT*, 21 Apr.

1955, on the British Thompson-Houston Company opening in Larne.

57 Isles and Cuthbert, *Economic Survey of Northern Ireland*, 35, 281; see also a long article on this in *BNL*, 29 Aug. 1957.

58 Hart, 'From Smokestacks to Service Economy', 88–92; *BNL*, Jan. 1952, reporting on a shortage of steel and a thousand workers laid off at the shipyard, the biggest jump in unemployment since the end of the war (*BT*, 28 Jan. 1952; also *UYB* (1953), 189), 10.4 per cent; 'Bleak Outlook for Shipyard', *BWT*, 24 Feb. 1961, and *BWT*, 14 Apr. 1961, on protest marches by shipyard workers against redundancies; Marc Mulholland, *Northern Ireland at the Crossroads: Ulster Unionism in the O'Neill Years, 1960–9* (Basingstoke, 2000), 33, calls early 1963 'the peak of the unemployment crisis', the highest since 1952.

59 *BT*, 19 Dec. 1958; *IN*, 27 Jul. 1959; BDTUC, *Annual Report* (1953), 3, (1954), 5, (1959), 3, (1960), 3; Patterson, *Ireland Since 1939*, 141–3.

60 Minutes of meetings of board of Northern Ireland Housing Executive (PRONI, HE/2/1/1/2, 4 Apr. 1973): Charles Brett on the damage to the urban environment from the urban motorway, causing sterilisation of large areas of land and rendering it unsuitable for housing or industrial purposes. His committee thought phases 2 and 3 of the urban motorway should be abandoned and that 'their original unqualified support of the Urban Plan was mistaken'.

61 Ron Weiner, *The Rape and Plunder of the Shankill: Community Action,*

the *Belfast Experience* (Belfast, 1980), 94–5, 100–1.

62 Both BDTUC and NIHT reports reflect people's disquiet. See, for example, BDTUC, *Annual Report* (1963), 10 and NIHT, *Annual Report* (1965–6), 9; Morrison, 'Planning the City', 148–9.

63 D.A. Singleton, in 'Belfast Housing Renewal Strategy: A Comment', *Housing Review* (Mar.–Apr. 1983), 42, shows redevelopment had been 'a traumatic experience' in the past; Housing Executive – Belfast Household Survey (PRONI, CENT/1/8/27, 1978) describes the overall decline in Belfast population (huge in the inner city and west Belfast but third-highest in north Belfast, including Bellevue Ward).

64 Brett, *Housing a Divided Community*, 36.

9. Politics, Normal and Otherwise

1 Tom Harrison, Ulster Outlooks (Sussex University, MO2101/13–14, 20 May 1944).

2 See Kynaston, *Smoke in the Valley*, 21–2, 48–51, 79–81, 135, 299.

3 Brendan Lynn, *Holding the Ground: the Nationalist Party in Northern Ireland, 1945–72* (Aldershot, 1997), 25.

4 Paddy Devlin, *Straight Left: An Autobiography* (Belfast, 1994), 73.

5 Field-Neill Survey, 80. The average spend on newspapers was 11d., against 2s. on stamps – i.e. more than double.

6 Fred Boal and Alan Robinson, 'Close Together and Far Apart', *Community Forum*, no. 3 (1972), 7–8, shows the *IN* read by 83 per

cent in a Belfast working-class Catholic area, but the *BNL* not 'widely' read in the working-class Protestant Shankill area, being more middle class in its appeal. The *BT* had a cross-community readership.

7 Even after such appointments, the BBC was still largely Protestant/unionist-dominated far into the 1970s, though it emerges well from a new study of how it operated during the Troubles: Robert J. Savage, *The BBC's 'Irish Troubles': Television, Conflict and Northern Ireland* (Manchester, 2015), 124, 160 and ch. 3.

8 Rex Cathcart, *The Most Contrary Region: The BBC in Northern Ireland 1924–1984* (Belfast, 1984), 175.

9 Ibid., 162.

10 Ibid., 177.

11 Ibid., 187.

12 Ibid., also 109–29, 146–7, 247. *See also* Henderson, *Brum*, 50 and 60 for the problem of the 'which religion' question on application forms.

13 Belfast Central Library, press cuttings, 40, 55, the 1958 elections, reporting half the house returned unopposed. Sir Norman Stronge, speaker of the house, had not had to fight an election since he was returned unopposed in 1938.

14 *IN*, 19 Oct. 1945.

15 Walker, *History of the Ulster Unionist Party*, 147–8. See also Henry Patterson and Eric Kaufmann, *Unionism and Orangeism in Northern Ireland Since 1945: The Decline of the Loyal Family* (Manchester, 2007) for the power Orangeism had within the party and its constant rejection

of any conciliation of the Catholic minority, particularly 63–4, for a public row in 1959 showing the 'limits of liberal Unionism'.

16 The march had been banned by the home affairs minister, George Hanna, with full cabinet approval. See *BWT*, 23 Apr. 1954, containing a speech by Brookeborough at Lurgan, criticising the Orange march through nationalist Annalong, though the *IW*, 1 May 1954, claims he never gave the conciliatory lines of the speech distributed to the press and puts a different spin on it.

17 *IN*, 5 Feb. 1952 and *BWT*, 6 Feb. 1952, reporting flags at half-mast in Dublin; *BWT*, 26 Dec. 1952, 17 Apr. 1953, describing outrage in Éire at the queen's title, but reporting that the ambassador would attend the coronation; *NW*, 16 Feb. 1952, reporting that two services were held for members of the Northern Ireland civil service, a Catholic one attended by six to seven hundred people.

18 *IW*, 7 Mar. 1953; lots of positive reports about Princess Elizabeth in *IN*, e.g. May 1948, 1 May 1953 and 2–3 Jun. 1953. See also Conn McCluskey, *Up Off Their Knees: A Commentary on the Civil Rights Movement in Northern Ireland* (Belfast, 1989), 7; Elliott, *Catholics of Ulster*, 400–1.

19 *IW*, 30 Jan. 1953: Cardinal D'Alton's comments in *IN*, 2 Jun. 1953.

20 *BWT*, 8 Mar. 1957; 'No Surrender', *BT*, 8 Aug. 1958.

21 *BT*, 19–23 Aug. 1958 and Rowel Friers cartoon, *BT*, 29 Aug. 1958. The script for *The Bonefire* is in

the Linen Hall Library's Theatre Collection. It is certainly very critical of Orangeism's virulent anti-popery and the way the 'frenzy of fire and drumming' on the eleventh night can turn the spectators into a murderous 'crazy crowd'.

22 *BT*, 29 Jan. 1960, quoting approvingly a *Times* review; also *BT*, 19–23 and 27–8 Jan. 1960 and Rowel Friers cartoon, *BT*, 23 Jan. 1960. Attracting a Friers cartoon was a true sign of impact.

23 *BT*, 15 Aug. 1958.

24 See, for example, *BWT*, 8 Jan. 1954, 30 Apr. 1954, 24 Feb. 1956 and *BT*, 13 Jul. 1955; Andrew Gailey, *Crying in the Wilderness: Jack Sayers – a Liberal Editor in Ulster, 1939–69* (Belfast, 1995), 47–8.

25 Bloomfield, *Stormont in Crisis*, 79.

26 *BT*, 21 Dec. 1945; 827 people had been detained since 1938.

27 *BT*, 9 Sept. and 31 Dec. 1948; 1950 overview, *BWT*, 5 Jan. 1951.

28 *NW*, 30 Nov. 1950; *BT*, 30 Dec. 1950.

29 *BWT*, 5 Jan. 1951, 23 Feb. 1951.

30 *BWT*, 24 Aug. 1951.

31 *BT*, 23 Jun. 1958.

32 *IW*, 30 Feb. 1954.

33 Speech to the Cromac Unionist Association, *BWT*, 28 Jan. 1955.

34 *BWT*, 26 Jan. 1956; Cardinal D'Alton's Christmas message condemning the IRA, *BWT*, 28 Dec. 1956; *BWT*, 11 Jan. 1957; Bishop of Clogher's condemnations, *BWT*, 13 Apr. 1959.

35 *BT*, 2–7 Feb. 1963, including de Valera's thank you to the RUC.

36 *BNL*, 5 Apr. 1954; *BWT*, 16 Jan.
    1959; *BT*, 14 Jan. 1959, 6 and 15
    Feb. 1959.

37 *IN*, 7 Apr. 1948.

38 Patterson and Kaufmann, *Unionism
    and Orangeism*, 20.

39 Editorial, 'Labour and Partition',
    BNL, 8 Apr. 1953.

40 Sydney Elliott, *Northern Ireland
    Parliamentary Election Results,
    1921–1972* (Chichester, 1973), 28,
    35–50; Aaron Edwards, *A History
    of the Northern Ireland Labour Party:
    Democratic Socialism and Sectarianism*
    (Manchester, 2009), 70–2; Speech
    by Brian Faulkner, *BWT*, 20 Feb.
    1959, in which he also points to
    nationalists voting for the NILP.
    See also Cathcart, *Most Contrary
    Region*, 188: it was for this election
    that the BBC finally won its long
    battle to persuade unionists to
    participate in election broadcasting
    (even if they remained pretty
    intransigent). Things improved in
    future election broadcasts.

41 However, unionists still dominated,
    with 37 MPs, against 8 nationalist
    and 6 for various labour (all
    Belfast), though Belfast was
    different, with 7 non-unionist
    against 10 unionist: Elliott, *Election
    Results*, 93, 123: Budge and
    O'Leary, *Belfast: Approach to Crisis*,
    207–27.

42 Editorial, 'Unionism's Way Ahead',
    BT, 1 Apr. 1958; Gailey, *Crying
    in the Wilderness*, 48–63. Sayers
    had displeased the UUC with
    his editorial and he was to find
    that even unionists he thought
    moderate were reluctant to be seen
    as such within the party.

43 *BWT*, 2 and 9 Jan. 1959; *BT*, 15
    Feb. 1959.

44 *BWT*, 27 Feb. 1959, 10 Apr. 1959,
    1 May 1959; P.J. McLoughlin,
    *John Hume and the Revision of Irish
    Nationalism* (Manchester, 2010),
    9–10; Lynn, *Holding the Ground*,
    141–5.

45 *BWT*, 13 and 27 Nov. 1959; *NW*,
    20 Nov. 1959; Patterson and
    Kaufmann, *Unionism and Orangeism*,
    63–4.

46 *IN*, 16 and 21 Nov. 1959, also 11
    Oct. 1959; *NW*, 20 Nov. 1959.

47 Diary of Sir Basil Brooke, first
    Viscount Brookeborough (PRONI,
    D3004/D/45, 4 Nov. 1959), also
    entries for 10 Nov., 26 Nov. and
    7 Dec. 1959; Lynn, *Holding the
    Ground*, 156–61.

48 Ibid.; *BT*, 31 Dec. 1962 and 5 Jan.
    1963 and 'Year of Conciliatory
    Breezes', *BT*, 28 Dec. 1963, though
    BT, 1 Jan. 1963, suggests that talks
    were unlikely to succeed.

49 *Larne Times*, 13 Feb. 1958.

50 *BT*, 1 Apr. 1958; Edwards, *Northern
    Ireland Labour Party*, 141–2; *BT*,
    1 Apr. 1958, on plans to contest
    all twenty-one seats on the new
    Newtownabbey Urban District
    Council.

51 Edwards, *Northern Ireland Labour
    Party*, 160–3.

52 Mulholland, *Northern Ireland at the
    Crossroads*, 44–5.

53 Editorial, 'Give and Take', *BT*, 31
    Mar. 1955; *BWT*, 22 Apr. and 13
    May 1955. By 1957, however, the
    mainstream press was not making
    much of the notorious Fethard
    boycott of Protestants: see *BWT*,
    28 Jun. 1957, also *BNL*, 11 Jul.
    1957, on Catholics protesting about
    Fethard. But Northern Ireland
    has its own version – Dungiven

Catholic residents boycotting Protestant shops because of a controversial Orange parade and a union flag put in Catholic church grounds: *NW*, 12 Jul. 1958.

54 BDTUC, *Annual Report* (1964), 6–7.

55 Edwards, *Northern Ireland Labour Party*, 130, quoting Robert Bingham, an NILP councillor in Castlereagh.

56 Ibid., 119–32, 141–5; Paul Arthur, in *Special Relationships: Britain, Ireland and the Northern Ireland Problem* (Belfast, 2000), 162, argues that the NILP's fate was sealed by poor organisation, as well as having little foothold outside Belfast.

57 *IN*, 11 Apr. 1966, reporting on the Toomebridge event.

58 Mulholland, *Northern Ireland at the Crossroads*, 97–8, 113–14.

59 David McKittrick, Seamus Kelters, Brian Feeney and Chris Thornton, *Lost Lives: The Stories of the Men, Women, and Children who Died as a Result of the Northern Ireland Troubles* (Edinburgh, 2001), 25–9.

60 *BT*, 27 Jun. 1966; McKittrick *et al.*, *Lost Lives*, 29. Reflecting back on 1966, the moderate press and civic and religious leaders spoke of its 'chilling moments of revelation of hatred and thuggery hidden not far below the surface', and its lessons for the moderate majority: *BT*, 2–4 Jan. 1967.

61 Fergal Tobin, *The Best of Decades: Ireland in the Nineteen Sixties* (Dublin, 1996), 200; Review of 1967, *BT*, 29 Dec. 1967.

62 Austin Currie, *All Hell Will Break Loose* (Dublin, 2004), 42, 58, on the optimism in the air in the

early 1960s, particularly with O'Neill's arrival, and of the author's time at QUB, when he learnt to understand unionism.

63 *BWT*, 9 Mar. and 27 Apr. 1962.

64 Sarah Nelson, *Ulster's Uncertain Defenders: Protestant Political, Paramilitary and Community Groups and the Northern Ireland Conflict* (Belfast, 1984), 49–53.

65 Bloomfield, *Stormont in Crisis*, 78. See also Faulkner's conclusion in Brian Faulkner, *Memoirs of a Statesman* (London, 1978), 53; Tobin, *Best of Decades*, 92–4, and on a 'kind of casual, reflexive bigotry' in the Unionist Party, 93–4.

66 Nelson, *Ulster's Uncertain Defenders*, 53.

10. Troubled Community

1 Roy McFadden, 'Fire Bomb', *A Watching Brief: Poems* (Belfast, 1979), 43. Although actually written about the Belfast Blitz, this poem stands in well for the way many also thought about the Troubles.

2 Ironically the NIHT's demise was officially marked in the hotel just as it, too, was closing (NIPC, Linen Hall Library, press cuttings, 620): *IN*, 1 Oct. 1971.

3 Patricia Craig, *Bookworm: A Memoir of Childhood Reading* (Bantry, 2015), 127.

4 *BT*, 8 May 1974.

5 NIHT, *Annual Report* (1970–1), 21. This was the NIHT's final report.

6 *East Antrim Times*, 10 and 17 Sept. 1971, 31 Mar. and 15 Sept. 1972; Patterson, *Ireland Since 1939*, 225–30.

7 John Darby, Geoff Norris and Northern Ireland CRC, *Intimidation in Housing* (Belfast, 1974), 3; 'AB' squatting files (PRONI, HE/2/8/1–4, 1987–8).

8 Darby *et al.*, *Intimidation in Housing*, appendix a–b; Michael Poole, 'Riot Displacement in 1969', *Fortnight*, no. 22 (Aug. 1971), 9–11; Darby, *Intimidation and the Control of Conflict*, 58.

9 CRC Research Unit, *Flight: A Report on Population Movement in Belfast during August 1971* (Belfast, 1971), which shows that it is still north-west Belfast experiencing most movement; *East Antrim Times*, 12 Aug., 27 Aug., 3 Sept., 17 Sept. and 29 Sept. 1971.

10 Darby *et al.*, *Intimidation in Housing*, 27–30, 34–7; *IN*, 1 Apr. 1974. A Newtownabbey Urban District Council deputation, led by Alliance councillor John Drysdale, went to see the secretary of state, Merlyn Rees, about intimidation in the area, particularly of Catholics. By then the Northern Ireland Office was conducting an inquiry into the conduct of the RUC at the Whiteabbey station. NIPC, Linen Hall Library, press cuttings, 614 Housing: Letters from Rathcoole residents, *IN*, 3 Nov. 1972. *IN*, 1 Apr. 1974, in which the parish priest commented that Catholics lived in these Protestant areas because they did not want to be part of a ghetto and would prefer to stay.

11 *East Antrim Times*, 4 Feb. 1972.

12 CRC: Camplisson's report (PRONI, CREL/5/2/1, 1 Jul. 1971); Newtownabbey Urban District Council minutes: Bawnmore Tenants' Association's campaign for a community centre (PRONI, LA/59/2CA/14, 1971); '100 Children in "No Play" Protest', *BT*, 27 Jul. 1971: 'they marched waving placards and tennis racquets from Bawnmore to Newtownabbey Town Hall last night and surrounded it during council meeting, protesting at the lack of playing facilities'. The 1971 census showed Newtownabbey and west Belfast having the highest number of young adults (aged fifteen to thirty-four) in the Belfast urban area: see Paul A. Compton, *Northern Ireland: A Census Atlas* (Dublin, 1978), 57.

13 CRC: Camplisson's report (PRONI, CREL/5/2/1, 1 Jul. 1971), 6.

14 CRC: North Belfast Group – reports (PRONI, CREL/5/2/1, Aug.–Oct. 1971); Minutes of first to seventy-seventh meetings of Chairman's Committee of Northern Ireland Housing Executive (PRONI, HE/2/1/3/1, 15 Oct. 1975), 164, showing those on the emergency housing list given priority over locals, with the problem noted above.

15 McKittrick *et al.*, *Lost Lives*, 328–30; CAIN, *Sutton Index of Deaths* (1969–2001), cain.ulst.ac.uk/sutton/, 7 Apr. 1972. Uninvolved residents on the estate were to pay a high price in sectarian murders by loyalist paramilitaries.

16 Camplisson, Memo to chairman (PRONI, CREL/1/3/36, n.d.).

17 Camplisson to Rowlands (PRONI, CREL/1/3/36, 1 Mar. 1973); F.W. Boal, P. Doherty and D.G. Pringle, 'Social Problems in the Belfast Urban Area: An Exploratory Analysis', Department of

Notes

Geography, Queen Mary College, University of London, Occasional Paper No. 12 (Jan. 1978), which was based on a study carried out for the CRC, Sept. 1973; Minutes of Police Liaison Committee (PRONI, LA/172/2/1/2, 22 Oct. 1975) expressed 'grave concern at increase of juvenile drinking'.

18 I deduce this from Camplisson's reports up to 1973, where he is reporting issues with neighbouring Graymount, considered a UDA stronghold, but not the White City, though Tartan gangs had definitely recruited there as early as December 1971. See CRC: North Belfast office – correspondence (PRONI, CREL/1/3/36, 1971–3).

19 Nelson, *Ulster's Uncertain Defenders*, 117.

20 Ibid., 117–19.

21 John Dunlop, Roy Adams and Tom Toner, *Report of the Project Team, May 2002: North Belfast Community Action Project* (Belfast, 2002), 142.

22 McKittrick *et al.*, *Lost Lives*, 1,046; *IN*, 30 Mar. 1974.

23 McKittrick *et al.*, *Lost Lives*, 3,046.

24 Ibid., 2,522; *IN*, 3 Mar. 1983. Constable McCormack was an easy target. From the local mixed area of Elmfield in nearby Glengormley/Bellevue, he (perhaps foolishly) carried out this duty alone at the same time every weekday.

25 See, for example, *IN*, 16 Jan. 1976.

26 CAIN, *Subversion in the UDR (Ulster Defence Regiment), by British Military Intelligence* (1973), cain.ulst.ac.uk/publicrecords/1973/subversion_in_the_udr.htm#annexe; *East Antrim Times*, 22

Oct. 1971: the UDR in the area had the biggest number of recruits in the province. As part-timers, its members paid a high price during the Troubles.

27 Northern Ireland Statistics and Research Agency, *Northern Ireland Neighbourhood Information Service*, www.ninis2.nisra.gov.uk; CAIN, *Sutton Index of Deaths* (1969–2001), cain.ulst.ac.uk/sutton/; Martin Melaugh, *Housing and Religion in Northern Ireland* (Coleraine, 1994), Section 3. A 1976 map produced by the director of Military Survey, Ministry of Defence, has the Whitewell area 30–40 per cent Catholic and Whitehouse 40–60 per cent: Northern Ireland Religious Areas: Scale 1:250,000, Ministry of Defence, London (QUB School of Geography, Archaeology and Paleoecology Map Library, 1976).

28 I.G. Shuttleworth and C.D. Lloyd, *Mapping Segregation in Belfast: Northern Ireland Housing Executive Estates, Belfast – Northern Ireland Housing Executive* (Belfast, 2007), 22, 38, 47.

29 'The Plight of Catholics in Newtownabbey' (PRONI, D3564/2/16, 1974). This document was part of a campaign by Catholic clerics Fr Denis Faul and Fr Raymond Murray to highlight sectarianism in the RUC and appeared in their *The RUC: The Black and Blue Book* (Cavan, 1975), 87–90. The White City does not appear in the CRC's 1974 report, Darby *et al.*, *Intimidation in Housing*, though Rathcoole and adjacent areas do.

30 Darby, *Intimidation and the Control of Conflict*, 140.

31 NIHE, *Annual Report* (1973–4), 7.

32 NIHT, *Annual Report* (1969–70), 10.

33 Brett, *Housing a Divided Community*, 41; NIHT, Manual of Housing Management (NIHE Library, 009827, 1965), amendment to paragraph 340, 8 Oct. 1968: a facility for payment by Giro was first introduced at this time, but the White City was not included at this point; Minutes of meetings of board of Northern Ireland Housing Executive (PRONI, HE/2/1/1/2, 7 Feb. 1973), on payment of rents by Giro in view of armed robberies; Singleton, 'Belfast Housing Renewal Strategy', 41, on the decline in housing conditions magnified by the Troubles and how paramilitaries were now empowering groups to stop redevelopment. The NIPC press cuttings (614) contain a huge amount on squatting, particularly *BT*, 1 Feb. 1973, and the 'chancers' using the Troubles and rent strikes as a cover to get better houses. See also, for rent arrears, rarely a problem in NIHT days: Special meeting of Newtownabbey Borough Council (PRONI, LA/172/2/2/4, 19 Jan. 1981), 1,885–6.

34 NIHE, *Seventh Report* (1977–8), 15. Local community associations also assisted in the decline in squatting – see NIHE, *Sixth Report* (1976–7), 1; the Housing Executive had to accept a role for local tenants' associations, which also included paramilitaries – see *BT*, 24 Jun. 1974, on this and the UDA role in Newtownabbey; see NIPC, Linen Hall Library, press cuttings (614) and *BT*, 2 Nov. 1972 on housing figures.

35 Brett, *Housing a Divided Community*, 70–1.

36 Padraig O'Malley, *Biting at the Grave: The Irish Hunger Strikes and the Politics of Despair* (Belfast, 1990), 283–4; Tom Cunningham, 'Introduction', *Stella Maris Secondary School*, stellamarissecondary.com, a very good history of the school and times.

37 McKittrick *et al.*, *Lost Lives*, 884–6; Jack Holland, 'The Voices of Loyalist Extremism', *Hibernia*, 25 Jun. 1975.

38 CAIN, *Sutton Index of Deaths* (1969–2001), cain.ulst.ac.uk/ sutton/; John Gray, in his forthcoming *Upon the Belfast Mountain: The Annals of Ben Madigan or the Cave Hill*, speaks of two other IRA murders there, that of fifteen-year-old Bernard Taggart, who had a mental age of eight, in November 1973, and foreman gardener Julian Patrick Connolly in 1981; *East Antrim Times*, 24 May 1974, on the Ulster Workers' Council strike, of which it is very critical – the newspaper was still consciously cross-community.

39 Brett, *Housing a Divided Community*, frontispiece and end-piece: 'Belfast Urban Area, Autumn, 1985'.

40 Housing Executive Research Unit, *Greater Whitewell Community Survey*, 17.

41 *IN*, 8 Jul. 2003.

42 *BT*, 14 and 29 Jul. 1997.

43 *Sunday Tribune*, 26 Jun. 2005.

44 Belfast Interface Project, *Belfast Interfaces: Security Barriers and Defensive Use of Space* (Belfast, 2012), 112–15; Neil Jarman,

Notes

Demography, Development and Disorder: Changing Patterns of Interface Areas (Belfast, 2004), paragraphs 24, 49.

45 *Sunday Tribune*, 26 Jun. 2005.

46 Eric Cownie (ed.), *The Whitewell Youth Mediation Project: Engaging with Disaffected Youths in an Interface Context, a Case Study* (Belfast, 2008), 47.

47 Dunlop *et al.*, *North Belfast Community Action Project*, 8.

48 Ibid.

49 Cownie (ed.), *Whitewell Youth Mediation Project*, 29.

50 *BT*, 21 and 23 Mar. 2005; Lee Reynolds, 'Do As We Say Not As We Do?', *Slugger O'Toole*, 5 May 2006, sluggerotoole. com/2006/05/05/do_as_we_ say_not_as_we_do, on an Easter republican parade in paramilitary gear on the Whitewell Road.

51 Cownie (ed.), *Whitewell Youth Mediation Project*, 36.

52 Ibid., 47.

53 Ibid., 34.

54 'Roads in Northern Ireland Affected by Flag Protests', *BBC News*, 11 Jan. 2013, www.bbc. co.uk/news/uk-northern-ireland-20985522 (accessed Aug. 2017).

Afterword

1 'Castle', *Belfast City Council Elections 1997*, gi0rtn.tripod.com/ belfast/97castle.html.

2 The castle has survived, according to John Gray, in his forthcoming *Upon the Belfast Mountain*, 'years of neglect' by Belfast Corporation and efforts 'to hive it off' to private

enterprise with plans for a luxury hotel in 1969.

3 Antrim County Council: minute book, quarterly and annual meetings (PRONI, LA/1/2/ GB/59, 12 Feb. 1958) – North Approach Road, diversion of Longlands Road, vesting order.

4 'Bonfire Gatherers in Cowardly Graffiti Threat', *North Belfast News*, 27 Jun. 2015, which blames a small number of dissident republicans in the area: 'However it is understood other than a handful of individuals they have little or no support.'

5 Alyn, *Sound of Anthems*, 30–3.

6 This is the conclusion of Dunlop *et al.*, *North Belfast Community Action Project* (Belfast, 2002), 7, 10, 20, 125.

7 Brendan Murtagh, 'Integrated Social Housing in Northern Ireland', *Housing Studies*, vol. 16, no. 6 (2001), 778–9, also found lower rates of intimidation and Troubles-related deaths on mixed estates.

8 Christel McMullan, 'Island or Bridge? An Ethnographic Study of an Integrated School in Northern Ireland' (PhD thesis, QUB, 2003).

9 *IN*, 11 Jul. 2015 and 26 Oct. 2015.

10 James Anderson and Ian Shuttleworth, 'Sectarian Demography, Territoriality and Political Development in Northern Ireland', *Political Geography*, vol. 17, no. 2 (1998), 198–201.

11 Executive Office, *Together: Building a United Community Strategy* (2013), www.executiveoffice-ni.gov.uk/ publications/together-building-united-community-strategy, 3. For this section I commissioned a report from Liverpool Institute of Irish Studies postgraduate,

Elizabeth De Young, who argues that this policy document does not emphasise a specific community-relations remit: Elizabeth De Young, 'The State of Integrated Housing' (unpublished report, 2016), 7–8.

12 Jonny Byrne, Ulf Hansson and John Bell, *Shared Living: Mixed Residential Communities in Northern Ireland* (Belfast, 2006), 20, 124, 128.

13 Executive Office, *Together: Building a United Community Strategy* (2013), www.executiveoffice-ni.gov.uk/ publications/together-building-united-community-strategy.

14 *BT*, 17 Jul. 1956.

15 Transcript of Cameron's meeting with NIHT representatives (PRONI, GOV/2/1/197, 2 Jul. 1969).

Bibliography

PUBLISHED SOURCES

'1969: The Housing Crisis', supplement to *Build* (Apr. 1969).

Akenson, D.H., *Education and Enmity: The Control of Schooling in Northern Ireland, 1920–50* (Newton Abbot, 1973).

Alexander, Neal, *Ciaran Carson: Space, Place, Writing* (Liverpool, 2010).

Allen, Nicholas and Aaron Kelly (eds), *The Cities of Belfast* (Dublin, 2003).

Alyn, Marjory, *The Sound of Anthems* (London, 1983).

Anderson, Don, *Oaklee: The First 30 Years* (Belfast, 2010).

Anderson, James and Ian Shuttleworth, 'Sectarian Demography, Territoriality and Political Development in Northern Ireland', *Political Geography*, vol. 17, no. 2 (1998).

Antrim County Health Committee, *Medical Officer's Report for the Year 1957* (Ballycastle, 1957).

Annual report. 3rd, 1950 on the Health of County Antrim (Belfast, 1951).

Arthur, Paul, *Special Relationships: Britain, Ireland and the Northern Ireland Problem* (Belfast, 2000).

Bardon, Jonathan, *A History of Ulster* (Belfast, 1992).

Barton, Brian, *The Belfast Blitz: The City in the War Years* (Belfast, 2015).

Belfast and District Trades Union Council, *Annual Reports* (Belfast, 1948–74).

Belfast Interface Project, *Belfast Interfaces: Security Barriers and Defensive Use of Space* (Belfast, 2012).

Belfast Official Industrial Handbook (Belfast, 1952).

Belfast Street Directory (Belfast, 1949–57).

Bender, Barbara (ed.), *Landscape: Politics and Perspectives* (Oxford, 1993).

Benes, Jaromir and Marek Zvelebil, 'Historical Interactive Landscape in the Heart of Europe: The Case of Bohemia', in Peter J. Ucko and Robert Layton (eds), *The Archaeology and Anthropology of Landscape: Shaping your Landscape* (London, 1999).

Benn, George, *A History of the Town of Belfast from the Earliest Times to the Close of the Eighteenth Century* (London, 1877).

Beringer, T.R.O., 'The Throne Hospital: A Short History', *Ulster Medical Journal*, vol. 67, no. 2 (Nov. 1998).

Bigger, F.C. and J.S. Crone (eds), *In Remembrance: Articles and Sketches, Biographical, Historical, Topographical by Francis Joseph Bigger* (Dublin, 1927).

Bird, Eric L., 'The Work of the Northern Ireland Housing Trust', *Journal of the Royal Institute of British Architects* (Nov. 1949).

Birrell, Derek, Alan Murie and J.G. Calvert, 'Housing Policy in Northern Ireland: Facts and Findings', *Community Forum*, no. 2 (1972).

Blake, John W., *Northern Ireland in the Second World War* (Belfast, 1956).

Bloomfield, Ken, *Stormont in Crisis: A Memoir* (Belfast, 1994).

Boal, Frederick W., P. Doherty and D.G. Pringle, 'Social Problems in the Belfast Urban Area: An Exploratory Analysis', Department of Geography, Queen Mary College, University of London, Occasional Paper No. 12 (Jan. 1978).

Boal, Frederick W. and Alan Robinson, 'Close Together and Far Apart', *Community Forum*, no. 3 (1972).

Boal, Frederick W. and Stephen A. Royle (eds), *Enduring City: Belfast in the Twentieth Century* (Belfast, 2006).

Bosi, Lorenzo and Simon Prince, 'Writing the Sixties into Northern Ireland and Northern Ireland into the Sixties', *The Sixties*, vol. 2, no. 2 (2009).

Breathnach, Caoimhghín S. and John B. Moynihan, 'Brice Clarke (1895–1975) and the Control of Tuberculosis in Northern Ireland', *Ulster Medical Journal*, vol. 78, no. 3 (2009).

Brett, C.B.E., *Housing a Divided Community* (Dublin, 1986).

Brett, David, 'Geologies of Site and Settlement', in Nicholas Allen and Aaron Kelly (eds), *The Cities of Belfast* (Dublin, 2003).

Browne, Reginald and National Federation of Housing Societies, *The Housing Society Movement in Britain* (London, 1943).

Budge, Ian and Cornelius O'Leary, *Belfast: Approach to Crisis – a Study of Belfast Politics 1613–1970* (London, 1973).

Building Design Partnership, *Belfast Urban Area Interim Planning Policy* (Belfast, 1967).

Byrne, Jonny, Ulf Hansson and John Bell, *Shared Living: Mixed Residential Communities in Northern Ireland* (Belfast, 2006).

Cameron, John and Northern Ireland Government, *Disturbances in Northern Ireland: Report of the Commission Appointed by the Governor of Northern Ireland* (Belfast, 1969).

Bibliography

Cameron, Stephen, *Death in the North Channel: The Loss of the* Princess Victoria, *January 1953* (Newtownards, 2002).

Campbell, John, *Memories of York Street* (Belfast, 1991).

Carnwath, Thomas, *Report to the Special Committee of Belfast Corporation on the Municipal Health Services of the City* (Belfast, 1941).

Cathcart, Rex, *The Most Contrary Region: The BBC in Northern Ireland 1924–1984* (Belfast, 1984).

Cole, Tim, '(Re)visiting Auschwitz: (Re)encountering the Holocaust in its Landscapes', *Cultural History*, vol. 2, no. 2 (2013).

Community Relations Commission Research Unit, *Flight: A Report on Population Movement in Belfast during August 1971* (Belfast, 1971).

Compton, Paul A., *Northern Ireland: A Census Atlas* (Dublin, 1978).

Connolly, S.J. (ed.), *Belfast 400: People, Place and History* (Liverpool, 2012).

Cownie, Eric (ed.), *The Whitewell Youth Mediation Project: Engaging with Disaffected Youths in an Interface Context, a Case Study* (Belfast, 2008).

Craig, Patricia, 'Village Voices', in Frederick W. Boal and Stephen A. Royle (eds), *Enduring City: Belfast in the Twentieth Century* (Belfast, 2006).

————, *Bookworm: A Memoir of Childhood Reading* (Bantry, 2015).

Currie, Austin, *All Hell Will Break Loose* (Dublin, 2004).

D'Orbán, P.T., 'Baby Stealing', *British Medical Journal*, vol. 2, no. 5, 814 (1972).

Darby, John, *Intimidation and the Control of Conflict in Northern Ireland* (Syracuse, 1986).

Darby, John, Geoff Norris and Northern Ireland Community Relations Commission, *Intimidation in Housing* (Belfast, 1974).

Darley, Gillian, *Octavia Hill* (London, 1990).

Day, Angélique and Patrick McWilliams (eds), *Ordnance Survey Memoirs of Ireland, vol. 2: Parishes of County Antrim I, 1838–9* (Belfast, 1990).

Debord, Guy, 'Introduction to a Critique of Urban Geography', in Harald Bauder and Salvatore Engel-Di Mauro (eds), *Critical Geographies: A Collection of Readings* (Kelowna, B.C., 2008).

Devlin, Paddy, *Straight Left: An Autobiography* (Belfast, 1994).

De Young, Elizabeth, 'The State of Integrated Housing' (unpublished report, 2016).

Dickson, David, *Dublin: The Making of a Capital City* (London, 2014).

Ditch, John, *Social Policy in Northern Ireland between 1939 and 1950* (Aldershot, 1988).

Doherty, James, *Post 381: The Memoirs of a Belfast Air Raid Warden* (Belfast, 1989).

Dubourdieu, John, *Statistical Survey of the County of Antrim* (Dublin, 1812).

Duncan, James S., Nuala C. Johnson and Richard H. Schein (eds), *A Companion to Cultural Geography* (Oxford, 2004).

Dunlop, John, Roy Adams and Tom Toner, *Report of the Project Team, May 2002: North Belfast Community Action Project* (Belfast, 2002).

Edwards, Aaron, *A History of the Northern Ireland Labour Party: Democratic Socialism and Sectarianism* (Manchester, 2009).

Elliott, Marianne, *When God Took Sides: Religion and Identity in Ireland – Unfinished History* (Oxford, 2009).

———, *The Catholics of Ulster: A History* (London, 2000).

Elliott, Sydney, *Northern Ireland Parliamentary Election Results, 1921–1972* (Chichester, 1973).

Faul, Denis and Raymond Murray, *The RUC: The Black and Blue Book* (Cavan, 1975).

Faulkner, Brian, *Memoirs of a Statesman* (London, 1978).

Ferriter, Diarmaid, *The Transformation of Ireland 1900–2000* (London, 2004).

Field, Dorita E. and Desmond G. Neill, *A Survey of New Housing Estates in Belfast: A Social and Economic Study of the Estates Built by the Northern Ireland Housing Trust in the Belfast Area 1945–1954* (Belfast, 1957).

Fisk, Robert, *In Time of War: Ireland, Ulster and the Price of Neutrality, 1939–45* (Dublin, 1983).

Fleming, George, *Magennis VC: The Story of Northern Ireland's Only Winner of the Victoria Cross* (Dublin, 1998).

Gailey, Andrew, *Crying in the Wilderness: Jack Sayers – a Liberal Editor in Ulster, 1939–69* (Belfast, 1995).

Gallagher, Eric, *At Points of Need: The Story of the Belfast Central Mission, Grosvenor Hall, 1889–1989* (Belfast, 1989).

Bibliography

Gardiner, Juliet, *The Blitz: The British Under Attack* (London, 2010).

———, *Wartime: Britain 1939–1945* (London, 2004).

Gill, Conrad, *The Rise of the Irish Linen Industry* (Oxford, 1925 [reprinted 1964]).

Girvan, Sean, *Cavehill: A Short Illustrated History* (Belfast, 1994).

Graham, Donald and North Belfast Community Resource Centre, *WhiteCity: Crumbling Orlits* (Belfast, 1986).

Gray, John, 'New Future for the Floral Hall', *The Cave Hill Campaigner* (Summer 2011).

———, *The Great Cave Hill Right of Way Case* (Belfast, 2010).

Grimshaw, William, *Incidents Recalled: Or, Sketches from Memory* (Philadelphia, PA, 1848).

Hägerstrand, T., 'Presence and Absence: A Look at Conceptual Choices and Bodily Necessities', *Regional Studies*, vol 18, no. 5 (1984).

Hanley, Lynsey, *Estates: An Intimate History* (London, 2007).

Hanna, Erika, *Modern Dublin: Urban Change and the Irish Past, 1957–1973* (Oxford, 2013).

Hart, Mark, 'From Smokestacks to Service Economy: Foundations for a Competitive City?', in Frederick W. Boal and Stephen A. Royle (eds), *Enduring City: Belfast in the Twentieth Century* (Belfast, 2006).

Hayward, Richard, *Ulster and the City of Belfast* (Ballycastle, 1950).

Heenan, Deirdre and Anne Marie Gray, 'Administration in Ireland: The Significance of Public Bodies', *Studies: An Irish Quarterly Review*, vol. 89, no. 356 (winter 2000).

Henderson, Brum, *Brum: A Life in Television* (Belfast, 2003).

Hennessy, Peter, *Having It So Good: Britain in the Fifties* (London, 2006).

Hepburn, A.C., *A Past Apart: Studies in the History of Catholic Belfast, 1850–1950* (Belfast, 1996).

Hill, Octavia, *Octavia Hill's Letters to Fellow Workers 1872–1911: Together with an Account of the Walmer Street Industrial Experiment* (Robert Whelan, ed.) (London, 2005).

Housing in Northern Ireland: Interim Report of the Planning Advisory Board (Belfast, 1944).

Hunter, Jack, *The Loss of the Princess Victoria* (2nd ed., Stranraer, 2010).

Isles, K.S. and N. Cuthbert, *An Economic Survey of Northern Ireland* (Belfast, 1957).

Jarman, Neil, *Demography, Development and Disorder: Changing Patterns of Interface Areas* (Belfast, 2004).

Jones, Emrys, *A Social Geography of Belfast* (London, 1960).

———, 'Belfast: A Survey of the City', in British Association for the Advancement of Science, *Belfast in its Regional Setting: A Scientific Survey* (Belfast, 1952).

Jones, Greta, *'Captain of All These Men of Death': The History of Tuberculosis in Nineteenth and Twentieth Century Ireland* (Amsterdam, 2001).

Juvenile Delinquency: Interim Report of the Northern Ireland Child Welfare Council (Belfast, 1954).

Kynaston, David, *Family Britain 1951–57* (London, 2009).

———, *Austerity Britain 1948–51: Smoke in the Valley* (London, 2008).

———, *Austerity Britain 1945–48: A World to Build* (London, 2007).

Lambkin, Romie, *My Time in the War: An Irishwoman's Diary* (Dublin, 1992).

Lynn, Brendan, *Holding the Ground: the Nationalist Party in Northern Ireland, 1945–72* (Aldershot, 1997).

Lyons, F.S.L., 'The Twentieth Century', in T.W. Moody and J.C. Beckett (eds), *Ulster Since 1800: Second Series – a Social Survey* (London, 1957).

Maginnis, Hilary, 'Some Belfast Business Families and Their Houses', *North Irish Roots*, vol. 13, no. 2 (2002).

Maguire, W.A., *Belfast: A History* (Lancaster, 2009).

Mahon, Derek, *New Collected Poems* (Gallery, 2011).

Martin, Peter, 'Social Policy and Social Change Since 1914', in Liam Kennedy and Philip Ollerenshaw (eds), *Ulster Since 1600: Politics, Economy, and Society* (Oxford, 2013).

Matthew, Robert H. and Northern Ireland Ministry of Health and Local Government, *Belfast Regional Survey and Plan, 1962: A Report Prepared for the Government of Northern Ireland by Sir Robert H. Matthew* (Belfast, 1964).

McCloone, Martin (ed.), *Culture, Identity and Broadcasting in Ireland: Local Issues, Global Perspectives – Proceedings of the Cultural Traditions Group/Media Studies UUC Symposium, 21 February, 1991* (Belfast, 1991).

McCluskey, Conn, *Up Off Their Knees: A Commentary on the Civil Rights Movement in Northern Ireland* (Belfast, 1989).

McFadden, Roy, 'Fire Bomb', *A Watching Brief: Poems* (Belfast, 1979).

McFetridge, Stewart, *Bellevue: Belfast's Mountain Playground – Things You Didn't Know or Had Forgotten* (Belfast, 1995).

McGrath, Michael, *The Catholic Church and Catholic Schools in Northern Ireland: The Price of Faith* (Dublin, 2000).

McIntosh, Gillian, *The Force of Culture: Unionist Identities in Contemporary Ireland* (Cork, 1999).

McKittrick, David, Seamus Kelters, Brian Feeney and Chris Thornton, *Lost Lives: The Stories of the Men, Women, and Children who Died as a Result of the Northern Ireland Troubles* (Edinburgh, 2001).

McLoughlin, P.J., *John Hume and the Revision of Irish Nationalism* (Manchester, 2010).

McMullan, Christel, 'Island or Bridge? An Ethnographic Study of an Integrated School in Northern Ireland' (PhD thesis, QUB, 2003).

McNeill, Mary, *The Life and Times of Mary Ann McCracken, 1770–1866: A Belfast Panorama* (Dublin, 1960).

McNeilly, Norman, *Exactly 50 Years: The Belfast Education Authority and Its Work (1923–73)* (Belfast, 1974).

Megaw, R.D. and Northern Ireland Ministry of Home Affairs, *Report of Enquiry into the Housing Schemes of Belfast Corporation* (Belfast, 1926).

Meinig, D.W. (ed.), *The Interpretation of Ordinary Landscapes: Geographical Essays* (Oxford, 1979).

Melaugh, Martin, *Housing and Religion in Northern Ireland* (Coleraine, 1994).

Milligan, Alice, *Poems by Alice Milligan: Selected and Edited with an Introduction by Henry Mangan* (Henry Mangan, ed.) (Dublin, 1954).

Mitchell, Frank and Michael Ryan, *Reading the Irish Landscape* (3rd ed., Dublin, 1997).

Moody, T.W. and J.C. Beckett (eds), *Ulster Since 1800: Second Series – a Social Survey* (London, 1957).

Moran, Joe, *Armchair Nation: An Intimate History of Britain in Front of the TV* (London, 2014).

Morin, Karen M., 'Landscape: Representing and Interpreting the World', in Sarah Holloway, Stephen P. Rice and Gill Valentine (eds), *Key Concepts in Geography* (2nd ed., London, 2009).

Morrisson, Bill, 'Planning the City; Planning the Region', in Frederick W. Boal and Stephen A. Royle (eds), *Enduring City: Belfast in the Twentieth Century* (Belfast, 2006).

Mulholland, Marc, *Northern Ireland at the Crossroads: Ulster Unionism in the O'Neill Years, 1960–9* (Basingstoke, 2000).

Murie, A., W.D. Birell, P.A.R. Hillard and D. Roche, 'Housing Policy Between the Wars: Northern Ireland, England and Wales', *Social Policy and Administration*, vol. 5, no. 4 (Oct. 1971).

Murtagh, Brendan, 'Ethno-Religious Segregation in Post-Conflict Belfast', *Built Environment*, vol. 37, no. 2 (2011).

———, 'Integrated Social Housing in Northern Ireland', *Housing Studies*, vol. 16, no. 6 (2001).

Nelson, Sarah, *Ulster's Uncertain Defenders: Protestant Political, Paramilitary and Community Groups and the Northern Ireland Conflict* (Belfast, 1984).

Northern Ireland Housing Executive, *Annual Reports* (1973–2001).

Northern Ireland Housing Trust, *Annual Reports* (1945–71).

Northern Ireland Ministry of Health and Local Government, *Inspector's Report on Belfast Corporation Housing Allocations Inquiry* (Belfast, 1954).

Northern Ireland Planning Commission, *Planning Proposals for the Belfast Area: Interim (Second) Report of the Planning Commission* (Belfast, 1945).

Northern Ireland: Planning for Prosperity (supplement to *Advertisers Weekly*, no. 4) (1956).

O'Byrne, Cathal, *As I Roved Out* (Belfast, 1946).

O'Connell, Sean, 'An Age of Conservative Modernity, 1914–1968', in S.J. Connolly (ed.), *Belfast 400: People, Place and History* (Liverpool, 2012).

O'Connor, Fionnuala, *In Search of a State: Catholics in Northern Ireland* (Belfast, 1993).

O'Laverty, J., *An Historical Account of the Diocese of Down and Connor, Ancient and Modern* (5 vols, Dublin, 1878–95).

Oliver, John A., *Working at Stormont: Memoirs* (Dublin, 1978).

O'Malley, Padraig, *Biting at the Grave: The Irish Hunger Strikes and the Politics of Despair* (Belfast, 1990).

Patterson, Henry, *Ireland Since 1939: The Persistence of Conflict* (Dublin, 2006).

Patterson, Henry and Eric Kaufmann, *Unionism and Orangeism in Northern Ireland Since 1945: The Decline of the Loyal Family* (Manchester, 2007).

Poole, Michael, 'Riot Displacement in 1969', *Fortnight*, no. 22 (Aug. 1971).

Privilege, John, 'The Northern Ireland Government and the Welfare State, 1942–8: The Case of Health Provision', *Irish Historical Studies*, vol. 39, no. 155 (May 2015).

Proctor, E.K., *Belfast Scenery in Thirty Views* (Belfast, 1832).

'Report of the HCT Seminar on 7 December 1983', *Housing Review*, vol. 33, no. 2 (Mar.–Apr. 1984).

Report on the Health of the County Borough of Belfast for the Year 1947, by the Medical Officer for Belfast (Belfast, 1948).

Report on the Health of the County Borough of Belfast for the Year 1949 (Belfast, 1950).

Road Communications in Northern Ireland: Interim Report (Belfast, 1946).

Savage, Robert J., *The BBC's 'Irish Troubles': Television, Conflict and Northern Ireland* (Manchester, 2015).

Scott, Peter, 'Visible and Invisible Walls: Suburbanisation and the Social Filtering of Working-Class Communities in Interwar Britain' (discussion paper, Reading, 2004).

Shea, Patrick, *Voices and the Sound of Drums: An Irish Autobiography* (Belfast, 1983).

Shearman, Hugh, *Ulster* (London, 1949).

Shirlow, Peter and Brendan Murtagh, *Belfast: Segregation, Violence and the City* (London, 2006).

Shuttleworth, I.G. and C.D. Lloyd, *Mapping Segregation in Belfast: Northern Ireland Housing Executive Estates, Belfast – Northern Ireland Housing Executive* (Belfast, 2007).

Simon, Ben, *Voices from Cave Hill* (Belfast, 2010).

Singleton, D.A., 'Belfast Housing Renewal Strategy: A Comment', *Housing Review* (Mar.–Apr. 1983).

Smyth, Peter, *Changing Times: Life in 1950s Northern Ireland* (Newtownards, 2012).

The City of Belfast Official Handbook (London [1950]).

Tobin, Fergal, *The Best of Decades: Ireland in the Nineteen Sixties* (Dublin, 1996).

Ulster Unionist Council, *Southern Ireland: State or Church?* (pamphlet, Belfast, 1951).

Ulster Year Book (1949–65).

Walker, Graham, *A History of the Ulster Unionist Party: Protest, Pragmatism and Pessimism* (Manchester, 2004).

Walsh, Maurice, 'Media and Culture in Ireland, 1960–2008', in Richard Bourke and Ian McBride (eds), *The Princeton History of Modern Ireland* (Princeton, 2016).

Weiner, Ron, *The Rape and Plunder of the Shankill: Community Action, the Belfast Experience* (Belfast, 1980).

Whyte, John, *Interpreting Northern Ireland* (Oxford, 1990).

Young, Robert M. (ed.), *Historical Notices of Old Belfast and Its Vicinity* (Belfast, 1896).

NEWSPAPERS

Belfast Central Library, press cuttings

Belfast Gazette

Belfast News Letter

Belfast Telegraph

Belfast Weekly Telegraph

East Antrim Times/Larne Times

Empire News and Sunday Chronicle

The Herald

Ireland's Saturday Night

Irish Independent

Irish News

Irish Times

Irish Weekly

Larne Times

Newtownabbey Times

North Belfast News

Northern Ireland Political Collection, Linen Hall Library, press cuttings

Northern Whig

The People

Picture Post

Sunday Life
Sunday Tribune
Ulster Herald

ARCHIVE RESOURCES

The National Archives (UK)

CJ3/60: Investigation into discrimination on religious grounds in Northern Ireland: report by Home Office, especially covering local authority housing and employment practises [*sic*], with proposals for further action (1969).

CJ4/156: Housing Executive (Northern Ireland) Act 1971: passage through Northern Ireland Parliament (1970–2).

CJ4/624: Community Relations Commission: aims and work (1971–4).

T233/442: Northern Ireland Housing Trust: formation and financing (1944–50).

Northern Ireland Housing Executive Library (now closed)

009827, Northern Ireland Housing Trust, Manual of Housing Management (1965).

HT.2.NORT, Northern Ireland Housing Trust (1968).

Public Record Office of Northern Ireland

Note: I was surprised at the difficulty in locating and using housing-related records in PRONI and elsewhere. In the transfer from the Housing Trust to the Housing Executive, records seem to have been either lost or destroyed. In PRONI many housing records remained unopened – not because of their sensitive nature, but because they have not yet been vetted or were lost in the system.

CAB/9/B/6/4–5: Cabinet Secretariat: housing – ex-servicemen, Irish Sailors Soldiers Land Trust (1931–68).

CAB/9/B/89/3: Cabinet Secretariat: housing, proposed legislation (1938–48).

CAB/9/C/65/5: Cabinet Secretariat: health service in Northern Ireland (1966–70).

CAB/9/C/65/7: Cabinet Secretariat: Mater hospital – position of Mater hospital (1951–65).

CAB/9/N/4/17: Cabinet Secretariat: housing allocation (1946–56).

CENT/1/8/27: Housing Executive – Belfast Household Survey (1978).

COM/63/1/290: Provision of housing (Housing Trust and local authorities) (1944–52).

COM/63/1/389: Northern Ireland Housing Trust: survey of housing needs in rural areas (1948–50).

CR1/76/E/6, CR1/76/E/8: Preachers' book of Whitehouse Church of Ireland parish, Co. Antrim (1924–76).

CR1/76/G/5: Magazine of Whitehouse Church of Ireland parish, Co. Antrim (1948).

CREL/1/3/36: Community Relations Commission: North Belfast office – correspondence (1971–3).

CREL/1/4/10: Community Relations Commission: local office – 359 Antrim Road, Belfast (1972).

CREL/3/7/1: Community Relations Commission: community development and community relations in Northern Ireland – some proposals (1974).

CREL/5/2/1: Community Relations Commission: North Belfast Group – reports (1971–2).

CREL/5/2/3: Community Relations Commission: expansion proposals (1973).

CREL/6/36–7: Community Relations Commission: press cuttings – social malaise in Belfast (1974).

CREL/6/37: Community Relations Commission: press cuttings – intimidation in housing (1974).

D1327/15/14: Ulster Unionist Council: file containing documents relating to the Housing Sub-Committee (1950–1).

D2086/AA/4: Minute book of the Belfast Council of Social Welfare (1938–52).

D2156/1: A map of Belfast Lough with a plan of the town of Belfast … by … James Lawson (1789).

D2742: William Ward notebooks (1941–8).

D3004/D/45: Diary of Sir Basil Brooke, first Viscount Brookeborough (1956–63).

D3303/14/1–11: Papers of Charles E.B. Brett (1948–79).

D3521/5: Abstract of title of the executors of the will of the late Robert Grimshaw (1871).

D3564/2/16: The Plight of Catholics in Newtownabbey (1974).

D3761/1/1: A brief history of the Belfast Housing Aid Society (1964–79).

D4122/B/81: Bundle of nine photographs relating to Whitehouse (1930–60).

D4122/B/151: Bundle of ten photographs of Irish landscapes (1930–60).

DCR/1/106: Department of Community Relations, Newtownabbey Urban District Council: transcript of guidance (1970).

DCR/1/153: Winding up Department of Community Relations (1974–5).

DCR/1/164: Community Relations Representatives: review (1974–5).

DCR/1/166: Northern Ireland Community Relations Commission: minutes of meetings (1974–5).

DCR/1/175: Newtownabbey Advice Centre, 23 Bencrum Park, Rathcoole (1974–5).

DEV/9/51: Ministry of Development: slum dwellings, details of ministry's proposals (1962–5).

DEV/9/57: Ministry of Development: rented accommodation, schedules of Northern Ireland Housing Trust containing details of costs of (1962–8).

ED/13/1/2283: Ministry of Education: school provision: correspondence with Northern Ireland Housing Trust (1947–9).

FILM18/8, 'Challenge': Housing Trust promotional film (*c.* 1965).

FIN/12/2/15: Ministry of Finance: housing estate developments – authorisation (1947–50)

FIN/18/26/122: Housing: land purchase – Housing Trust application for vesting order, Carnmoney, Belfast (Whitewell), date of vesting order (21 Dec. 1945) (1945–57).

GOV/2/1/197: Cameron Commission: evidence submitted by Northern Ireland Housing Trust per F.W. Hornibrook (general manager), Belfast (1969).

HE/1: Housing Trust [reports] (n.d.).

HE/2/1/1/1–3, 18: Minutes of meetings of board of Northern Ireland Housing Executive (1971–87).

HE/2/1/3/1: Minutes of first to seventy-seventh meetings of Chairman's Committee of Northern Ireland Housing Executive (1973–8).

HE/2/1/13/1: Northern Ireland Housing Executive: chief executive's correspondence (1973–80).

HE/2/8/1–4: Northern Ireland Housing Executive: 'AB' squatting files (1987–8).

HE/2/6/1/3: Northern Ireland Housing Executive: Housing Condition Survey (1974).

HLG/1/4/2: Belfast County Borough Council: infectious diseases – measles (1930–47).

HLG/1/4/4: Welfare Services Bill – general policy (1947–8).

HLG/1/7/1: General statistical information on Health Committee (1949–50).

HLG/1/7/3: Health Services Act (Northern Ireland) 1948: Advisory Committee on the Maternity Services – statistics (1950–1).

HLG/1/14/7: Slum clearance: Committee on Ulster Folk Life and Traditions (1957–60).

HLG/3: HLG: Housing 'HG' files (1922–62).

HLG/3/10: War Damage Committee (1942–6).

HLG/4/18: Belfast County Borough Council: boundary extension (1938).

HLG/4/26: Audit Reports: Belfast Rural District Council (1941–58).

HLG/4/48: Belfast County Borough Council: Belfast Castle: papers concerning acquisition from earl of Shaftesbury (1935).

HLG/6/1/8: Temporary housing (bungalows) policy [1944–50].

HLG/6/1/11: War damage: compensation on dwellings affected by planning schemes (1944).

HLG/6/1/12: Controlled materials for housing schemes (1943–7).

HLG/6/1/13: Housing Act (Northern Ireland) (1945).

HLG/6/1/14: Building industry: questions (1946–9).

HLG/6/1/16: Re-erection of buildings destroyed by enemy action (1944–8).

HLG/6/1/18–19: Planning Branch – policy (1944).

HLG/6/1/24: Housing Trust: general papers (1947–50).

HLG/6/1/27: Housing Act (NI), 1944: general papers (1944).

HLG/6/5/2, 3A: Northern Ireland Housing Trust: minutes (1948).

HLG/6/5/4: Question of erection of flats on blitzed sites (1947–52).

HLG/6/8/2: Northern Ireland Housing Trust: minutes of proceedings (1951–2).

HLG/6/13/1: Housing of problem families (1956).

HLG/6/13/2: Compensation for compulsory purchase (1956).

HLG/6/18/2: Inquiry into Belfast Corporation (1961).

HLGP/4/2: Northern Ireland Housing Executive meetings: ministry and executive (1971–4).

HSS/27: Belfast Housing Inquiry (1953–4).

LA/1/2/GA/48: Antrim County Council: minute book, quarterly and annual meetings (1947–8).

LA/1/2/GB/59: Antrim County Council: minute book, quarterly and annual meetings (1958).

LA/172/2/1/2: Minutes of Police Liaison Committee (1975).

LA/172/2/2/4: Special meeting of Newtownabbey Borough Council (1981).

LA/7/3/B/16: Belfast Corporation/County Borough Council: file marked: 'Miscellaneous', mainly concerning housing issues (1944–63).

LA/7/3/E/13/2, 9: Belfast Corporation/County Borough Council: files relating to negotiations with the Northern Ireland Housing Trust (1957–64).

LA/7/3/E/13/7: Belfast Corporation/County Borough Council: file relating to miscellaneous housing matters (1960–5).

LA/7/12/AB/1: Belfast Corporation/County Borough Council: minute book of the [Special] Housing Committee (1948–53).

LA/7/12/AC/1: Belfast Corporation/County Borough Council: minute book of the Housing (Clearance and Re-development) Committee (1957–62).

LA/59/2F/23, 26 and LA/59/2FA/24–5: Newtownabbey Urban District Council [formerly Belfast Rural District Council]: Belfast Rural District Council minutes (1946–52).

LA/59/2CA: Newtownabbey Urban District Council minutes (1958–73).

OS/1/56/2: Ordnance Survey: first edition 6" (1:10560) maps: Ballygolan, parish of Templepatrick (1833 or 1855, revised 1857).

OS/6/1/57/1A–6: Ordnance Survey: County Series 6" (1:10560) maps: Antrim sheet (1832–3).

SCH/362/1/5: Register (female), Greencastle national/public elementary school and later from 1938, St Mary's (Star of the Sea) public elementary/primary school, Belfast (1937–48).

SCH/362/5/2: Inspector's suggestion book (female), Greencastle national/public elementary school and later from 1938, St Mary's (Star of the Sea) public elementary/primary school, Belfast (1936–54).

SCH/362/5/3: Inspector's suggestion book (male), Greencastle national/public elementary school and later from 1938, St Mary's (Star of the Sea) public elementary/primary school, Belfast (1947–56).

SCH/1198/1/3: Register (male) of Holy Family Boys national/public elementary/primary school, Belfast (1940–55).

SO/1A/229: Housing and Local Government: list of staff employed by the Northern Ireland Housing Trust (1945).

SO/1A/255: Housing and Local Government: list of staff employed by the Northern Ireland Housing Trust on 31st March 1947 (1947).

T1319/1: Abstract of title to lands in Ballygolan, Drumnadrough and Skegoneill, County Antrim, Thompson family (1823–99).

T3756: Account of German air-raid on Veryan Gardens, Belfast (1941).

VAL/1B/115A: Valuation records: parish of Carnmoney, first valuation, Ballgolan(d) (1836).

VAL/8/344: Valuation records: Northern Ireland Housing Trust – miscellaneous information (1946–63).

VAL/8/408–9: Valuation records: Housing Trust, Poor Law valuation (1946–58).

VAL/8/410: Valuation records: Part 3: Housing Trust – first appeals, housing (1949–58).

VAL/8/415: Valuation records: Housing Trust – Whitewell site (1945–65).

VAL/8/435: Valuation records: health services – question of Commissioners of Valuation undertaking valuation of property taken over by various authorities and boards (1949–54).

VAL/12/B/5/2A:Valuation records: electoral division of Ballygolan, Rural District of Belfast (1923–9).

VAL/12/B/5/12A–J:Valuation records: Belfast Union: electoral division of Whitehouse, parish of Carnmoney (1862–1929).

VAL/14/A/50:Valuation records: Belfast Ward, Bellevue, rate valuations (1975).

Queen's University Belfast McClay Library Special Collections
QUB/J/1/7: D.G. Neill Collection (1941–95).

Queen's University Belfast School of Geography, Archaeology and Paleoecology Map Library
Ordnance Survey 6" County Series, County Antrim, sheet 57, 6th edition (1936–8).

Ordnance Survey 1:10,000 Series, sheet 114 (1975).

Ordnance Survey 1:2,500 Series, sheet 114-13 (1965).

Northern Ireland Religious Areas: Scale 1:250,000, Ministry of Defence, London (1976).

Ordnance Survey 1:1,250 Series, sheet 114-13SE4 (1989).

RTÉ Archives
PXD3/18477: *Stolen Babies* (21 Sept. 2009).

Registry of Deeds, Dublin
369/538/249691, 432/66/280034, 432/322/280738, 619/467/425914, 646/69/443054: Grimshaw leases, (1786–1812).

Sussex University, Mass Observation Archive
MO1306, Americans in Ireland (1942).

MO2101, Tom Harrison, Ulster Outlooks (1944).

MO2505 and 5462, Moya Woodside, Diary (1940–1).

MO5245, D.M. Bates, Diary (1941).

Ulster Folk and Transport Museum: BBC Northern Ireland Community Archive

668–9: *The McCooeys* (only three episodes survive) (1948–55).

1691: *For Your Benefit*: interviews with Brian Dunn, chairman of the White City Tenants' Association, and Donald Graham, author of the report *White City: Crumbling Orlits* (Feb. 1986).

3214: *The Easter of the Bombs* (Jan. 1974).

3701: *Consumer Desk*: the Northern Ireland Housing Executive and Orlits (Oct. 1986).

8033: *Recollections*: *Sammy Barr* (who ran the Flamingo Ball Room) (Aug. 1989).

8037: *Recollections*: interview with Dave Glover (Jul. 1989).

8530: *Recollections: Paddy Hopkirk* (who grew up Whitehouse) (Jun. 1990).

WEB RESOURCES

Belfast Forum, www.belfastforum.co.uk

'Castle', *Belfast City Council Elections 1997*, gi0rtn.tripod.com/belfast/97castle.html

Conflict Archive on the Internet (University of Ulster), *Subversion in the UDR (Ulster Defence Regiment), by British Military Intelligence* (1973), cain.ulst.ac.uk/publicrecords/1973/subversion_in_the_udr.htm#annexe

Conflict Archive on the Internet (University of Ulster), *Sutton Index of Deaths* (1969–2001), cain.ulst.ac.uk/sutton/

Culture Northern Ireland: Belfast Galleries, www.belfastgalleries.com

Cunningham, Tom, 'Introduction', *Stella Maris Secondary School*, stellamarissecondary.com

Executive Office, *Together: Building a United Community Strategy* (2013), www.executiveoffice-ni.gov.uk/publications/together-building-united-community-strategy

Formation of the Northern Ireland Tuberculosis Authority, supplement to *Ulster Medical Journal*, vol. 58 (1989), 30–41, www.ncbi.nlm.nih.gov/pmc/articles/PMC2448157/pdf/ulstermedj00082–0030

Housing Executive Research Unit, *Greater Whitewell Community Survey* (2014), www.nihe.gov.uk/greater_whitewell_shared_community_survey.pdf

McCoy, Jayne, 'Homes Scandal?', *Diary of a Sutton Councillor* (2012), jaynemccoysblog.wordpress.com/tag/orlit-homes/

Bibliography

'No Place Like Home', *Burton Latimer Heritage Society* (1987), www.burtonlatimer.info/history/proposed-demolition-orlits.html

Northern Ireland Parliamentary Debates: 50 Years of Northern Ireland Parliamentary Debates Online (Belfast, 2006), http://stormont-papers.ahds.ac.uk

Northern Ireland Statistics and Research Agency, *Northern Ireland Neighbourhood Information Service*, www.ninis2.nisra.gov.uk

Smith, Mark K., 'Octavia Hill: Housing, Space and Social Reform', *The Encyclopaedia of Informal Education* (2008), www.infed.org/thinkers/octavia_hill.htm

Acknowledgements

This book started out as an attempt to capture the memories of the first residents of the White City housing estate. It is dedicated to the half-dozen who became my earliest, and thereafter most consistent, informants. Sheila Burns, Anna Pearson and Shane McAteer have passed away since; Flo Kelsey, Brian Dunn and Gerry Mulholland have remained as stalwarts, and Flo in particular carries the history of the estate in her head, since she first moved there in 1949.

Other key people who deserve thanks are John Dunlop, Moira Morrow, my sisters, Geraldine Walsh and Eleanor Dent, Linda Taylor, Lizzy Welshman, May Doherty, former neighbours, the Brooks sisters – May, Enie and Nessie – as well as Stephen and Mike Smith, Norah Van Puten, Philomena McAteer, Anne McAteer, Anna Magee, Geraldine Kane, Pat Rogers, Ultán Gillen, Trevor Parkhill, Maurice Hayes, Mark Langhammer, Lindsey Earner-Byrne, Joe Camplisson, Eileen Gordon, Tony Gallagher, Pete Shirlow, Kevin Bean, Viola Segeroth, Nick Jackson, Diane Urquhart and Graham Walker. I am grateful to representatives of the various housing authorities: Sean McKenna, Joel Kingham, Margaret Gibson and Tony Kennedy from the Housing Executive; Sylvia Doran, Mai Moore and Ian Elliott from the housing associations; Brian French and Carrie Poole of the Northern Ireland Statistics and Research Agency. Thanks are due to my publisher, Blackstaff Press, particularly Patsy Horton, and my editor, Alicia McAuley, and to staff at the various libraries and archives, especially: Ursula Mitchell and Lisa Coyle-McClurg at Queen's University Belfast; Gary McMahon, Marion Molloy, Wesley Geddis, John Rea and Marie Lennon at the Public Record Office of Northern Ireland; Angela Mackeys and Sarah Steenson at Belfast Central Library; Alistair Gordon at the Linen Hall Library; Niamh MacNamara, BBC archivist at the Ulster Folk and Transport Museum; and staff at the Down and Conor Diocesan Archives, Somerton Road, Belfast.

Elizabeth de Young, Marisa McGlinchy and Sam Manning provided expert research assistance. Brian Walker, Paul Arthur and John Gray valiantly read the entire script and Roy Foster and Ian

McBride supported the undertaking from its inception.

The project was funded by the Leverhulme Trust, for whose understanding when there were difficulties I am truly grateful.

Family and friends bear quite a burden in supporting obsessive writers. My most consistent and long-lasting support, muse and best critic – my husband, Trevor Elliott – passed away as I was researching *Hearthlands*, and my son, Marc Elliott, has had to assume part of that difficult mantle, but close friends have been there too, particularly Anne Lawrence and Annie Gwyn.

The author and publisher gratefully acknowledge permission to include the following copyright material:

Alyn, Marjory, *The Sound of Anthems* (London, 1983), Copyright © 1983, Marjory Alyn. Reproduced by permission of Hodder and Stoughton Limited; and St Martin's Press Ltd., London, copyright © 1983 by Marjory Alyn.

Mahon, Derek, 'Spring in Belfast' from *New Collected Poems* (2011) is reprinted by kind permission of The Gallery Press. www.gallerypress.com

McFadden, Roy, 'Fire Bomb' from *A Watching Brief: Poems* (1979) is reprinted by kind permission of McFadden estate.

Photographs are the author's own, apart from where indicated. Including:

'Housing Trust plan for the Whitewell estate', VAL/8/415 © Public Record Office of Northern Ireland. Plan reproduced by kind permission of the Deputy Keeper of the Records, Public Record Office of Northern Ireland

'M2 under construction', reproduced by kind permission of T. Jackson McCormick via Wesley Johnston.

'Map of Ballygolan area, 1901', reproduced by permission of OSNI and Land & Property Services © Crown copyright and database right.

Acknowledgements

'Map of Bellevue ward', reproduced by permission of OSNI and Land & Property Services © Crown copyright and database right.

'Northern Ireland Housing Trust's catchment areas', reproduced by kind permission of the Northern Ireland Housing Executive.

'Northern Ireland Religious Areas, 1976' Ministry of Defence. © Crown Copyright 2017. Reproduced under the terms of the Open Government Licence http://www.nationalarchives.gov.uk/doc/opengovernment-licence/version/2/. With thanks to The Map Library, School of Natural and Built Environment, Queen's University Belfast.

'Phase one of the M2, October 1966', INF/7A/12/9 © Public Record Office of Northern Ireland. Photograph reproduced by kind permission of the Deputy Keeper of the Records, Public Record Office of Northern Ireland.

'White City and Throneview, 1949', reproduced by kind permission of the Northern Ireland Housing Executive.

Every effort has been made to trace and contact copyright holders before publication. If notified, the publisher will rectify any errors or omissions at the earliest opportunity.

Index

Index

Index

Index

Index

Index

McKenna, Seán, 143
McKibbin, Frederick, 55, 56
McLarnon, Gerald, 153
McMillen, Marion, 94
McNamee, Eoin, 87
McSparran, J.P., 151
Mercy primary school, Belfast, 120
Merston Gardens, Belfast, 41
Methodist Church, 18
Middleton, Colin, 1
Midgley, Harry, 43, 118, 125
Midland Hotel, Belfast, 51
Mill Dam, Belfast, 20, 188
Mill Road, Belfast, 19, 20, 128, 140
Ministry of Commerce, 137
Ministry of Community Relations, 81
Ministry of Development, 100, 137
Ministry of Education, 117, 118, 125, 126
Ministry of Finance, 35
Ministry of Health and Local Government,
    26, 31, 32, 34, 41, 43, 44, 46, 53, 58, 77,
    117, 126, 127, 137
Ministry of Home Affairs, 59
Ministry of Labour, 34, 145
Ministry of Supply, 33
Monaghan, Rinty, 109, 110
Monkstown, County Antrim, 75, 145, 166,
    173
Montgomery, Field Marshal, 109
Montgomery, John, 180
Moody, T.W., 150
Moore, Clayton, 154
Moore, Thomas, 104
Morrison, Bill, 135, 137, 138
Morrow, Moira, viii, 76, 111, 114–15, 138
Moss, Stirling, 82
Mossley, County Antrim, 145
Mount Lydia, Belfast, 56
Mount Vernon, Belfast, 126, 168
Mulderg Drive, Belfast, 41, 178
Mulholland, Gerry, viii–ix, 68, 75–6, 77, 79,
    89, 95, 102, 106, 108, 120, 138
Murphy, Mary Anne, 20
Murray, Ruby, 104
Musgrave Street, Belfast, 92

Napoleon, 8–9
Napoleon's Nose. *See* McArt's Fort, Belfast.
Nash, Andrew, 9
National Health Service (NHS), 117,
    127, 128, 130. *See also* public health in
    Northern Ireland; welfare state.
Nationalist Party, 148, 157
Navarra Place, Belfast, 55, 76, 144, 178

Neill, Desmond, 150. *See also* Field-Neill
    Survey.
Nelson, Sarah, 163, 170
Nelson, Thomas, 45
New Lodge, Belfast, 168
Newcastle upon Tyne, England, 89
Newcastle, County Down, 115
Newington, Belfast, 49, 67, 84, 120
Newry, County Down, 93
Newtownabbey, County Antrim, 53,
    133–6, 139, 158, 159, 165, 166, 167, 168,
    170, 173, 175, 179
Newtownards, County Down, 135
Nightingale, Florence, 80
North Brunswick Street, Dublin, 93
North Queen Street, Belfast, 67
North Road, Belfast, 92
North Street, Belfast, 114
Northern Ireland Civil Rights Association,
    162
Northern Ireland Housing Executive, 46,
    141, 142–4, 146, 173, 174, 175, 177,
    179, 191
Northern Ireland Housing Trust, 1, 2, 21,
    22–46, 54, 55, 56, 57–9, 60–3, 64, 65, 67,
    68, 69–74, 76, 77–81, 82, 83, 90, 99–101,
    113, 117, 118, 120, 121, 131, 132, 134,
    136, 139–40, 141, 142, 143, 144, 145,
    165, 174, 176, 189, 192
    allocation of houses, xi, 29, 35, 39,
        42–6, 64–6, 82, 139, 144
    establishment of, xi, 27–35, 41
    funding of, 29–30, 32, 40, 81
    housing managers, 23, 29, 30, 37–9,
        42, 44, 66, 67, 69, 78–81, 99, 139,
        143. *See also* Hill, Octavia.
Northern Ireland Labour Party (NILP), 26,
    52, 150, 157, 158, 159, 170
Northern Ireland Tuberculosis Authority,
    127
Nutt's Corner, County Antrim, 87

Oates, Gerry, 109–10
O'Brien, Sir Lucius, 22, 24, 26, 32–3, 34,
    35, 36, 43, 45, 66
O'Connor, Mary, 91
Old Cavehill Road, Belfast, 6, 10
Old Lodge, Belfast, ix
Old Throne Park, Belfast, 178
Oldpark Road, Belfast, 168
Oliver, John, 25–6, 32, 43, 46, 47, 52, 63,
    127, 136, 137
O'Malley, Padraig, 176
O'Neill, Captain Terence, 44, 154, 162

257

Index